THIRD EDITION

… one of the finest training manuals for divorce mediators available on the market … issues are laid out in a manner that makes them accessible to the intending practitioner as well as the academic or experienced mediator.

SPIDR News

Anyone who takes the profession seriously should buy it.

Family Law

Marian Roberts' book is the first to provide the basis of solid knowledge in the UK and for that reason alone should be on every trainer's "must buy" list … Mediation in Family Disputes should not, however, merely be seen as a training tool. It has a message for a wider audience, particularly the mediation sceptics.

Family Mediation

… a valuable resource …

ChildRIGHT

… very well written with material clearly explained.

D1334626

For Simon
For Adam and Sara
For my parents

Mediation in Family Disputes
Principles of Practice

Third Edition

MARIAN ROBERTS

ASHGATE

Published by
Ashgate Publishing Limited
Gower House
Croft Road
Aldershot
Hampshire GU11 3HR
England

Ashgate Publishing Company
Suite 420
101 Cherry Street
Burlington, VT 05401-4405
USA

www.ashgate.com

British Library Cataloguing in Publication Data
Roberts, Marian
    Mediation in family disputes : principles of practice. -
    3rd ed.
    1. Divorce mediation - England 2. Domestic relations -
    England 3. Divorce - Law and legislation - England
    4. Divorce mediation - Wales 5. Domestic relations - Wales
    6. Divorce - Law and legislation - Wales
    I. Title
    346.4'2'0166

Library of Congress Cataloging-in-Publication Data
Roberts, Marian.
    Mediation in family disputes : principles of practice / by Marian Roberts.
-- 3rd ed.
       p. cm.
    Includes bibliographical references and index.
    ISBN 978-0-7546-4619-8 (hardback)
    ISBN 978-0-7546-4624-2 (paperback)
  1. Family mediation--Great Britain. 2. Dispute resolution (Law)--Great Britain. I. Title.

KD750.R63 2008
346.4101'5--dc22

2008002621

ISBN 978 0 7546 4619 8 (hardback)
ISBN 978 0 7546 4624 2 (paperback)

Mixed Sources
Product group from well-managed forests and other controlled sources
www.fsc.org Cert no. SGS-COC-2482
© 1996 Forest Stewardship Council
FSC

Printed and bound in Great Britain by
TJ International Ltd, Padstow, Cornwall

Contents

List of cases

A. v. *A. (Children's Shared Residence Order)* [1994] 1 FLR 669 CA
A. v. *A. (Shared Residence Order)* [2004] 1 FLR 1195
Re A.B. (No.2) [1995] 1 FLR 351 (WALL J.)
Re B. (A Minor) (Contact) (Interim Order) [1994] 2 FLR 269
Balfour v. *Balfour* [1919] 2 KB 571
Beales v. *Beales* [1972] 2 All ER 667
Bowman v. *Fels* [2005] EWCA CIV 226
Browne v. *Pritchard* [1975] 3 All ER 721
Caffell v. *Caffell* [1984] 5 FLR 169 CA
Camm v. *Camm* [1983] 13 Fam. Law 112
Charman v. *Charman* [2007] EWCA CIV 503
D. v. *D. (Shared Residence Order)* [2001] 1FLR 495
Re D. (A Minor) (Contact: Mother's Hostility) [1993] 2 FLR. 1 CA
Re D. (A Minor) (Justices' Decision Review) [1977] Fam. 158
Re D. (Minors) (Conciliation: Privilege) [1993] 1 FLR 934 CA (SIR THOMAS BINGHAM J)
Dipper v. *Dipper* [1980] 2 All ER 722
Edgar v. *Edgar* [1980] 3 All ER. 887
Fielding v. *Fielding* [1978] 1 All E.R. 267
Re G. (A Minor) (Parental Responsibility Order) [1994] 1 FLR 504 CA
Re G. (Parental Responsibility: Education) [1994] 2 FLR 964 (GLIDEWELL LJ)
Gillick v. *West Norfolk and Wisbech* AHA [1986] AC 112
H. v. *H.* [2007] EWHC 459 (Fam)
Re H. (Conciliation: Welfare Reports) [1986] 1 FLR 476 (EWBANK J)
Re H. (Minors) (Access) [1992] 1 FLR. 148
Re H. (Minors) (Illegitimate Children: Father: Parental Rights) (No.2) [1991] 1FLR 214 CA
Re H. (Minors) (Prohibited Steps Order) [1995] *The Times,* 8 February 1995, CA
Halsey v. *Milton Keynes General NHS Trust* [2004] 1 WLR 3002

Henley v. *Henley* [1955] 1 All ER 590
Hurst v. *Hurst* [1984] 5 FLR 867 CA
Jessel v. *Jessel* [1979] 1 WLR 1148
Jussa v. *Jussa* [1972] 2 All ER 600
M. v. *M.* [1973] 2 All ER 81
M. v. *M. (Pre-nuptial Agreement)* [2002] 1FLR 654
Re M. (A Minor) (Contact: Conditions) [1994] 1 FLR 272
McFarlane v. *McFarlane* [2006] UKHL 24, [2006] 1FLR 1186
McTaggart v. *McTaggart* [1948] 2 All ER 755 (DENNING LJ)
Merritt v. *Merritt* [1970] 2 All ER 760
Mesher v. *Mesher* [1980] 1 All ER 126 CA
Miller v. *Miller* [2006] UKHL 24, [2006] 1FLR 1186
Mole v. *Mole* [1950] 2 All ER 329 CA
Re P. (A Minor) (Education) [1992] 1 FLR 316 (BUTLER-SLOSS LJ)
Pais v. *Pais* [1970] 3 All ER 491
Re R. (A Minor) (Contact) [1993] 2 FLR 762 (BUTLER-SLOSS LJ)
Re R. [1995] 1 FLR 716
Richards v. *Richards* [1984] AC 174
Riley v. *Riley* [1986] 2 FLR 429
Robinson v. *Robinson* [1983] 1 All ER 391
Rossi v. *Rossi* [2006] EWHC 1482 (Fam)
S. v. *O.* [1978] 8 Fam. Law 11
S. v. *S.* [1962] 2 All ER 816
Re S. (Minors) (Custody) [1992] Fam. Law 148
Re S. (Parental Responsibility) [1995] *The Times*, 24 February, CA (WARD LJ)
Theodoropoulos v. *Theodoropoulos* [1963] 2 All ER 772
Re W. (A Minor) (Consent to Medical Treatment) [1993] 1 FLR 1
Re W. (A Minor) (Contact) [1994] 2 FLR 441 CA
White v. *White* [2000] 2 FLR 981
Wright v. *Wright* [1980] 2 FLR 276

Table of statutes

Preface to third edition

In the past decade, mediation has become an institutionalized, officially endorsed and expanding mode of decision-making across many areas of social life. Mediation in family disputes, early on the scene, is now an established pathway in the current landscape of dispute resolution processes. Publicly funded by government, with a recognized potential to benefit a larger section of the public, family mediation is confirmed by academic research to provide the public with the opportunity to resolve family disputes more quickly and cheaply, and with less acrimony than the traditional litigation and court processes.

The consolidation of the professional practice of family mediation reflects its progress and creativity over the past decade – the remarkable achievement of the rich resource of quality assurance work of the UK College of Family Mediators exemplifies this, as does the application of mediation to a growing range of family conflict situations, such as international child abduction and the homeless young. However, the last decade has also seen the field threatened by turbulence and flux – for example, the move away from no-fault divorce associated with the demise of the Family Law Act 1996; the dominance of lawyer interests; external pressures arising from an overburdened family justice system; as well as structural tensions and conflicts of function within the field. It is essential yet again, to re-affirm the call for continuing vigilance in relation to the principles that distinguish mediation and inform its code of practice, policies and standards designed to protect the public.

This book seeks to place those core ethical and professional principles of practice at the centre of effective practice. This approach, focused mainly on issues arising from high conflict disputes over children (where the author has most experience), applies to all areas of decision-making arising from family separation and divorce, as well as to disputes arising in other family situations.

Mediators can be conceived of as contemporary practitioners of an ancient and universal craft. With accumulated experience, collegiality contributes significantly to the spirit and practice of craftsmanship as a vital source of learning and expertise. I want therefore to thank all those with whom I have worked over the years – at the South East London Family Mediation Bureau, during my ten years at National Family Mediation, and within the UK College of Family Mediators – for their contributions to the field. I want especially to pay tribute to the late Toni Gerard, an esteemed and dedicated colleague in all three domains, and a dear friend.

In particular, I want to say how grateful I am to Susan Tilley, solicitor and mediator, for the detailed care and precision of her extensive recommendations for updating and re-organizing Chapter 3 on the legal context of family mediation. Sara Roberts, counselling psychologist, was of great assistance in clarifying aspects of contemporary therapeutic understanding. Simon Roberts' scholarship, guidance and support over the years have been, as ever, invaluable. Again, responsibility for the views expressed in the book, for all its limitations, and for any errors, remains mine.

Marian Roberts
2008

Prologue[1]

... I simply wanted some kind of reasonableness to operate, recognizing the marriage had ended but seeking to achieve, you know, an ending in a reasonable manner. *Non-resident father*

One needs a neutral Guardian Angel to step in – someone not legal, not family, who has no vested interest but is very aware of both sides. *Mother with residence*

We thought there should be something in between two people talking and a court hearing. We thought there must be something in between, surely ... we didn't want something as drastic as court ... when it gets as far as court it's taken out of your hands. So we felt that wasn't satisfactory ... but the two, one to one, wasn't working. So we needed something in between. *Father with residence*

Well, we weren't talking really. We were very hostile to each other then. And I think we needed somebody to act as intermediary, to break the ice and to get us talking. *Non-resident mother*

---

1   Quotes of those who experienced mediation (see Davis and Roberts, 1988).

1   What is family mediation?

> The varieties of dispute settlement, and the socially sanctioned choices in any culture, communicate the ideals people cherish, their perceptions of themselves, and the quality of their relationships with others. They indicate whether people wish to avoid or encourage conflict, suppress it, or resolve it amicably. Ultimately the most basic values of society are revealed in its dispute-settlement procedures. (Jerold Auerbach, 1983, pp. 3–4)

The emergence in Britain of mediation as a recognized approach to settling family disputes following family breakdown has been, in many ways, a remarkable development. Its adoption in the late 1970s involved a new and evolving application of an ancient method of settling quarrels, perhaps better suited than any other to the special characteristics of family disputes.

Mediation is also based on certain values that have justified its use, both for the disputants as well as for those who have chosen to become mediators. These are exemplified in the comparison of the way people are treated under existing forms of intervention:

> It strikes me that if you have some kind of grading scale for your institutions, like courts, schools, and hospitals, as to which gave the participants the most adult setting, it might be interesting to see how different institutions rank. Are you told what to do or asked what you want to do? Are you made to wait or is your time valued? Are you allowed to know what is going on or are you kept in the dark? Are you powerful or powerless? Are decisions made for you or do you get to make the decisions? Are you treated as a human being or are those qualities not considered? One of the things that strikes me in mediation is that it comes out much higher on that scale than many of our institutions and I think that is why it works. (Davis, 1984, p. 54)

This standard of respect has lain at the core of the principles of mediation practice. Respect for the parties' authority and capacity to make their own decisions has been paramount in mediation as has been respect therefore

1

for their perceptions and values. This fundamental ethic of respect has been seen to be essential for the mediator to have proper regard for the right of the parties, whatever the difficulties, to be the architects of their own agreements, and for party competence and control, as the distinguishing characteristic of mediation, to have any meaning. Norms of fairness, mutual respect and equity of exchange have informed the expectations of adult behaviour that have underpinned the practice of mediation (Fuller, 1971; Rubin and Brown, 1975). These expectations have been perceived to be of most value precisely because of the recognition that circumstances may be bringing out the 'worst' in people, who may perhaps have become victims of their own 'powerful infantile feelings which divorce itself may catalyse' (Brown and Day Sclater, 1999, p. 154). However laid low by circumstances and personal vulnerability, people were not to be regarded as incapable or ill. Mediation, in offering a calm, safe forum for reasonable exchange could provide the opportunity for retaining or regaining control over their own affairs and for encouraging self-determination and autonomy.

Decision-making capacity is what has defined this standard of adulthood and is therefore what has distinguished mediation both from other forms of dispute resolution (such as lawyer negotiation and adjudication) and from other forms of professional intervention (such as social work). The affirmation of the decision-making authority of the parties derives from a tradition of humanist ideas about equality and liberty, which accord respect for the inherent dignity, privacy and autonomy of the individual person (for example, Lukes, 1973). Sennett (2003, p. 262) distils the connection between equality, autonomy and respect in this way:

> Rather than an equality of understanding, autonomy means accepting in others what one does not understand about them. In so doing, the fact of their autonomy is treated as equal to your own. The grant of autonomy dignifies the weak or the outsider; to make this grant to others in turn strengthens one's own character.

The early growth of family mediation in Britain can be seen as a later manifestation of that revival of alternative approaches to conflict and dispute that occurred in the US, in the community justice movement in particular, arising from the social movement of the 1960s, of the 'new consciousness' that challenged traditional attitudes and values in the context of dispute resolution (a process memorably observed by Reich in *The Greening of America*, 1970). The values of mediation exemplified the spirit of the time – the importance of respect, dignity, fairness, justice, reciprocity, individual participation, consensus and party control. The resurrection of these values countered a dominant, prevailing value system characterized by adversarial processes, impersonality, lawyer control and rule-centred authoritarian command.

It is fair to say too that the story of the modern growth of mediation, incorporating mediation in the context of family disputes, can be described in different ways (Roberts, 2006):

- as a response to the 'evolutionary demise' of 'conventional forms of institutionalised searches for justice, in the form of the courts and trial ... because they are failing to satisfy modern requirements for voice, justice and conflict resolution' (Menkel-Meadow, 2004, p. 100);
- as symptomatic of the changing nature of state power in late capitalism, manifesting both in the radically transformed nature of the courts developing new strategies of dispute settlement and in the expansion of government outwards to co-opt and shape a hitherto 'private' sphere of negotiation;
- as the struggle for recognition of a new professional group offering an innovative and different way of managing family conflict and disputes, one involving the re-discovery of a universal and ancient triadic process;
- as a movement of recovery on the part of lawyers, fearing competition and seeking to protect their traditional monopoly of control over dispute resolution.

Aspects of all these interpretations inform this account of the family mediation story.

Until relatively recently, there was a limited choice open to a couple (married or cohabiting) for sorting out their differences in the wake of the dissolution of their relationship. They could negotiate together and make their own decisions on the vital and interrelated issues that confronted them on parting – issues relating to the children, their home, the distribution of their financial assets (and debts), maintenance and the divorce itself. Some couples, perhaps managing on their own or with the help of the local vicar, doctor, respected friend or family member, might work out mutually satisfactory arrangements. Although there are no figures available, many couples appear not to manage to engage in face-to-face discussions, let alone discussion free from the tumult of anger, bullying and rowing. Perhaps, in many cases, matters are just left unresolved to the satisfaction of none of those involved, especially the children (Mitchell, 1985).

The traditional approach in most cases has been for each partner to consult their own lawyer and for the two lawyers to negotiate on their clients' behalf, reach agreement if possible or, if not, hand over to a judge the responsibility of making decisions. The judge makes an order that is imposed on the parties on the basis of the facts before him.

For couples unable to reach agreement on their own, the only alternative therefore was to transfer responsibility for negotiating and decision-making to third parties, namely lawyers and/or judges. Then another choice became available. With the establishment in 1978 of the first family mediation service in Britain, the opportunity now existed for separating and divorcing couples unable or unwilling to manage entirely on their own, yet not wishing to relinquish responsibility for making their own decisions, to meet together on neutral territory and, with the help of a third party – the mediator – seek to work out and mutually agree their own arrangements by means of a negotiating process structured to achieve this. Two crucial differences characterized this transformation: first, the location of decision-making authority lay with the parties; and second, the parties themselves were the negotiators.

So mediation emerged to fill a space hitherto unoccupied, which none of the existing services, welfare, advisory or therapeutic on the one hand or lawyers and the courts on the other, could in their nature have filled. Mediatory intervention could not in its nature be a substitute for these other interventions. For example, mediation generally presupposes the parties obtaining independent legal advice whenever necessary. Being properly appraised about relevant legal matters is vitally important if people are to participate in negotiation in an informed and fair way. Notwithstanding the changing nature of the contemporary court, manifesting hybrid processes and diversion procedures that encourage settlement rather than adjudication as the court's primary function, mediation continues to remain a discrete and autonomous intervention separate from and independent of the court. Counselling or therapeutic help may also enable a party to engage more effectively in negotiation by alleviating incapacitating emotional stress. Given the common subject matter that is the focus of these various services, the consequences of family breakdown, the need for clarity about the nature and purpose of different forms of interventions is critical if confusion is to be avoided and the interests of the public protected. Therefore, the specific and unique contribution of mediation has to be distinguished from these other forms of intervention, offering quite different kinds of help.

The development in the late 1970s of mediation in the sphere of family disputes (as well as in the field of community and neighbourhood quarrels) in the UK, and a decade earlier in the US, represents the modern discovery of a mode of dispute resolution that has a long-established anthropological and historical heritage (Roberts, 1979; Rwezaura, 1984; Acland, 1995). With its long-established and cross-cultural practice experience (the 'second oldest profession'!, Kolb, 1985) and a large and distinguished body of knowledge, mediation has been readily adaptable to the specific conditions of joint decision-making in the context of family breakdown. Those working in this field can learn much about the theory and practice of mediation from the writings of those early researchers who studied it first hand and came to understand its processes and the role of the mediator cross-culturally on the basis of their empirical observations (for example, Douglas, 1957, 1962; Stevens, 1963; Gulliver, 1979).

In the early years, handbooks for family mediators were used as a primary resource for practitioners and, until relatively recently, were few in number and were from North America (for example, Coogler, 1978; Haynes, 1981; Lemmon, 1985; Saposnek, 1985). While these contained many valuable insights for the practising mediator, they were of limited use in Britain. In the first place, the American focus was primarily on the resolution of property and financial disputes (Coogler, 1978; Haynes, 1981) when that of the British was initially primarily, though not exclusively, on disputes involving children. Second, where the focus was on children, the authors had grafted mediation on to their practice of family therapy and their approach to mediation therefore reflected this professional appropriation (for example, Saposnek, 1985). Haynes' handbook (1993) on all issues of mediation, adapted by Fisher and Greenslade to the British legal, social and cultural context, was designed to be used in conjunction with associated training, professional regulation and insurance. Today, North American influences continue to dominate the mediation literature (for example, the 'transformative' approach to mediation[1]) but with limited impact on practice in Britain (Roberts, 2007).

Mediation across fields of practice is now an established landmark on the dispute resolution map. Family mediation, in particular, has emerged from its innovative, empirical grass roots as an autonomous professional practice independent of other professional interventions in the field of separation and divorce, such as therapy, counselling, social work and legal practice. Mediators come to mediation from different professional backgrounds and are trained in different settings. No existing professional background can claim any monopoly of expertise in this field (SPIDR, 1989). Styles of practice and practice models vary. The areas of family mediation practice have expanded beyond those arising from divorce and separation and include child protection, child abduction, the homeless young and other kinds of the family dispute (for example, inter-generational family matters).

Family mediation now has statutory recognition, public funding and official encouragement. Family mediation practice in Britain is governed furthermore by European legal instruments (in particular, Recommendation No. R (98) 1 1998) and government-sanctioned quality assurance standards covering both individual practice competence and quality assurance standards relating to the provision and delivery of legally-aided family mediation services (Mediation Quality Mark, 2002). In addition, there is government endorsement of professional self-regulation and the upholding of uniform national standards for all family mediators. The UK College of Family Mediators, in setting and monitoring standards of training and practice for its members (those family mediators who meet its standards

---

1   See, for example, Bush and Folger (2005).

whatever their profession of origin or sector of provision – for-profit or not-for-profit), is the only national membership body solely fulfilling a regulatory function.

The institutional context within which family mediation is practised creates its own challenges. The court, changing in nature and hybrid in character itself, refers increasing numbers of intractable cases to out-of-court family mediation providers. The court welfare service (now re-organized as the Children and Family Court Advisory and Support Service – CAFCASS) has expanded and redefined the roles of its officers to embrace larger, more diverse and often incompatible professional functions (social work, therapeutic, mediatory and adjudicatory) and an interchangeable and undefined terminology – 'assessment', 'casework', 'report writing', 'intensive dispute resolution', 'intensive case management', 'relationship management' and 'roundtable discussions' (CAFCASS Consultation Paper, 2005). It is not surprising that CAFCASS has difficulty even identifying the 'right name' for its practitioners so multiple are the tasks it aspires to perform (CAFCASS Consultation paper, 2005, s. 47).

New external pressures impose unrealistic and inappropriate demands on family mediation – providing for the unmet needs of children coping with family breakdown; funding pressures for quicker, cheaper results; diversionary pressures to reduce court lists; and the pressures of co-option by government to meet targets and satisfy professional agendas that have nothing to do with the objectives of family mediation.

These radical and complex transformations over such a short period highlight a growing necessity for a rigorous approach to clarity of understanding about the nature and distinctive features of the mediation process as well as its essential professional and ethical operating principles. Where change and fluidity in adjacent professional boundaries create a lack of clarity as to what intervention is contemplated, the potential for confusion in the public is magnified. It is therefore incumbent on family mediators not only to represent their primary goals and how to achieve them with conceptual and professional clarity, but, just as important, to practise with a knowledge of the limitations of the processes and of their role. Only then can there be practice of a kind that has proper regard for priorities and boundaries and which is likely to be appropriately applied and therefore effective.

Mediators do not claim mediation to be a panacea or the primary determinant of successful resolution. Many factors, personal, social, economic, as well as time itself, are influential. Kressel (1985, p. 4) has appraised the challenges involved in the settlement of divorce disputes as follows:

> The orchestration of a constructive process of divorce negotiation must be considered one of the most demanding tasks that rational beings are expected to perform.

The actual practice of mediation in family disputes is recognized to be gruelling as well as creative intellectually, emotionally and imaginatively. The dynamics of the process are fraught and many-layered. With the need for clarity greater than ever about what mediation is and can achieve, as well as the limitations and obstacles that might render its use inappropriate, the scale of the task requires mediators to adopt a modest approach with a full awareness of the obstacles.

Defining mediation

Mediation is a form of intervention in which a third party, the mediator, assists the parties to a dispute to negotiate over the issues that divide them. The mediator has no stake in the dispute and is not identified with any of the competing interests involved. The mediator has no power to impose a settlement on the parties, who retain authority for making their own decisions.

The terms 'mediation' and 'conciliation' were often used interchangeably in Britain in the context of family disputes. They have different definitions in a labour-relations context where mediation is associated with the making of formal recommendations (ACAS publication, para. 29). 'Conciliation', however, has been used loosely to embrace a general approach to mitigating the harmful effects of family conflict. It used to cover a range of differing practices that were part of court procedure as well as the voluntary and statutory services operating independently of the court. 'Conciliation' has been used to describe the conciliatory approaches of court personnel, such as in the preparation of welfare reports by court reporting officers, as well as the constructive bilateral negotiations conducted by some lawyers negotiating on behalf of their clients. In addition, the Family Law Bar Association set up what it called a Conciliation Board, which was in fact a document-based scheme of arbitration to settle disputes over property and finance. As in the US a couple of decades earlier, 'conciliation' in the United Kingdom became a 'buzzword' covering an array of different conflict intervention processes and styles. For the public, the misunderstanding was compounded by the frequent confusion of conciliation with reconciliation, the reuniting of estranged couples. Therefore, for the purpose of clarity, the term mediation was adopted in the late 1980s because of its precise reference to a specific form of third-party intervention in the settling of disputes (in the family arena). The object of the process is consensual joint decision-making, authority for which is retained by the parties themselves.

What is mediation?

> The most important point to remember when discussing mediation is that it is nothing more or less than a device for facilitating the negotiation process. Negotiations can and do occur without a mediator but mediation can never occur in the absence of negotiation. (Cormick, 1981)

These words, while written in connection with environmental mediation, are no less apposite in the context of family mediation. Negotiation involves processes of communication, information exchange and learning. These are the means by which the dispute of the parties is placed, gradually, in a context of increasing knowledge about all the circumstances, pressures, feelings, attitudes, perceptions and needs that surround the dispute (Gulliver, 1979). Because this knowledge leads to improved understanding there is likely to be a lessening of competition and hostility and therefore an adjustment and modification of expectations, demands and preferences. A brief and final bargaining stage may be included once all the groundwork of communication and learning has been accomplished.

It is where the terms 'negotiation' and 'bargaining' are used interchangeably that misunderstanding can be created. A failure to distinguish between the two could lead to the view that negotiation is too limited a process to accommodate the special circumstances of family breakdown, such as heightened feelings of distress and the needs of the children (for example, Shepherd et al., 1984, p. 21). It has been asserted, for example, that 'a straightforward bargaining model risks treating the children as inanimate possessions' (Robinson and Parkinson, 1985, p. 375). It has been argued therefore that you have to look to insights of the family systems approach and the techniques of family therapy in order to cater adequately for the special needs of those undergoing divorce or separation. It is also the reason why the 'negotiation/bargaining' phase is relegated to a relatively minor and late phase in the conciliation process (Fisher, 1986).

Bargaining and negotiation are not synonymous. Bargaining, associated with the cut and thrust of the marketplace, refers to the series of offers and counter offers, demands and counter demands, the 'trading' of concessions, which may have limited applicability in the family context, as parents themselves would be the first to protest. Negotiation, on the other hand, much broader in scope and encompassing exchanges of communication and learning, can accommodate a bargaining phase late on in the negotiation process, useful as a mopping up operation, when the splitting of differences and the pooling of losses occurs (Douglas, 1957, 1962). As Douglas' research illustrates, parties to negotiation do not begin to split their differences until they have reached agreement on the crucial negotiation points.

If negotiation is successful, this learning process can lead to greater co-ordination, even possibly co-operation, between the parties, resulting in a mutually agreed outcome (see Gulliver, 1970, p. 20). Negotiation is all about learning. The parties begin to learn more about each other and their dispute. This necessarily involves knowledge about the context of the dispute, including relevant aspects of the past, feelings, ethical concerns about fairness and 'justice', and the impact on others, particularly children, who may be central to the dispute. In mediation, the parties also learn to negotiate, and so to talk instead of fight. As has been observed in another context, although also involving marital stress, 'persons mutually at odds are apt to cut each other off intentionally or otherwise from the very information that might lead to a healing of their differences' (Mayer and Timms, 1970, p. 88).

In very simple terms therefore, mediation is about getting the parties to talk to one another again. Talking is, after all, one of the most important means of avoiding trouble (Roberts, 1979, p. 67). Talking can also provide an opportunity for the expression and release of strong feelings such as anger and bitterness. The therapeutic effects of the expression of powerful emotion however, have to be delicately balanced against the harmful effects of saying too much. Some things are better left unsaid. Secondly, talking provides the means of discussing an end to the dispute and of reaching a settlement. Before the break-up, the family made its own decisions on the important matters that affected it and settled its disputes in its own way (Maidment, 1984). Except in cases of risk to the health and well-being of children, the autonomy of this 'self-contained disputing arena' is not questioned (Dingwall and Eekelaar, 1986, p. 55). Conflict and distress interrupt the capacity to communicate so that, at a time when it is difficult for people to talk to one another but also when it is imperative for vital decisions to be made, re-establishing communication becomes of paramount importance.

This leads us briefly to outline the role of the mediator in the process of negotiation. If, as we have seen, the essence of the process is the communication exchange between the parties, we see too that the mediator's task is to facilitate this exchange. The mediator's role therefore is auxiliary to that of the parties. Indirectly and unobtrusively, the mediator should clarify and focus on the parties' own negotiations and assist them in finding areas of agreement. This requires a skilled exercise of creativity and control without being either passive or directive.

The main objectives of the mediator are briefly the following:

- to re-establish contact between the parties;
- to provide a neutral forum where the parties may meet face to face;
- to provide within that forum an impartial presence supportive of negotiation;

- to facilitate the exchange of information between the parties within a structured framework;
- to help the parties to examine their common interests and objectives and the possibilities for reaching agreements that are practicable, mutually acceptable and beneficial to themselves and their children.

The core characteristics of mediation

It is universally accepted that the process of mediation has four fundamental and universal characteristics (McCrory, 1981, p. 56):

- the impartiality of the mediator;
- the voluntariness of the process (because the mediator has no power to impose an outcome);
- the confidentiality of the relationship between the mediator and the parties;
- the procedural flexibility available to the mediator.

It is these characteristics that make mediation as a method of dispute settlement of value to disputants. In view of the circumstances that frequently threaten the integrity of these defining characteristics (that of the voluntariness of the process in particular), their significance cannot be overestimated. Professor McCrory goes as far as to say that if these characteristics are altered or if one or more is absent, then the process cannot be characterized legitimately as mediation. These characteristics will be examined in more detail in the following chapters.

The premises of mediation

There are three requirements without which mediation cannot occur.

A willingness to co-operate

Without a modicum of willingness to co-operate, however reluctant, a mediated solution will not be possible. If people understand what mediation involves and enter the process voluntarily, they do so being prepared at least to attempt to negotiate. This does not mean that there need be an absence, or low levels, of conflict or hostility. Conflict, often high, is a normal feature of family disputes that are successfully mediated. North American comparative research shows, for example, that those reaching agreement on all issues relating to their divorce are not more co-operative than other subgroups studied (Kelly, 2004). In consumer research in Britain (Davis and Roberts, 1988) it was found that although some people did not believe co-operation would be possible because of the degree of hostility, they were prepared to try mediation, and often managed to reach agreement on specific issues even against a background of continuing conflict. In many cases, this willingness to co-operate may be overlaid by other perhaps competing motives. One party, for example, may hope for a reconciliation and seek to use mediation initially, at any rate, to pursue that object. One party may want to use the occasion to resume fighting. If there is no desire to co-operate at all, then mediation becomes impossible.

Competence

The presumption of the competence of the parties to make their own decisions themselves is fundamental to mediation. However laid low people may be by stressful circumstances and personal vulnerability, they do not cease to be capable, other than in exceptional situations. In fact mediation, in offering the parties the opportunity of taking control of their own affairs, may provide them with the very means of encouraging self-determination and autonomy and of enhancing adult and parental responsibility (Folberg, 1984). The implicit expectations of mediation – reasonableness, adult behaviour and mutual respect – are of most value precisely because circumstances may be bringing out the worst in people who may be behaving childishly and selfishly, may be aware of it and its effect on their children and yet have been unable hitherto to do anything about it.

This presumption of competence includes the premise that parents love their children, know their children best and are best able to decide what is in their interests, even though they may genuinely differ in their views about this. Their agreement over the arrangements for their children can be regarded as the best safeguard for the children's welfare.[2] Research confirms the central detrimental impact of continuing parental conflict on children (Wallerstein and Kelly, 1980; Cockett and Tripp, 1994; O'Quigley, 1999).

There is no evidence to support the view that only the better educated can benefit from mediated negotiation. Whatever their social, economic or educational background, most people, given the opportunity, have the capacity to articulate their concerns and wishes, engage in discussion and make their own decisions.

---

2   A contrary view is posited by some that agreement *per se* may be damaging to the interests of children (see Chapter 10).

Equality of bargaining power

Even where there is a presumption of competence, mediation may be inappropriate in certain circumstances and especially where differences of power between the parties are substantial. The mediator has a fundamental ethical responsibility to end a mediation session where it appears that unfairness would result because of the exercise of duress by one party over another or where cultural or other considerations deny a party the capacity to negotiate in their own right at all. Good practice dictates that, in most cases, suitability for mediation could be determined prior to mediation by effective screening procedures (see Chapters 7, 11; and on the need of mediators themselves to avoid the coercive exercise of power, see Chapters 2 and 7).

Distinguishing mediation from other forms of intervention

Two elements are involved in learning about mediation. First, there is the positive aspect, acquiring knowledge of the nature and purpose of mediation and of the role and functions of the mediator. Second, there is the disassociation of assumption (for example, the lawyer's assumption that disputants are adversaries or the therapist's assumption that conflict between individuals requires diagnosis and treatment) and practices necessary for those seeking to make the transformation from their original or existing profession into the new role of mediator, a transformation that is the primary goal of any mediation training. This involves understanding what has been described as the new philosophical map of mediation and its landmarks, landmarks that are different from those of the familiar professional map but which may cover the same territory, in this context that of family breakdown. This requires, therefore, clarity about the ways in which mediation differs from existing interventions, particularly those engaged in addressing problems arising from separation and divorce, which may appear at first sight to be similar – for example, conciliatory negotiations of lawyers; settlement-seeking by court reporting officers; welfare interventions by social workers; interventions into family functioning by family therapists; and the focus on personal and interpersonal dynamics of counsellors and psychotherapists.

Arbitration and adjudication

What distinguishes mediation from other forms of dispute settlement is, as we have seen, the location of decision-making authority. In mediation, authority for decision-making lies with the parties themselves. Arbitration and adjudication, on the other hand, both involve an appeal to a third party to impose a decision because the parties themselves cannot agree. In arbitration, the parties invite the arbitrator to make this decision and agree to honour the decision even though it is not legally binding. The difference between arbitration and mediation has been described in this way:

> Mediation is a form of peacemaking in which an outsider to a dispute intervenes on his own or accepts the invitation of disputing parties to assist them in reaching agreement. Whereas under arbitration the parties agree in advance to accept the decision of the arbitrator, no matter how unpalatable his judgment may appear when it is rendered, in mediation the parties maintain at every point in the proceedings, up to the very end, the prerogative of declaring the mediator 'persona non grata'. (Douglas, 1957, p. 70)

In adjudication, the judge imposes his decision not by invitation of the parties but by virtue of the office from which he derives his authority (Roberts, 1979). Adjudication usually follows a hearing attended by formal rules and procedures and the parties are represented by professional advocates. The order made by the judge is in favour of one of the parties, who is regarded as the winner. The loser is legally bound by the order, the implementation of which carries all the authority and sanction of the court.

One professional mediator has summed up the differences between the processes as follows:

- mediation 'involves helping people to decide for themselves';
- adjudication and arbitration 'involves helping people by deciding for them' (A.S. Meyer, Chairman, New York State Mediation Board, 1960, p. 164).

Negotiation by lawyers

Mediation must be distinguished from those negotiations, however conciliatory, typically conducted by lawyers. Many matrimonial disputes are formally settled by legal advisers advising and representing the parties. These bilateral negotiation processes are conducted by professionals (whether solicitors or barristers) who act on their clients' behalf. The parties are not present nor therefore do they participate in the negotiations, the pace, substance and tone of which is controlled by the lawyers.[3] In

---

3   A new approach to lawyers negotiating family disputes is one called 'collaborative family law'. Derived from North America, this involves lawyers, their clients (couples mainly) and other professionals (such as counsellors) working together in round-table meetings to negotiate financial and other agreements outside the litigation and court process. A feature of this approach is that 'collaborative' lawyers agree not to be involved in any subsequent litigation that might ensue in

comparison, in mediation the parties conduct the negotiations themselves and reach their own agreements with the help of the mediator (see Chapter 3 for the distinction between the giving of advice, which is contrary to the mediator's role, and that of information, which is acceptable).

Empirical research on lawyer negotiations is limited, most studies being based on self-reports of lawyers (often self-serving) following completed negotiations. Observational studies of actual negotiations are rare. North American research on divorce negotiations has found these to be 'depressingly consistent' with negotiations in a variety of legal contexts (Menkel-Meadow, 1993a, p. 369). Findings showed a desire not to bargain too hard and to settle cases quickly for the 'going rate'. This was the case especially where lawyers were 'repeat players' with each other and sought to reach 'standardized solutions'. There was little evidence of problem-solving or focusing on the individual needs and interests of particular clients. The general evidence is that cases settle quickly with little 'negotiation intensity' (often settling on the basis of first offers) or bargaining of either a principled or unprincipled nature, as both sides try 'to cut a quick deal' that is often 'fairer' to the lawyers' payment incentives than to particular clients (Menkel-Meadow, 1993b, p. 371).

In the UK, notwithstanding the increasing resort to alternative dispute resolution processes, a majority of matrimonial legal disputes are still dealt with by means of lawyer negotiations, which take place in private (see Chapter 11 for discussion of the impact of power imbalances on lawyer negotiation) and occur largely within the framework of litigation (Davis et al., 1994; Roberts, 1995a).

While a minority of family lawyers do undoubtedly exacerbate conflict, the combativeness of lawyers should not be exaggerated. The Code of Practice of Resolution (formerly the Solicitors Family Law Association), for example, reflects an awareness of the impact family solicitors have on relations between their clients and recognizes the need for solicitors to adopt conciliatory and settlement-making approaches in the interests of all the parties, including the children. The Code of Practice, which sets out the principles and good practice guidelines of a constructive approach to dealing with family law matters, has been incorporated in the Law Society's Family Law Protocol and endorsed by the courts. All family solicitors who are members of Resolution are expected to adhere to the Code unless the law, professional rules or clear client instructions contradict it (Walsh, 2006).

---

the same case should 'collaborative lawyering' fail to resolve the issues. The first British collaborative family law group trained in the approach (of over a hundred in England and Wales) was established in 2004.

Mediation and social work

Differences between mediation and social work may appear less obvious perhaps than the differences between mediation and the processes of the adversary legal system, but they are no less significant.

Location of authority

The source of the social worker's authority has three possible locations: the employing agency, the law (for example, in the case of probation officers) and the professional expertise derived from a specialist body of knowledge and skill.

The authority of the mediator derives from a tacit understanding between the parties and the mediator. The parties consent to participate with the mediator in the mediation process. The mediator is only there with the permission of the parties. To the extent that they are aware of their right not to participate if they so choose, the parties retain ultimate control. The attributes and the skills of the mediator in promoting communication and assisting decision-making is a second source of authority. Furthermore, as Professor Fuller (1971, p. 315) has pointed out, one must not ignore the fact that 'the mediator's power may largely derive from the simple fact that he is there and that his help is badly needed'. The mediator's authority therefore may derive as much from the 'urgency' of the situation as from any special gifts of the mediator.

Self-determination

The ideal of self-determination as one of social work's fundamental values (McDermott, 1975) may appear superficially to resemble the 'party control' that is the central tenet of mediation. Self-determination in social work practice, however, refers primarily to the way the client may participate in the solution to problems and to the fact that the social worker will refrain from interfering except 'in essentials' (McDermott, 1975, p. 144, quoting Alan Keith-Lucas). The client, in other words, is subject to the ultimate controlling authority vested in the social worker. The use of the term 'client' itself underlines the dependence inherent in the social work relationship, implying as it does an inability to identify one's own needs or to discriminate between a range of possibilities (Mayer and Timms, 1970).

Self-determination is also used to refer to an increase in psychological insight gained by the client into his own needs and motives as a means towards, or condition of, furthering his own development (McDermott, 1975).

The precepts of mediation are, in contrast, the competence of the parties to define their disputes and assert their own meanings, their right and power to make their own decisions and the opportunity to do so. The mediator is subject to their authority, not vice versa.

Expertise

The expertise of social workers is claimed to lie in the body of knowledge and skills from which their professional authority derives. In mediation in family disputes, the expertise of the mediator lies in a method of dispute resolution that recognizes and protects the right of the parties to make their own decisions in matters over which they are expert, for example, their own children's lives. Where the parties themselves lack the requisite expertise necessary for informed decision-making (for example, legal, tax, welfare rights input), it is the responsibility of the mediator to ensure that this is included in the process. The expertise of the mediator, involving as it does no authority to impose an outcome or to give advice, determines the unique, even paradoxical nature of the professional relationship of the mediator with the parties. Only in the most exceptional circumstances should mediators find it necessary to contemplate asserting superior authority and use their specialist knowledge (for example, on child development) in order to influence the direction of negotiations.

Competence

The professional ideology of social workers is one properly focused on concerns about child welfare and child protection, the domain of public law where parental competence may be appropriately challenged by the state. This may be contrasted with the sphere of mediated decision-making under the private law (such as in relation to issues arising from separation and divorce) where parental competence is not legally challenged and there is a presumption of party competence. The parties to mediation and their children – to apply the Finer Report (1974, para. 4.285) – should not be seen as 'clients' and still less as 'patients' or 'objects of assistance' but rather as 'subjects of rights'. There is a view that the tensions and sorrows of divorce may result in a 'diminished capacity to the parent' (Wallerstein and Kelly, 1980, p. 36). A preoccupation with one's own troubles, however, is not a disqualification from competence to negotiate nor a good reason to relinquish decision-making responsibility to others. The goals both of social work and of mediation would be distorted in the latter intervention, being deployed as a means of extending surveillance over separating or divorcing couples and their families under the guise of 'child protection'.

Impartiality

Alliances between social workers and their clients are frequently established as one of the ways of building up trusting relationships. A mediator, however, must remain impartial between the two parties to the dispute and never form or be perceived to form an alliance with one or the other.

Assessments

Whatever the limitations of objective assessment in a child-care context (Sutton, 1981), assessments are made by social workers as part of the process of determining strategies of treatment or action.

The concept of assessment is inappropriate in mediation, first because of its inseparability from the treatment, which is carried out on its basis: 'assessment is impossible without treatment; treatment is an assessment' (Sutton, 1981, p. 69); secondly because it inevitably shifts the locus of knowledge and therefore of power from the parties, to the person making the assessment (for example, Walker, 1986). Assessments in social work are also confidential. In mediation everything is out in the open. If a record is kept, it is of the bare facts and outcome and is not withheld from the parties. In fact, some mediators encourage the parties to record such details themselves (see also Chapter 9).

Short-term work

One of the features of family mediation is that it is time-limited. On average, children-only issues are mediated in one to three sessions and four to six sessions cover all issues – that is, financial, property as well as children issues. The short-term focus of the work is, on the whole, in contrast with the longer term nature of social work, involving as it often does the building up of relationships between the social worker and their client. Some social work is, of course, short-term or 'task-centred', for example the provision of material assistance, though even a request for material help may be interpreted by some social workers as the 'presenting' problem (Mayer and Timms, 1970).

Focusing on the future

Broadly speaking, the mediation process looks to the future for it is recognized that the past cannot be negotiated over.[4] As Gulliver (1979) demonstrates, change is intrinsic to the dynamic process of exploration that negotiations involve. The mediation process itself involves a movement away from sterile interpersonal quarrelling and recrimination toward an examination of future options. While information about the past may well be relevant to an understanding of the dispute and should not be excluded, it should, in any event, come from the parties themselves. The mediator is not concerned to examine what went wrong. There may often, therefore, have to be a deliberate steering away from the minefield of the past over which there will inevitably be differences of perspective. The facts of the past can only be adjudicated over (see Chapter 2). In social work practice, on the other hand, the case history, by definition retrospective in outlook, is an important tool for making judgements and determining strategies for the present and future.

Until 1989, when the principle of openness in relation to assessment, decision-making and intervention was implemented by giving social work clients the right of access to any personal information held on file, the case history was the property of the professionals and was not available to those it discussed. While this change of attitude and approach to openness was welcomed as a most significant development in social work, the low number of clients who have requested access has raised questions. Several reasons for this have been suggested, including the number of grounds for excluding clients from access (for example, exemptions to protect sources of information and third parties), fears that files can be edited, lack of knowledge of the right of access to personal files, and difficulties of access for family members.

The Family Group Conference (FGC)

Since being first piloted in Britain in the 1990s, the family group conference is a social work practice approach of growing application by local authorities in public law child-care cases where there is a plan or decision to be made about a child's welfare. There are now many FGC projects specialising in addressing a range of problems associated with child welfare and protection – youth offending, domestic abuse, school truancy and exclusions and other child protection concerns. The objective of the FGC is to secure the

---

4   It is accepted that the subject of mediation and its relation to the dimension of the past and its association with issues of 'justice', is more complex and controversial than is stated here (see Chapter 11 for further discussion).

co-operation of the family in planning for the future protection and well-being of the child. It may be that the FGC is a useful tool for avoiding the issue of court proceedings, although it can also be recommended by the court to take place during proceedings. The FGC does not replace or remove the need for a child protection conference where that is necessary and it can be of value in enabling an outline child protection plan to become a fully developed one (Walsh, 2006).

At a family group conference, the wider family (this can include friends) can meet together and receive specific information from the relevant agencies about the concerns and the needs of the child concerned and why a decision about future arrangements for the child is required. Participants in the FGC are given time on their own to make a decision that protects and promotes the child's welfare subject to whatever 'baseline' condition the referring agency may stipulate. The decision may include identifying family and community support to enable the child to remain with his/her parents, identifying a placement of the child with the wider family if remaining with the parents is not possible, or, where a kinship placement is not possible, allowing the wider family to support a plan for the child (Walsh, 2006).

The FGC is designed to be an inclusive and effective way of involving the wider family in the decision-making process, giving them and the child a voice in the arrangements being made. In that respect, there may be similarities with the decision-making process of mediation in the context of public law cases. While these processes are not mutually exclusive and may well supplement one another, there are important basic differences between FGCs and mediation:

- FGCs are not designed to resolve disputes and are not appropriate therefore in those cases where antagonism exists between social workers and the family, thus making it difficult for there to be co-operation between them.
- FGCs may be inappropriate when the problems that exist arise from conflict between birth families and foster or adoptive parents. Mediation may be a more suitable process in such circumstances, for its specific aims are to reduce conflict, open a dialogue between the parties and focus attention on the child.
- In Britain, FGCs operate as schemes set up by local authorities. The decisions of the FGCs about the child's future have to remain within the framework of previous decisions taken by the local authority. This role was confirmed in a government paper, which stated: 'FGCs do not replace or remove the need of child protection conferences which should always be held when the relevant criteria are met' and 'Where there are child protection concerns, they should be developed and

implemented under the auspices of the ACPC'[5] (Alternative Dispute Resolution Project Final Report, 1998).

Mediation and advice, guidance, counselling and psychotherapy

Mediation as a dispute resolution negotiation process differs in a number of respects – goals, rationale, process and method, and theoretical assumptions – from the spectrum of extensive therapeutic interventions that range from the brief, task-centred intervention of practical advice-giving and guidance (approximately one to three sessions) to the more extended intervention of counselling (approximately six to ten sessions) and psychotherapy (extending perhaps to three years) with a less circumscribed focus and possibly a more intangible outcome. These interventions each therefore 'vary in their therapeutic scope, appropriateness and degree of required sustained commitment' (Palmer and McMahon, 2006, p. 103). Whatever the label, all these interventions, notwithstanding the complexity of an extensive and growing range of practice approaches and a variety of theoretical frameworks, reveal broadly similar common features.

- They are treatment interventions operating in the field of mental health.
- All share an intention to help people think, feel, behave and relate differently.
- All aspire to work from a common set of values, in particular the adoption by the intervener of a non-judgmental and empathic stance, which combines with an essential quality of listening ability and skill 'to assist their clients in developing insight into their problems to help them make appropriate changes in their lives' (Bor and Palmer, 2002, p. 25).
- A key factor in all these interventions is the central therapeutic role and function of the helping relationship. Emphasis on the significance and role of the relationship varies. This relationship may be deployed either as the sole means of effecting therapeutic change, as in the psychoanalytic or person-centred approach, or as the vehicle of change, as in the cognitive-behavioural approach (Bor and Palmer, 2002; Palmer and McMahon, 2006). Effectiveness lies in the *quality* of the helping relationship – more, that is, than the application of specific treatment regimes.

---

5   Department of Health Consultation Paper (1998), *Working Together to Safeguard Children: New Government Proposals for Inter-Agency Co-operation*, 7.15, 7.16.

- Whatever the therapeutic framework, the therapeutic process covers recognizable stages – a critical assessment stage (whether formal or informal, comprehensive or minimal) and a diagnosis stage (incorporating history-taking) leading to the choice of the most effective therapeutic intervention.
- Each practice approach or model is based on the core assumptions it makes about the nature of the human condition. This forms the particular frame of reference that will influence the choice of treatment intervention: 'These assumptions will fundamentally colour the counsellor's beliefs about the nature of the problems for which people seek help, the type of intervention which should be offered and the significance and meaning of the relationship between [the counsellor] and the person [s/he] hope[s] to assist' (Palmer and McMahon, 2006, p. 14). Examples of the main theoretical traditions on which practice across these different therapeutic interventions draws (in complex ways) are the phenomenological/humanistic/existential strand, the psychoanalytic/psychodynamic strand and the cognitive behavioural strand (Woolfe et al., 2003).

Therapeutic intervention in the context of the family, rather than the individual (as above), is distinguished in more detail below, from mediation in the context of the family.

Mediation and family therapy

Mediation and family therapy are forms of intervention that also differ essentially in terms of their objectives, process and method, and theoretical assumptions. The need to clarify and distinguish these two areas of practice became pressing, particularly in the 1980s, when the danger emerged in Britain that the young plant of family mediation could be distorted by a graft of family therapy assumptions and techniques.[6] (For a full debate on this topic in *Mediation Quarterly*, see Roberts, 1992; Haynes, 1992; Amundson and Fong, 1993; also Walker and Robinson, 1992.)

Family therapy posits a theoretical dimension, that of the system, different from those of the therapeutic interventions related to the individual. Family therapy has been described as a way of 'conceptualizing the cause and cure of psychiatric problems' (Haley and Hoffman, 1967, p. v). In the view of the family therapist, the 'site of pathology' is the family rather than the individual and the set of relationships within which that individual is embedded (Minuchin, 1974). The scope of family therapy is wide. It involves

---

6   Another such danger emerged in the 1990s in respect of a similar 'bid for turf' by family lawyers.

not only 'a technical approach towards treatment … it is also a theoretical view of pathology giving rise to a whole range of treatment possibilities' (Walrond-Skinner, 1976, p. 6).

The primary objective of family therapy is to modify 'dysfunctional' behaviour. It does this by challenging and changing the organization of the family in such a way that the perceptions and experiences of the family members change (Minuchin, 1974, p. 13). The basic assumption of family therapy therefore is of dysfunction, possibly psychiatric, in the family that requires treatment.

As far as mediation is concerned, marital breakdown and the disputes that arise from it are not regarded as symptoms of psychopathology, nor are the parties regarded as suffering from incapacities that render therapeutic intervention necessary. Nor is it the object of mediation to challenge the perceptions of the parties. On the contrary, the parties are regarded as competent both to define the issues for themselves and to come to their own decisions. Their perceptions are seen as essential to an accurate understanding of their dispute and its context. The focus of mediation is a modest one, limited in most cases to the purpose of negotiated joint decision-making on the specific substantive issues in dispute. If the process and outcomes of mediation lead to a reduction of bitterness and conflict in the relationship between the parties, then the process can be therapeutic in the widest sense. That quality of improved understanding is one of most distinctive benefits of the process but it need not be its primary object.

The second fundamental difference between mediation and family therapy is that the therapist assumes a leadership role (Minuchin, 1974; Walrond-Skinner, 1976). The mediator does not. Whatever method of family therapy is adopted (Minuchin's structural approach, Haley's strategic approach, the Mental Research Institute's (Palo Alto Group) brief therapy, Epstein and Loos' dialogical constructivist approach or the Milan model of systemic family therapy), all adopt a mode of intervention that places the therapist as a knowing expert in a position of exceptional power in relation to the family. This result is deliberate, for as one leading family therapist has stated, it is only from a position of leadership that the therapist has the freedom to manipulate the therapeutic system: 'The therapeutic contract must recognize the therapist's position as an expert in experimental social manipulation' (Minuchin, 1974, p. 140). The systemic approach of the Milan method of family therapy exemplifies the leadership role of the therapist: 'When conducting the session the therapist must immediately demonstrate that he will lead it and dictate its form and pace' (Campbell et al., n.d., p. 16). Power also lies in the therapist's claim to have the monopoly on meaning. This monopoly involves explaining the problem in terms of the therapist's conceptual framework, which determines the diagnosis and method of treatment.

The mediator, on the other hand, affirms the supremacy of the parties' meanings and decision-making authority. The parties' control over the definition of the issues is fundamental to their control over the decision-making process and its outcome. One of the first tasks of the mediator is to gain an understanding of the issues as they are perceived by the parties themselves. This means giving paramount worth to the perceptions, feelings and meanings of the parties. The mediator can have no privileged perspective on how to view and interpret experience. The skill of the mediator must lie in facilitating the crucial exchanges of accurate and constructive information that lead, through adjustments of expectations and preferences, to greater understanding, co-ordination and order, and eventually to a settlement of the dispute (Gulliver, 1979). The mediator's expertise lies, therefore, in ensuring that the capacity of the parties to take responsibility for their own affairs is recognized and protected.

General systems theory as applied to the analysis of the family has been developed in the context of family therapy (for example, Walrond-Skinner, 1976; see also Minuchin, 1974). Systems-thinking in its application to family mediation exemplifies this inextricable connection (Parkinson, 1986; James and Wilson, 1986).

In the 1980s it was argued that mediation practice could be fruitfully expanded by invoking the ideas and techniques of family systems thinking. It was claimed, in particular, that family systems theory contributed two valuable insights to the practice of family mediation:

- An integral aspect of family life was the interdependence of its members.
- Problems and tensions affecting one or more members of a family generally affected other members as well (Parkinson, 1986).

No one would deny the soundness of the observation that an individual does not live in a personal, social or cultural vacuum (Seidenberg, 1973). What could be challenged however, was that these axioms of common sense were peculiar to systems-thinking or family therapy. The stress and sorrow of individuals in conflict inevitably touches others – family members and especially children, friends and colleagues. An understanding of the impact of the legal, economic, political, social, gender, cultural, ethnic, family and psychological environment of any dispute between individuals, particularly one involving children, is fundamental to the discussions that occur in mediation. The mediation process itself involves an examination of the broader implications for the parties and their families of their differences, their common interests, the various possible courses of action and their consequences. In other words, the recognition of the relevance of the interactive process is not a monopoly of the systems approach. Nor could it be assumed that the best means of helping people to appreciate the inter-personal and socio-cultural considerations of their predicament was by means of a family systems framework and/or the application of family therapy techniques.

Not only are the assumptions, objectives and methods of these two models of intervention incompatible, there also seem to be a number of hazards associated with attempts to apply family therapy approaches to mediation.

First, the boundaries between family mediation and family therapy could become dangerously blurred. The negotiation and decision-making processes of mediation could become tainted with the stigma of family dysfunction and treatment associated with family therapy. Furthermore, the values of mediation, such as the respect for the parties' capacity to behave as reasonable adults, could be undermined. One example of this danger is evidenced in the statement of a leading North American therapist/mediator: 'In many ways the mediator must act as a parent figure to the parents since their struggles are often not unlike those of siblings squabbling over joint possessions' (Saposnek, 1985, p. 176).

Second, the terminology of family therapy could be imposed on mediation and its processes. The liberal and inexact use of the word 'system', for example, and the adoption of the language and typologies of family therapy (for example, the 'enmeshed', 'disengaged' and 'autistic' modes of classifying families) could be viewed as the colonizing attempt of one group of professionals, the family therapists, to appropriate mediation as an extension of their own activities, by means of the transforming processes of their specialist discourse.

Third, some practitioners have drawn a distinction between the use of family therapy techniques in *therapy* and their deployment in *mediation*. It has been argued that at a time of crisis and stress, such as attends family break-up, family therapy can offer a means of dealing with the underlying obstacles to rational communication. Family systems theory, in particular, is considered to be useful for dealing with intractable or irrational couples – those who are locked in destructive conflict. Haynes (1992), for example, while warning against resort to the family therapy toolbox when stuck as a mediator, outlines the conditions that should determine any application of such strategic interventions:

- an awareness of the specific strategy,
- an ability to predict the anticipated outcome of the strategy,
- the application of the strategy to the negotiating rather than the dynamic behaviour of the parties,
- an immediate return to mediation when that strategy has been implemented.

The determinist behavioural assumptions that have informed family systems thinking affect the techniques that are used to bring about change – for example, circular questioning, hypothesizing and paradoxical interventions. The systems view is that challenging and changing behaviour will lead to changes in perceptions and experience. This is the reverse of the process by means of which change is perceived to be brought about through learning and an improvement of understanding (see for example, Deutsch, 1973; Eckhoff, 1969; Gulliver, 1979; Stevens, 1963; Stulberg, 1981).

In a systems approach, the therapist seeks to effect a change in 'belief system' by means of changing the system's behavioural interaction. This requires the use of techniques designed to manipulate behaviour patterns in order to modify perceptions. These techniques are designed therefore to place the therapist in a position of power and are acknowledged to be intentionally manipulative, that is, covert (Campbell et al., n.d.; Minuchin, 1974; Walrond-Skinner, 1976). The application of such techniques in mediation (for example, family assessment, the questioning techniques of the Milan method and the use of one-way mirrors and concealed video-recorders) are not what the parties expect, and with or without their express knowledge and prior consent, they serve only to increase the controlling power and manipulative apparatus of the therapist/mediator.

Systems therapists have not aimed to engage the informed participation of their patients. As a result, the family remains essentially passive, unable to recognize the exact nature of the demands made upon it. In some cases, this may involve the therapist engaging in a covert adversarial power struggle with the family if they prove 'resistant' (Howard and Shepherd, 1987). Obviously there is a tension between this approach and the view that among the crucial characteristics that distinguish human beings is their capacity to form intentions, become aware of alternatives, make choices and acquire control over their own behaviour (Lukes, 1973). The presuppositions underlying a systems approach negate the significance of human intention in the interactive process (Watson, 1987). It is precisely this component of intention that is central to mediation. As such, the systems approach is incompatible with the assumptions and goals of mediation. As Lukes (1973, p. 133) notes: 'We cease to respect someone when we fail to treat him as an agent and a chooser, as a self from which actions and choices emanate'.

In the 1990s, the post-modern discussions of family therapy reflected a general move towards an awareness of the ethical implications of professional power and control and, in particular, a move away from open attempts to assert an expert role in the treatment process and towards working with families in a 'person-centred' way (for example, see Epstein and Loos, 1989; Goolishan and Anderson, 1992; Larner, 1995; Anderson, 2001; Street, 2003). A greater awareness was evident too that the focus on the family system could lead to the neglect of the impact of external social issues such as race, class and gender (Woolfe et al., 2003). Notwithstanding these theoretical shifts of paradigm (the main phases of which have been identified by Dallos and Draper, 2000), 'the features of this movement ... have continued in the same direction' (Street, 2003). The conceptual framework of family therapy continues to be one focused on context and interpersonal processes and, in practice, the degree to which opportunities for professional domination are reduced, must remain in doubt.

Finally, the therapist is concerned with the underlying dynamics of relationships. Therefore, there can be a tendency to regard the specific issues focused on in mediation as 'presenting' problems, symptoms of the more profound 'real' conflicts or problems (Kressel, 1985, p. 76). This view has three important implications for mediation:

- The insights of the therapist/mediator in deciding what is 'real' may be accorded greater validity than those of the parties.
- In the making of interpretations, there is a risk of escalating conflict and antagonizing the parties. Kressel (1985, p. 33) cites the example of a well-meaning divorce mediator who tried to break an impasse in negotiations over a custody dispute by suggesting to the husband that his inflexible bargaining position might be the product of his understandable hurt and anger at being rejected by his wife rather than because of any doubt about his wife's ability as a parent. The husband refuted this interpretation vehemently and accused the mediator of partiality and lack of understanding. Consumer research in Britain has confirmed that the parties resent such attempts at psychological interpretation, regarding them as presumptuous and often erroneous (Davis and Roberts, 1988). The therapist's traditional 'assumption of repressed feelings' may be inappropriate in mediation (Saposnek, 1985, p. 45). This assumption derives from the belief that some emotional catharsis is necessary if ambivalence or other unresolved feelings about the divorce are to be sorted out. Only then, it is argued, will constructive negotiation on the issues in dispute be possible. Although tension may be lowered by the expression of strong feeling, excessive emotional exchanges can be destructive and lead to a worsening of relationships and of the problem. Mediators usually discourage such expression of negative emotion for this reason. In any event, one at least of the parties will often refuse to discuss the emotional aspects of the break-up.

Even as an advocate of the therapeutic orientation in mediation, Kressel (1985, pp. 275–8) cautions against its application in practice:

- because of the demands it places on the diagnostic competence of the mediator,
- because of the complications it adds to the already difficult role of the mediator,
- because of the risks it runs of alienating the parties,
- because it is likely to be ineffective: long-standing patterns of relating cannot easily be changed by a short-term 'task focused' intervention.

In this context, Kressel (1985, p. 277) cites the advantages of the clarity, simplicity and 'time honoured interpretation of the mediator's role' – the modest profile of the mediator, the encouragement of the parties' autonomy and the avoidance of the adoption of standards of settlement foreign to the parties.

2 The emergence of family mediation

There is, in short, special appropriateness in taking a long, hard look at a social invention which has managed to transform the method of combat from destruction to construction without, in so doing, abridging the right ... to a forum in which ... differences can be worked over in the most vigorous and thorough fashion. (Douglas, 1957, p. 69)

Since the Second World War, there has been a steady increase in the number of divorces in Britain, although an increase has also occurred in many other Western countries. There are also large differentials in the level of divorce across Europe, with higher rates observed in Northern European countries, including Britain, and far lower levels in Southern European countries, such as Italy (where divorce became legal only in 1971). Demographers are unclear whether these differences represent different stages of transition or whether they are likely to persist. (Clarke and Berrington, 1999). While divorces in England and Wales increased rapidly following the enactment of the 1969 Divorce Law Reform Act in 1971, the number of divorces did fall between 1993 and 1994 from 165,000 to 158,000, representing the first fall since 1989 (Family Policy Studies Centre, 1996). Over that same period, the marriage rate also dropped dramatically, by 50 per cent. The divorce rate rose again in the mid-1990s reaching 161,000 in 1997 and then subsequently stabilized at a level of about three divorces per 1000 population, levelling out at below 150,000 a year (Joseph Rowntree Foundation, 2004). Estimates then indicated that 41 per cent of marriages in England and Wales would end in divorce, the highest divorce rate in the European Community (though still significantly lower than that seen in the United States), and about one in four newborn children would see their parents divorce. Figures from the Office for National Statistics confirm these estimates, showing that in 2004 the number of divorces increased to 167,116, the highest since 1996 and the fourth successive annual increase, although 7.2 per cent lower than the highest number of divorces, which peaked in 1993 at 180,018 (see

29

Walsh, 2006). It should be borne in mind that statistics refer to the number of decrees absolute granted and do not take into account marriages that are extant although in difficulty, and couples who have separated but are not divorced (Clarke and Berrington, 1999). Current estimates suggest that two thirds of those divorcing and a substantial and increasing number (precise figures unknown) of those who separate after living together have children under 16 (Hunt with Roberts, 2004).[1]

The rise in divorce has to be seen in the context too of the many changes that now affect family life – not only do increasing numbers of couples live together outside marriage but British society is increasingly secular, pluralistic, multi-cultural and ethnically diverse, same-sex relationships can be accorded legal recognition, and many children are born as a result of technological advances in reproductive science rather than 'naturally' (Munby, 2005).

Notwithstanding the 'normality' of divorce and separation in British society, for all those directly affected it is a crisis, painful and uniquely personal and considered to be, after bereavement, the second most stressful life event. The ending of intimate ties unleashes powerful emotions, such as feelings of loss, betrayal, rejection, failure, grief, anger and guilt, as well as relief and a sense of victory. At the same time, harsh and exhausting changes in the circumstances of daily life are often precipitated, resulting not infrequently in lowered standards of living, financial hardship and ill-health. These changes, such as moving house, having less money and increased child care responsibilities, would be demanding at the best of times. Yet, notwithstanding the heavy pressures and personal distress that family members may be labouring under, there is a risk that in these circumstances the emotional instability or irrationality of divorcing or separating individuals may be exaggerated (Kressel, 1985). Selfish, even destructive, behaviour should not be give greater emphasis than those qualities of courage, resilience, strength and forbearance that are also shown both by adults and by children in these testing times (Burgoyne, 1984).

Many writers (Bohannan, 1971; Wallerstein and Kelly, 1980; Haynes, 1981; Kressel, 1985; Clulow, 1995) acknowledge that divorce is not simply an event marked by the legal 'rite of passage' that obtaining a decree absolute involves, but 'a complex social phenomenon as well as a complex personal experience' (Bohannan, 1971, p. 33). In what he terms 'the six stations of divorce', Bohannan describes the overlapping experiences that constitute, in varying order and degrees of intensity, the processes involved in divorce. He describes these as follows:

---

1   It is estimated that 28 per cent of children will be affected by divorce before the age of 16. Statistics show that, in 2001, 146,914 children in England and Wales experienced parental divorce, 68 per cent of them aged ten or less and 24 per cent under five (Hunt with Roberts, 2004).

1. the *emotional divorce* characterized by feelings of hurt, anger, loss of attraction and trust;
2. the *legal divorce*, which creates re-marriageability;
3. the *economic divorce* which marks the re-organization of the financial and property arrangements;
4. the *'co-parental' divorce* which involves matters of residence of and contact with children and which produces, in his view, the most enduring pain of divorce; for example, in the way parents have to come to terms with the realization that there can be no 'clean break' where there are children, and that, bar situations of moral and physical danger, the relationship between one parent and the child ceases to be any business of the other parent;
5. the *community divorce*, which covers the impact of divorce on the social life of divorcees, for example the way married friends treat divorcees and the organizations available to meet the needs of information and friendship of divorced people;
6. the *'psychic' divorce*, which describes the means by which individual autonomy is recovered. This is thought to be the most difficult yet the most constructive achievement of all.

A high incidence of divorce and separation is now accepted as an inevitable fact of life. The concerns of policy makers and researchers about rising rates of divorce and separation have focused not on divorce itself but on the post-divorce period, especially on the need to mitigate some of the harmful consequences of divorce, particularly for children. Research has highlighted the numbers of children who are affected by family breakdown and the 'harm' they may suffer – emotional, educational, social and behavioural – with implications for their future well-being (Rogers and Pryor, 1998). On the other hand, recent large-scale studies (for example, Hetherington and Kelly, 2002) indicate that 'a majority of children cope reasonably well with family re-ordering and continue to function in the normal range' and current research that explores children's own views, opens new perspectives on children's lives (Wade and Smart, 2002, p. 1). In respect of the impact of parental separation for instance, a view of children as passive victims of their social circumstances has been challenged by one where children are seen to be 'active social agents' capable of thinking for themselves and acting upon and influencing their circumstances (Wade and Smart, 2002, p. 1).

Two government committee reports exemplified early concerns about the social impact of divorce and separation by espousing a new spirit in which family breakdown should be viewed. The Finer Report (1974, para. 4.313) affirmed the need to 'civilize' the consequences of breakdown by recommending that the 'winding up' of marriage failure should be accomplished by the couple making the most rational and efficient arrangements for their own and their children's future. The Report first gave public recognition to the idea of conciliation in family disputes, which it defined as:

> the process of engendering common sense, reasonableness and agreement in dealing with the consequences of estrangement ... assisting the parties to deal with the consequences of the established breakdown of their marriage, whether resulting in a divorce or a separation, by reaching agreements or giving consents or reducing the area of conflict upon custody, support, access to and education of the children, financial provision, the disposition of the matrimonial home, lawyers' fees and every other matter arising from the breakdown which calls for a decision on future arrangements. (Finer Report, 1974, paras 4.305 and 4.288)

The idea of conciliation contained in the Finer Report thus expressed this fresh approach to family breakdown in terms of two objectives. First, that it should be approached in a quiet restrained way with the least possible bitterness and fighting; and second, that the parties themselves should take primary responsibility for resolving their own disputes (Roberts, 1983a). The Booth Report (1985, para. 3.10) reinforced these recommendations:

> It is of the essence of conciliation that responsibility remains at all times with the parties themselves to identify and seek agreement on all the issues arising from the breakdown of their relationship.

From the 1930s until 1971, the terms 'conciliation' and 'reconciliation' had been used inter-changeably in English family law to refer to the repair of failing relationships (Dingwall and Eekelaar, 1988). Then, in a Practice Direction on Matrimonial Conciliation issued in 1971 by the President of the Family Division, conciliation was distinguished for the first time, both from reconciliation and from the preparation of welfare reports for the court (Parkinson, 1983). It is in the context of industrial relations, however, that conciliation as a form of alternative dispute resolution has had the longest history, dating from the Conciliation Act 1896.

Following the Booth Report, continuing concern both about the current prevalence of divorce and that the divorce process was making things worse for couples and their children, resulted in the publication in 1988 by the Law Commission of 'Facing the Future – A discussion Paper on the Ground for Divorce' (Law Com. No. 170). The Law Commission's findings were that the present law was confusing and unjust and fulfilled none of its original objectives, namely the support of marriages with a chance of survival and, secondly, the decent burial of those marriages that were dead, with the minimum of bitterness, embarrassment and humiliation. Extensive consultation with professional groups and representative sectors of the public plus additional research endorsed the findings of Law Com. No. 170, and the Law Commission went on to publish its Divorce Reform Proposals, 'Family Law and the Ground for Divorce' (Law Com. No. 192) in 1990. These included two further objectives of a 'good' divorce law:

- to encourage as far as possible the amicable resolution of practical issues relating to the couple's home, finances and children and the proper discharge of their responsibilities to one another and their children;
- to minimize the harm that the children may suffer both at the time and in the future and to promote so far as possible the continued sharing of parental responsibility for them (Law Commission, 1990, p. 2); this objective was fundamental also to the Children Act 1989.

The Law Commission Report recommended that irretrievable breakdown of marriage remains the sole ground for divorce. In a radical departure from the existing law, the Report and its accompanying draft Bill introduced, with the overwhelming support of the vast majority of consultees, the period of consideration and reflection – the 'cooling off' period or breathing space – as a new way of demonstrating irretrievable breakdown of marriage. Within this period of consideration and reflection, the parties' own responsibility for decision-making was given central emphasis. The other radical innovation of the proposals was the incorporation of mediation as 'an important element in developing a new and more constructive approach to the problems of marital breakdown and divorce' (Law Commission, 1990, para. 7.24). These proposals were subsequently incorporated into the Green Paper, the White Paper on Divorce Reform (both of which were titled *Looking to the Future: Mediation and the Ground for Divorce*) and then the proposed Family Law Act 1996. Despite the hope that the Family Law Act promised for introducing a 'good' divorce law, those divorce reform sections were not enacted. (For further discussion on the Family Law Act and on other legal developments, see Chapter 3.)

In the last decade, notwithstanding its shelving of the Family Law Act 1996, the government has sought to shift family justice in directions aimed at improving the welfare of children and protecting vulnerable people at stressful times (see for example, numerous consultation papers, working papers and reports,[2] and legislation[3]). One such direction is towards 'early dispute resolution' with family disputes arising from divorce and separation kept away from the courts and within the domain of decision-making by couples themselves wherever possible (The Private Law Programme, 2004; Walsh, 2006).

---

2   One notable example is the Report to the Lord Chancellor of the Children Act Sub-Committee (CASC) of the Advisory Board on Family Law in 2003. This Report, *Making Contact Work*, followed extensive interdisciplinary consultation.

3   The Adoption and Children Act 2002 and the Children Act 2004.

As in North America, two themes, often intertwined, can be discerned informing the impetus behind official enthusiasm for mediation in family disputes and in the civil justice system in Britain (Woolf, 1995). The 'warm theme' celebrates mediation as a potentially superior method of dispute resolution and refers to the 'impulse to replace adversary conflict by a process of conciliation to bring the parties into mutual accord' (Galanter, 1984, p. 2). The 'cool theme' emphasizes administrative efficiency and cost-savings (for example, in the reduction of court hearings or welfare reports) at a time when matrimonial disputes account for two thirds of the civil legal aid outlay[4] and the civil justice system has been indicted by its own most senior judge as being too expensive, too slow, too complex and too unequal (Woolf, 1995).

The advantages of mediation in family disputes

There has long been consensus that mediation can offer a number of advantages over conventional legal approaches to the resolution of family disputes, particularly where children are concerned (see Chapter 10 for a more detailed discussion of this topic in respect of children). First, the decisions in mediation are made by those who have to live with them, rather than by some third party, however wise and well-meaning. The retention of control over their own affairs can also assist the parties in their recovery of self-respect and dignity. Although there may appear to be temporary relief in legal experts taking over problems, the limitations of this can soon become apparent. While the law can provide protection from individual aggression or state intrusion, 'it also encourages the isolation that makes protection necessary' (Auerbach, 1983, p. 13). Furthermore,

> [a]lthough a lawyer can provide reassuring guidance, in loco parentis, the price of protection is still dependence. Even as a dangerous adversary is fended off, the judge looms as a menacing authority figure, empowered to divest a litigant of property or liberty. Autonomy vanishes as mysteriously as the smile of the Cheshire cat. (Auerbach, 1983, p. viii)

The parties, locked into a relationship of dependence, can find themselves more lacking in control than ever.

Second, a mediated agreement, because it is voluntarily consented to, is more likely to be satisfactory to the parties and therefore to be adhered to by them (Emery, 1994). Even where no agreement is reached, mediation

---

4   Latest figures contrast the average cost of legal aid in a non-mediated case, £1,682, with that of a mediated case, £752, with a saving of £930 per case (National Audit Office Report, 2007).

as a process can be of value in providing the parties with improved opportunities for communication.

In addition, mediation can be seen to straddle traditional professional boundaries in its accommodation of the multi-dimensional aspects of family disputes – legal, ethical, emotional and practical. The negotiation process has intrinsic scope for the requisite flexibility and creativity: '[i]t would be difficult to point to another thoroughly pragmatic development in the national scene making use of keener psychological insights' (Douglas, 1962, p. 3). The legal process, in comparison, is limited by the fact that it recognizes only legal norms and cannot therefore fulfil the psychological or ethical requirements as well as the requirements of legal justice for the parties and their children (Saposnek, 1983).[5] Mediation, on the other hand, allows the parties to draw up their own agendas and define issues in their own terms, incorporating what might be important to them, ethically or emotionally, however irrelevant these may be in law.

The opportunity provided in mediation for the expression of feelings can be an important advantage over the legal system, although if this is excessive or prolonged it could seriously impede rational exchange and lead to a deterioration of relations, rather than any improvement. This is not to suggest that mediation deals with the emotional side of divorce, and lawyers with its rational side. Rational decision-making is the objective of mediation, achieving this by means of what has been termed its 'person-oriented' perspective rather than by the 'act-orientation' of litigation (Fuller, 1971; see also Chapter 6 for an exploration of Simmel's view (Simmel, 1908a, trans. 1955) of the role of the mediator in realizing the principle of reason and objectivity in order to transform conflict).

One of the special features of family disputes involving children is that there are usually (though not necessarily only) two disputants involved – the parents in most cases. Fuller's analysis of mediation appraises 'the dyad' as the 'home ground' of the mediation process (Fuller, 1971, p. 310). Another special feature is that the parents are bound together through their children in a continuing and interdependent relationship, whether they like it or not (that is, unlike a relationship that involves only a brief interaction occasioned by a one-off encounter, such as a car accident or business transaction).

> The two parties are locked in a relationship that is virtually one of 'bilateral monopoly'; each is dependent for its very existence on some collaboration with the other. (Fuller, 1971, p. 310)

---

5   Yet it has also been argued that the adversarial legal system correlates with an oppositional stance necessary for some in making sense of their experience of divorce (Day Sclater, 1999).

This relationship creates the 'internal pull towards cohesion', which mediation by its nature presupposes (Fuller, 1971, p. 314). In family disputes the 'heavy interdependence' occasioned by this intermeshing of interests is likely to be of an intensity sufficient to induce in the parents a willingness, however minimal or reluctant, to collaborate in the mediation effort and reach some sort of accommodation (Fuller, 1971, p. 310). This is because the parties' common interests (namely their children) may be seen or may come to be seen as more important than who is right or who is wrong. This creates a strong pressure to follow the Confucian 'middle road', a tradition that embodies the duty of everyone, as his or her first obligation, to achieve harmony with others and with nature (Shapiro, 1981).

The mediation process is, in essence, forward-looking (but see also Chapter 11). Whereas the judge looks backwards to events of the past and makes a judgement on those facts in terms of the legal norms connected with them, the mediator looks forwards to a consideration of future options and the consequences of alternative courses of action (Eckhoff, 1969). That is what makes the mediation process singularly appropriate to the negotiation of family disputes concerning children, where future child care arrangements have to be determined over several years and where co-ordination between the parents is necessary to achieve this (Sander, 1984). This is in contrast to the powerful but once-and-for-all nature of court decision-making. While it should be noted that family jurisdiction is different in kind from other jurisdictions in that it is almost entirely discretionary, it is still the judge who decides.

There are dangers in failing to acknowledge sufficiently that family proceedings are, to a large extent, conducted on an inquisitorial basis, as well as in exaggerating the destructive influence of lawyers. Nevertheless the adversary mould of western legal systems does inevitably encourage competitive rather than co-operative attitudes and exchanges. Lawyers traditionally are expected to act as partisans, championing their own client's interests. Limited disclosure, communication through third parties, the translation of everyday language into legal discourse, the transformation of the client's objectives into legal categories plus the win/lose nature of the judge's order – all these processes impede not only a search for truth but any expression of concern for the person on the other side (Gilligan, 1982). The process of mediation, in comparison, can facilitate direct communication and confidentiality of exchange both of which are more likely to reduce misunderstanding and conflict and nurture a potential for co-operation that might not otherwise be realized. More practically, evidence indicates that disputes are resolved more quickly in mediation than by adversarial means with costs more predictable and cheaper than either lawyer negotiation or adjudication (Emery et al., 1991; Walker et al., 1994; Glasser, 1994; McCarthy and Walker, 1996a; National Audit Office Report, 2007).

Any agreement reflects arrangements at a particular moment. But circumstances and minds do change. Mediation not only enables specific practical disputes to be settled. It can also be an important 'learning experience' (Sander, 1984, p. xiii). The parties can learn how to negotiate more effectively together, and by means of this improved capacity to negotiate, better manage future differences themselves in the longer term, modifying or making new arrangements in accordance with changing circumstances (Davis and Roberts, 1988). Research concludes that reaching agreements in mediation is a vital component in the making and maintaining of co-operative relationships between divorcing parents (McCarthy and Walker, 1996b).

The intact family – whatever its form at a given historical moment – usually makes decisions without interference (except in the rare case of risk of harm to a child). Where conversations have been disrupted by family breakdown, mediation can enable these to be resumed, not only between the parties but also across generations – for example, between grandparents and fathers or mothers in relation to contact over grandchildren – thus sustaining the 'private ordering' domain. Family break-up should not become an excuse for external agencies to interfere and take control. (See Chapter 10 for discussion of children's rights and representation.)

Competing tensions within family mediation

Mediation is practised in a political, legal, ethical and economic environment. This inevitably gives rise to a number of tensions that affect a mediator's practice.

Political pressures

With the exception of the reservations of a minority of academics and feminists (for example, Freeman, 1984; Davis and Bader, 1985; Roberts, 1983a, 1986; Bottomley, 1984, 1985; Matthews, 1988; Piper, 1993), enthusiasm for mediation in Britain has not been troubled by the more widespread criticisms that emerged in the US in the 1980s (for example, Abel, 1982; Auerbach, 1983; Fiss, 1984). Examining the political implications of 'informal justice', findings there suggested that, in some cases, alternative dispute agencies such as small claims courts and landlord and tenant courts, have served to divert the legitimate claims of the more vulnerable groups in society (the poor, blacks and women) away from legal channels into forms of second-class justice that lacked the safeguards of due process and increased covert state regulation. It has been claimed that while 'informal justice' processed the small claims and minor disputes of the poor, justice according to law was reserved for the rich. This concern has been focused on the public mediation programmes, though not specifically on family mediation. Ironically, concern is also directed at private fee for service family mediation, which, it is claimed, has been available only to the rich (Folberg and Taylor, 1984).

Family mediation in Britain, particularly in the light of recent developments in family law, cannot escape these concerns. Davis and Bader (1985) first highlighted the pressures and powerlessness experienced by the parties in the context of 'conciliation' on court premises. Practice Direction [1986] 16 Fam. Law 286 of the Principal Divorce Registry was the first to direct judges and registrars to consider referring contested cases to local mediation services where these existed. Early fears that these independent, out-of-court mediation services risked incorporation within the judicial system were thankfully unfounded. Public funding for independent family mediation provision became a reality for the first time when mediation was proposed as the main plank of divorce reform (Family Law Act 1996) accompanied by Government proposals for legal aid reform (Green Paper, *Legal Aid: Targeting Need*, 1995; White Paper, *Striking the Balance: The Future of Legal Aid in England and Wales*, June 1996). The consequent risks were clear. The potential for increased numbers of couples being encouraged to use mediation as the officially preferred approach to dispute resolution could result in inappropriate pressurization to mediate, on legal aid recipients in particular, as well as in inappropriate cases being referred to mediation. In addition, government funding, while bringing much needed financial security to struggling service providers, also imposed, inevitably, expectations of accountability and of performance defined in terms of effectiveness, and quantifiability in terms of Value for Money (VFM). Political tensions such as these have had to be addressed by mediators in the context of current practice, particularly in resisting back-door coercion into mediation and in meeting challenges to professional autonomy over policy, principles and quality assurance (see Roberts, 2005b).

Rights and responsibility

Mediators must be the first to acknowledge that the better informed both parties are, the better able they are to negotiate effectively. Knowledge of legal entitlements is an essential prerequisite for the mediation of family matters. However, individual rights associated as they are with the pursuit of legal interests, can exist in tension with a different ethic, that of collaboration, co-operation and mutual responsibility associated with mediation (Gilligan, 1982). Under the banner of children's rights and in particular Article 12 of the UN Convention on the Rights of the Child (the right of the child to express an opinion and to have that opinion taken into account), recent attempts to expand the role of welfare professionals in the private law proceedings of divorce, complicate the picture still further. (See Chapter 10 for further discussion.)

A mediated agreement, if it is to be fair and satisfactory to both parties, and in the children's interests, has somehow to balance the demands of these apparently competing approaches.

Objectives and reality

Kressel (1985, p. 204) has drawn attention to the lofty nature of the mediator's goals, the fulfilment of all of which would constitute no mean achievement. These aspirations apply in all fields of mediation practice, whether the dangerous and slow context of mediation in international disputes or the personal realm of family disputes (Roberts, 2007). In the context of family mediation these goals – difficult enough to meet at the best of times – have to be striven for in circumstances of enormous personal stress and practical, social and economic difficulty:

> With regard to the parties, the mediator is expected to establish and maintain trust and confidence; to demonstrate empathy and understanding for the positions of each side; to be highly expert on substantive and procedural issues, but to use that expertise to guide and counsel, not to impose personal views or take sides. With regard to the process, the mediator is expected to foster a procedure of dispute resolution: in which neither party gets all that it is asking, although neither ends up feeling humiliated or defeated; that engages all parties in an active process of give and take, albeit one that is sufficiently controlled so that the risks of conflict escalation are kept to the minimum; and that is based on an objective and realistic assessment of the forces and interests at play. With regard to the settlement, the mediator is expected to promote agreements; that both sides can defend publicly; that each can view as reasonably fair; and that lay the groundwork for improved interaction. (Kressel, 1985, p. 204)

Parental autonomy and state intervention

Officially, parental autonomy and private ordering are encouraged (see Chapter 3). But at the same time the court has a duty to protect the interests of children in matrimonial and other family proceedings in both contested and uncontested cases (Matrimonial Causes Act 1973, s. 41; Children Act 1989; Children and Adoption Act 2006). The Children Act 1989 removed the duty of district judges to make any judgment as to the satisfactoriness or otherwise of the arrangements for children at the Children's Appointment. Whether the court would use its power to refuse to accept an agreement made by the parties themselves has remained uncertain. There has been uncertainty too about the grounds on which the court's supervisory jurisdiction ought to be exercised (Maidment, 1984).

The principle of the best interests of the child as the first and paramount consideration guides the court in making decisions over children (Children

Act 1989, s. 1). While, as Richards has observed, it is a concept that few would object to, it is also a concept 'that allows for the maximum range of disagreement' because of the wide divergence of views (professional and parental) possible as to what does constitute the best interests of the child (Richards, 1994a, p. 260). This principle, while not one of the basic premises of mediation, nevertheless informs the legal and ethical framework within which decision-making in mediation takes place (Finer Report, 1974). The principle of party authority is, however, fundamental to mediation. Research findings (such as Lund, 1984; Wallerstein and Kelly, 1980) which show that the basis of what is best for the child can lie in agreement between parents, resolve (in practice) these tensions of principle.

The organizational framework within which mediation is practised

Many different organizational arrangements characterize the practice of mediation in Britain – whether in the independent, not-for-profit or private, for-profit, or court-associated sector of provision. Broadly speaking, a distinction can be drawn between services that are directly linked to the court and those that are independent of the court, based as they are in the community. In fact, the picture is more complex and the influence of the court more pervasive, intruding even into the practice of out-of-court services (for example in their accepting court referrals and in the presence of members of the judiciary on their management committees). Nevertheless, the degree of involvement in the judicial process is still a useful index for determining the fundamental differences in mediation provision.

Court-based settlement practices

A variety of practices, termed variously 'in-court conciliation', 'mediation', 'settlement-seeking' and 'dispute resolution', are conducted either at the direction of the court or occurring on the court premises as a form of dispute resolution used in the early stages of contested private law proceedings, such as residence or contact applications. The purpose of such meetings is to assist the parties in negotiating an agreement over the disputed issue without the need for further legal intervention. Many different schemes operate throughout the country at the preliminary First Appointment Hearing (the practice for final hearings is much more uniform nationally) making use of the combination of a CAFCASS officer (known as a Child and

Family Reporter (CFR)) and a district judge or magistrate (*Facilitation and Enforcement Group Final Report* – Lord Chancellor's Department, 2003). Historically, at least five such schemes have been identified in the county court (Ogus et al., 1987, p. 66). Three examples are explored below.[6]

The conciliation appointment before the registrar (now called the district judge) and the court welfare officer (now called the Child and Family Reporter)

Here, conciliation is an integral part of the legal process and took place under the authority of the registrar. The first experimental scheme of this kind was set up by Mr Registrar Parmeter at the Bristol County Court in 1977, in order to reduce the number of defended divorces. It was extended in 1978 to some custody and access disputes in undefended divorces. The appointment was to take place before affidavits were filed and before the case was set down for a full hearing. The parties and their solicitors would attend a meeting with the registrar and a welfare officer in order to clarify the exact nature of the dispute. If there seemed to be a prospect of agreement, the parties and the welfare officer would have a private discussion in another room for about 40 minutes. These discussions would be legally privileged and so could not be subsequently disclosed (Practice Direction [1982] 3 All ER 988). Should an agreement be reached the registrar would make an order giving effect to it. Otherwise he would give directions for the trial of the dispute.

Since then, several courts have introduced similar schemes including, in 1983, that at the Principal Registry of the Family Division. This scheme was extended to include referrals from a judge at the Children's Appointment. It is probably the only such scheme in the country where children over the age of nine are brought to the appointment. This is considered by judges and court officers to be useful for ascertaining the views of children at an early stage.

---

6   More recently, three models of in-court conciliation, differentiated by the degree of judicial control involved, have been compared in terms of their overall and relative effectiveness: an hour's meeting with a CAFCASS officer followed by a brief report to the district judge (low judicial control); the district judge leading negotiations in a court room with lawyers representing the parties (high judicial control); and the district judge initiating the process in chambers, the parties then negotiating with the CAFCASS officer, followed by a report to the judge (mixed judicial control) (Trinder et al., 2006).

Conciliation before a judge

Some judges sometimes attempt to mediate if both parties are present at the Children's Appointment (MCA 1973, s. 41) but they do not divest themselves of their judicial authority in assuming the mediatory role (see footnote 6).

Settlement-seeking by a court welfare officer during the preparation of a welfare report

The main traditional duties of court welfare officers have been their statutory duties to investigate and report, providing information to the court on matters relating to the welfare of children. Additional duties included the supervision of arrangements for children (James, 1988). The court welfare officer has occupied a position of formal authority as an officer of the court whose primary responsibility was to assist the judge (or magistrate) in judicial decision-making. The officer did this by acting as the 'eyes and ears' of the court, investigating all the circumstances and reporting back to the court so that an informed judgment could be made by the judge. This inevitably involved providing the judge with an account of the circumstances of the family concerned. In the 1980s, some court welfare officers, pursuing practices influenced by notions of systemic family therapy, saw their primary objective as effecting a change in the dysfunctional family, rather than meeting the requirements either of the judicial process (for determining parental disputes) or of the families and their perceptions of their needs (James and Hay, 1993). These court welfare officers (for example, Howard and Shepherd, 1982) denied that their reports to the court need include recommendations involving value judgments. While it must have been professionally desirable for the court welfare officer to avoid making a moral judgment on the conduct of the parents, a recommendation concerning the course of action to follow in the best interests of the child was unavoidable if the report was not to be useless as an aid to adjudication. Moreover, those practitioners, in claiming the right both to exercise their professional judgment independent of legal or judicial constraint as 'free floating professionals' (James and Hay, 1993, p. 119) and to use their power as court welfare officers to impose their methods on disputants, simultaneously sought both to deny and to exploit their statutory authority.

A conciliatory approach adopted by welfare officers in the course of their investigation duties may indeed bring about some, or even total agreement between the parties to a dispute. There are however fundamental differences of objective and practice in the tasks of welfare investigation and of mediation. First, the parties' participation in the court investigation is mandatory, depending not on their consent but on the need of the court to inform itself when called upon to make orders affecting children; in addition, discussions are not privileged. Nor is it possible for the court welfare officer to be impartial vis-à-vis the parties, for, in the absence of an informal agreement, the officer subsequently has to prepare an influential report in which his or her own opinions predominate. The principle of party competence of mediation is also subservient to the court welfare officer's statutory child protection function.

For all these reasons, attempts by a court welfare officer to mediate from this powerful position of formal authority tend to place the parties, especially if reluctant to agree, under considerable pressure at a time when they may already be feeling vulnerable and overawed by the formality and unfamiliarity of court proceedings and the atmosphere of the court. The dangers of coercion are compounded by those of manipulation in the covert use, at that time by some court welfare officers, of family therapy techniques (including the frequently secret use of one-way mirrors and video-recorders) often employed with neither the prior knowledge nor the consent of the parties, as a means of assessing families and their relationships (for example, Howard and Shepherd, 1982).

The Booth Committee (1985, para. 41.2) recommended strongly the separation of report-writing and mediation, going as far as to describe these two activities as 'so different as to be incompatible'. Mr Justice Ewbank (*Re H. (Conciliation: Welfare Reports)* [1986] 1 FLR 476) first gave this viewpoint judicial backing by stating:

> Conciliation and reporting as a court welfare officer are different functions. Conciliation is the helping of parties to resolve their disputes. The duty of the welfare officer is to help the court to resolve disputes that the parties are unable to resolve. Both functions are of great value but they are not functions which are to be mixed up. Probation officers who are involved in conciliation are not subsequently to investigate and write welfare officers' reports. This is a fundamental point which has been made on many occasions ...

Practice Direction [1986] 16 Fam. Law 286 of the Principal Registry of the Family Division officially endorsed the need for the separation of these two functions by directing that the same officer should not act both as report writer and as conciliator in the same case. Home Office policy confirmed this prohibition (National Standards for Probation Service Family Court Welfare Work, Home Office, 1994). This policy document attempted to clarify the respective functions of the court welfare officer. Section 4.3 on the purpose of the welfare report stated:

> Where in the course of preparing the report the court welfare officer identifies opportunities for helping the parties to reach agreement, these should be pursued in line with the general principle of promoting parental responsibility *but it is not*

the role of the court welfare officer to set out to resolve disputes when preparing a welfare report. (Emphasis added)

The court welfare officer may also have a settlement-seeking role in relation to Directions Appointments. These discussions are distinguished from mediation in that they are not privileged and are normally brief (Home Office, 1994, s. 5.23). Outcomes must be reported to the court (Home Office, 1994, sections 2.6 and 2. 7).

Research by Davis and Bader (1985) into the conciliation appointments at the Bristol County Court revealed that what in fact took place was a stressful encounter with the spouses, mostly in the overcrowded public waiting area of the court, under the threat that failure to agree would result in the imposition of further costs and delay. Solicitors spoke on behalf of their clients and there was little direct negotiation between the parties themselves. The parties' experience of in-court conciliation was therefore of a coercive and excluding process with little attention being paid to their own understanding and interpretations of their circumstances. From the standpoint of the courts, these appointments provided an efficient means of rationalizing cases, diverting them away from judicial hearings. Settlement-seeking pressures (including those from the parties' own solicitors) dominated at the expense of the quality of those settlements.

More recent research (Trinder et al., 2006) confirms many of these findings. They conclude, in particular, that the model of in-court conciliation deployed makes a significant difference both to the rate of agreement and to parental satisfaction with the process – the lower the degree of judicial control, the better the outcome. In addition, this research concludes that while in-court conciliation can result in a high agreement rate (76 per cent full or partial agreement) on contact issues over children (restoration, timetabling and quantity of contact) where judicial control was low, it had limited impact on those key co-parenting factors that make contact work (such as shared decision-making and the quality of the parental relationship), regardless of the model of in-court conciliation deployed (Trinder et al., 2006). Significant problems, such as those identified in the 1980s, are still associated with in-court conciliation – the short time available (45 minutes on average); the unsuitability of some cases; risk issues; the experience of pressurization and coercion; low levels of parental satisfaction; and uncertainty about the role children in the process (Trinder et al., 2006).

Recent data (CAFCASS Review Paper, 2003; CAFCASS Consultation Paper, 2005; Trinder et al., 2006) confirm earlier findings (such as James and Hay, 1993) about the lack of uniformity that characterizes in-court conciliation practice – nationally and locally, between areas, teams and individual officers. In its thematic review, Her Majesty's Magistrates Courts Service Inspectorate itself criticizes in-court conciliation for having 'no common definition that described, clarified or set limits to the schemes …' and primarily serving the interests of the courts in assisting efficient management of court lists, reducing reports and securing settlements (quoted in Kirby, 2006, p. 973). Findings highlight that this variety reflects divergent philosophical and theoretical views as to the objectives, values, functions and skills that should underpin this area of work. The lack of clarity as to overall aims and objectives and the absence of 'any coherent and evidentiary framework' within which court welfare work is located (James and Hay, 1993, p. 178), was addressed at that time by the introduction in 1994 of a policy of uniformity embodied in the Home Office's National Standards for Family Court Welfare Officers. While on the one hand James and Hay (1993, p. 119) stated 'there are as many approaches to court welfare work as there are court welfare officers', they also identified emerging common features of practice: for example, the pervasive influence in court welfare work of family therapy; the almost universal hostility to the court process and its perceived destructiveness; the concomitant view as to the importance of diverting disputants away from the court; a growing interest in issues of race, gender and power; and an increased focus on dispute resolution co-existing with the traditional investigative role.

This preference for 'dispute resolution' over traditional report-writing (an 'inefficient use of professional time') has intensified over the years (see CAFCASS Consultation Papers, 2000, 2004 and 2005, section 34). At the same time, the scope of 'dispute resolution' has expanded and become increasingly ill-defined, incorporating 'intensive dispute resolution', 'casework', 'intensive case management', 'relationship management', 'assessment', 'active problem-solving' and 'roundtable reunions' – terminology that is used interchangeably and lacks specification as to what professional intervention precisely is being contemplated. These CAFCASS strategy proposals of 2004 also fail to clarify the relationship between functions recognized to be incompatible if carried out by the same officer in the same case (see above). Moreover, in requiring disputants seeking legal determinations of their disputes to be subjected automatically, without consent or regard to legal entitlement, to social work and/or therapeutic interventions ('assessment', 'casework', and so on), these proposals resurrect those same grave concerns raised in the 1980s in response to the experiments carried out by some teams of divorce court welfare officers.[7]

---

7   Kirby (2006, pp. 970 and 973) usefully clarifies the nature of the professional intervention that is intended in respect of private law in-court dispute resolution as, on ceasing to be 'officers of the court' following the creation of CAFCASS, officers are now beginning 'to reclaim their social work heritage' in their primary task of protecting and promoting child welfare. He is careful to distinguish this activity from mediation – 'It is not mediation and should not be confused with it.'

As James (1988) pointed out, the development of in-court conciliation, ad hoc, local and piecemeal as it has been, was undeniably a major practice innovation new to probation work, which had traditionally been individual work rather than co-working in joint sessions. James (1988) referred then to the substantial confusion resulting from this development, surrounding not only the use of terminology, but also concepts, structures and management. 'Conciliation' had to be 'smuggled' into court welfare work for two reasons: (a) because of the absence of any authority to provide for or resource its development; and (b) because of the powerful and unanimous legal and judicial consensus supported by researchers such as Davis (1985), on the basic incompatibility between the use of conciliation/mediation and the task of welfare investigation. Recent CAFCASS proposals on in-court 'dispute resolution' do not describe this activity as 'mediation' nor do they make reference either to the relationship between the in-court conciliation and mediation or to the number of highly effective arrangements all over the country for making voluntary referrals from the court to independent or private mediation services. This omission may reflect the recognition that if what is practised *is* called 'mediation', the principles of voluntariness, confidentiality and impartiality apply as do the officially endorsed quality assurance standards governing family mediation practice (in respect of selection, training, qualifications, competence assessment, policies and practice guidelines and codes of practice). These requirements are the most rigorous in respect of the practice of publicly funded mediation. Significantly, those who experience mediation (whatever it may be called) in the context of the court, enjoy neither these protections of professional regulation nor that of caveat emptor, the most restricted protection of the market place. The North American SPIDR Commission (Society of Professionals in Dispute Resolution, 1989) affirmed that the less choice the parties have over process, programme or mediator, the greater the mandatory requirements for rigorous standards of training, qualifications and professional ethical conduct and discipline.

If differences between interventions are to be understood and respected and the boundaries of distinct processes kept clear, attempts at promoting legal settlement as part of court proceedings must be distinguished from the offer of mediation. That offer, if it is to be effective, needs to be kept independent of the court process and therefore of its coercive powers (Davis, 1985; Trinder et al., 2006; Kirby, 2006). Mediation is a privileged, confidential and voluntary process of dispute resolution. Where it is undertaken at the instigation of the court, cases need to be suitable and the parties need to give their fully informed consent. 'It may take place on court premises or elsewhere. Research suggests that mediation is more effective away from court premises' (Home Office, 1994, section 5.34). Furthermore, where court officials act as mediators, the parties are exposed inevitably to unsatisfactory pressures. There are dangers both of coercion in the mediation process and of impairment of judicial authority where these functions are combined (Roberts, 1986).

Out-of-court mediation provision

Following the publication of the Finer Report in 1974, the earliest offer of family mediation was provided in the out-of-court, independent, voluntary (or charitable) sector of provision. Support from the judiciary for these pioneering initiatives has been described as 'visionary' by one of their first managers, Mr Fred Gibbons of the South East London Family Mediation Bureau (Roberts, 2007, p. 203) The first of these out-of-court services was the Bristol Courts Family Conciliation Service (BCFCS) established in 1978 and funded by the Nuffield Foundation and other trusts (for a recent detailed account of the history of this service, see Parkinson, 2004). Initially a pre-court service, it was intended to complement in-court conciliation at the Bristol County Court. The use of 'courts' in its title was confusing for the BCFCS had no formal connection with the local courts (Parkinson, 1986). No doubt it was thought that this judicial association would lend greater authority and status to its activities and win the support (in the form of referrals) of the legal profession. This was ironic in view of the fact that the chief advantage of the service lay in its independence of the court.

The second full-time out-of-court service, the South East London Family Mediation Bureau (originally called the South East London Family Conciliation Bureau), was set up in 1979 in the Borough of Bromley. Funding was dependent on a variety of charitable and local authority sources as well as strong probation support. Administratively and financially linked to the Civil Work Unit of the Probation Service, it took great pains to demarcate and maintain clear information and professional boundaries in order to preserve its independence of the court. This was because its co-ordinator and a few of the early mediators were then also court welfare officers. The majority of the mediators were mainly drawn from a variety of professional backgrounds (legal, personnel, social work, psychology and counselling).

This interdisciplinary mix was unusual then as the mediators who first staffed the early out-of-court mediation services came primarily from professional backgrounds, in social work, counselling and therapy, which focused on child welfare and child protection work. That professional ideology and a Law Society determined to confine dispute resolution to the sphere of legal activity and therefore the control of lawyers, influenced the terms in which mediation in these early days was then perceived and tolerated, namely as a form of welfare activity primarily concerned with issues related to children.

Since then, the situation has been transformed and developments have been dramatic, organizationally, professionally, legally and politically. There are now 1,110 practising family mediators in England, Wales and Scotland and 197 organizations with a legal aid contract for family mediation work in England and Wales, both in the not-for-profit and private sectors including solicitors who practise as mediators (UKC Strategy Review, 2006a; NAO Report, 2007).

In the period October 2004 to March 2006 some 29,000 people who were funded through legal aid, attempted to resolve their disputes through mediation, only 20 per cent of those funded for family breakdown cases (excluding those involving domestic abuse).[8]

Family mediation is provided in the private and the not-for profit sector. In the latter sector there are some 51 Family Mediation Services (FMS) in England, Wales and Northern Ireland, forming an association under the umbrella of National Family Mediation (NFM), the main provider of not-for-profit, out-of-court family mediation in the country. In the 1990s, NFM, having clarified the nature and features of the core mediation process in its professional requirements (selection, training and accreditation), consolidated the distinctive environment of mediation in the context of family issues in its development of a range of quality assurance procedures, supervision training, and in devising policies and practice guidelines relating to the consultation of children in mediation, domestic abuse and cross-cultural practice. NFM currently has a network of 54 services, which represents 40 per cent of the mediation profession, and undertakes 50 per cent of publicly funded work (NFM, 2007).

All NFM services provide mediation on issues relating to children and the organization has prided itself on its focus on the importance of the perspective of children in parent discussions during the process of mediation. Services also offer All Issues Mediation (AIM) that is, the mediation of the detailed arrangements concerning financial, property, as well as children issues. Agreement rates are consistent with those in other countries, that is, 70 per cent of couples agree arrangements in respect of their children and 80 per cent reached agreement on all issues (Joseph Rowntree Foundation Research, 1994).

Until the advent in 1996 of the UK College of Family Mediators (the national professional standard-setting body for all family mediators whatever

---

8   In the same period, 120,000 family disputes involving finances and children were completed through bilateral lawyer negotiations or through court proceedings. A further 30,000 completed cases that were settled through the courts involved domestic abuse. Recent findings, highlighting the benefits of family mediation (less acrimony, cheaper and quicker), point to the substantial scope there exists for increasing the take-up of mediation and therefore for improving value for money in the legal aid budget (NAO Report, 2007).

their profession of origin or sector of provision), when the incompatible regulatory and provision functions were separated in accordance with recommended policy (see Council of Europe Recommendation, 1998; Lord Chancellor's ACLEC Report, 1999), the NFM professional framework provided the means by which uniform standards were set and monitored in the not-for-profit sector of provision. The achievement of these standards depended in practice upon the local service base, which recruited mediators, and provided the necessary infrastructure for securing referrals of cases and overseeing the quality and accountability of work by local supervision procedures. Moreover, the service base for the provision of family mediation ensured that a balance was maintained between the demand for mediation and the supply of mediators.

What characterized these early developments – the provision of an independent and dedicated mediation service base, in particular – was the struggle that had to occur for mediation to emerge and become recognized as a discrete activity distinct both from the practice of therapy and welfare professionalism and from legal practice and process. It was not until 1989 that mediation broke free from this confusing inheritance. In that year its distinctive nature and process, embodied in its own ancient tradition, was affirmed officially both in its incorporation as the basis of the first national mediation training programme (introduced by NFM) and in the definition in the Report from the Lord Chancellor on the costs and effectiveness of conciliation:

> The distinguishing feature [of mediation] should be *to enable couples to retain control of the decision-making process* consequent on separation or divorce, encouraging them to make their own agreements. (Conciliation Project Unit, 1989, para. 20.19, 358, emphasis added)

This clarification of the significant characteristic of mediation as a decision-making process was confirmed in the adoption in 1991 of new selection criteria for eligibility for training with the NFM. Aptitude for mediation, analysed and demonstrated via a range of specific performance-based selection exercises and procedures, became the primary determinant of suitability for training for mediation rather than any particular educational or professional qualification and experience. This was in line with the recommendations of the North American Society of Professionals in Dispute Resolution (SPIDR Report, 1989). The SPIDR Commission on Qualifications found that no particular type or degree of prior education or job experience was shown to be an effective predictor of success as a mediator, arbitrator or other professional 'neutral'. Terminological clarification ensued too when, by 1989, the term 'mediation' began to replace 'conciliation', preferred because of its greater precision.

In the mid 1980s, a private sector initiative, Solicitors in Mediation, the creation of a small group of solicitors and a social worker, was the precursor of a new body, the Family Mediators Association (FMA), which introduced training on all issues for mediators working in the private sector. The FMA, an association of individual practitioners (rather than of services), adopted a model of practice based on a lawyer and mental health professional co-working together. While this model proved to be expensive, it promoted a view of family mediation as consisting of a combination of the expertise of family law and of therapy, rather than one affirming mediation's own historical, cross-cultural heritage and distinctive body of knowledge. This approach perpetuated, unfortunately, the old 'mindset' that continued to muddy the waters of mediation and which reflected:

> a mental universe dominated by the now aging dyad of 'justice' and 'welfare' and while there is obviously nothing wrong with either 'justice' or 'welfare', mediation is about something else. It is primarily directed towards the support of private ordering in seeking to facilitate joint decision-making through party negotiations. (Roberts, 1993a)

The FMA's monopoly in the private sector was challenged by the growth of a number of lawyer-dominated training programmes, including those offered by the Solicitors Family Law Association (renamed Resolution) with the support of the Law Society, itself anxious to extend its remit over mediation. The risk to the public both of unregulated practice and of confusion arising from a proliferation of different and competing accreditation schemes were powerful reasons for the establishing a national professional body responsible for the setting and monitoring of uniform standards for all practitioners. This led to the creation in 1996 of the UK College of Family Mediators by the three main family mediation providers, National Family Mediation, Family Mediation Scotland and The Family Mediators Association (see Chapter 11).

Distinguishing features of independent mediation services compared with those annexed to the court

The main features distinguishing out-of-court mediation provision are set out below.

- Referrals come from many sources, which include self-referrals, Citizens' Advice Bureaux, solicitors, health workers, as well as the court and the court welfare service (CAFCASS).

- These schemes are not restricted to those involved in matrimonial proceedings. Unmarried couples and other family members, such as grandparents, also have access to them.
- Mediation is available at an early stage while couples may still be living under the same roof, before divorce petitions are filed or even before legal advice has been sought. Independent mediation is also available later on, long after legal proceedings are completed.
- Even the busiest independent services can offer appointments at short notice, of especial value in moments of crisis, for example if a teenager refuses to return home following a contact visit.[9]
- The length and number of sessions can be determined by the agency itself according to its own objectives and the particular needs of the consumers.
- Confidentiality can be more confidently assured in an out-of-court service, where there is less danger of the parties confusing the role of the mediator with that of court officials in cases where a report has also been ordered by the court.
- Mediation as practised in independent agencies can better ensure that the authority of the parties to determine their own arrangements over their own affairs in their own way is protected. This fundamental requirement of mediation cannot easily be reconciled with court-directed or court-annexed mediation where the ethos of the court, characterized as it is by the surrendering of decision-making authority to a judge, prevails and where the settlement-seeking experience is inevitably pressurized, often coerced.

---

9   The recent NAO survey (2007) reported that there is capacity among many mediators to take on more cases and that 94 per cent of mediators reported that the average waiting time for the first appointment was two weeks or less.

3 The legal context

> ... Marriages do break down and ... the civil legislator must take account of this fact and provide the best framework of law to cater for this. (The Lord Chancellor, House of Lords, Hansard, 30 November 1995, p. 704)

Radical changes in dispute resolution approaches now challenge the all-pervasive legal and 'adjudicative bias' that for so long conditioned thinking about dispute resolution in western society (Effron, 1989, p. 480; European Mediation Directive, 2008). Reliance on litigation and adjudication, now seen to be detrimental, in many cases, to the effective resolution particularly of family disputes, has disabled the public as well as legal professionals, from contemplating alternative dispute resolution processes, such as mediation, which have lacked the privileged position of adjudication in the legal process and which have existed outside the monopoly of control of legal professionals. Roberts and Palmer (2005, p. 3) have charted the manifold ways in which, over the last three decades, the distinctive culture of public disputing, characterized by its entrenched reliance on litigation and the courts, has undergone a transformation towards the emergence of a 'new world', at the heart of which 'lies a burgeoning culture and ideology of settlement'.[1]

Many decisions following family breakdown are negotiated between the parties themselves with or without the assistance of lawyers. The prevalence of this private negotiation was officially recognized and endorsed in relation to family conflict in the Finer Report (1974) followed by the Booth Report (1985).

---

1   'Settlement' is defined here 'in the general sense of the search for negotiated, consensual agreement as opposed to resort to a third-party decision ... While the rhetoric of voluntary agreement is retained, settlement in the lawyer's sense can well be, perhaps is typically, the culmination of a bruising process, characterized by secrecy and suspicion, in which one party's representatives have successfully wasted the other to the point at which the latter decides reluctantly, perhaps facing the inevitable, that he or she has got to give up' (Roberts and Palmer, 2005, p. 3, footnote 10).

This comparatively new approach, at that time, to the management of disputes in the field of family breakdown soon became an acknowledged part of legal policy and of the substantive law, culminating most recently in the Access to Justice Act 1999 (incorporating section 11 of the Family Law Act 1996), the Adoption and Children Act 2002 and the Children Act 2004. The proposals for divorce reform, while not surviving the demise of the Family Law Act 1996, accorded primary responsibility for decision-making to the parties and were therefore also in line with the Children Act 1989. The Children Act, in introducing its two innovatory principles of parental responsibility and non-intervention of the court, embodied for the first time a view of the public interest that was defined, certainly in the private law, in terms of settlement through agreement (Bainham, 1990). In presupposing that the public interest is best served by the facilitation of parental agreement, coupled with the discouragement of the intervention of the court, a premium is placed on mediation as part of this movement away from legal process and towards alternative dispute resolution processes.

This trend became apparent when the introduction of irretrievable breakdown as the sole ground for divorce (subject to proof of one of the five 'facts') officially removed the former fault basis of divorce (Matrimonial Causes Act 1973, s. 1). Furthermore, with the introduction in 1977 of the Special Procedure and the way undefended divorces are processed, the usual judicial decision-making function of the court was replaced. Although a decree nisi was awarded in open court and a decree absolute granted only if the court declared itself satisfied about the arrangements for the children, the privately negotiated settlements made by divorcing couples were in fact rubber stamped by the court (Davis et al., 1983). The court does of course still offer adjudication in disputes involving the decree, money and children to those who require it; but the large majority of cases are settled prior to trial and only a tiny percentage are concluded in adjudication.

Mediation is an essential part of this movement towards 'private ordering'. But all private negotiation in family matters, bilateral party negotiations, mediated negotiations or lawyer negotiations, take place within the 'shadow of the law' (as famously formulated by Mnookin and Kornhauser, 1979). In theory, this provides the 'defining context' within which mutual actions, expectations and decisions occur (Hamnett, 1977, p. 5). Strikingly, research has revealed that, in practice, so far as lawyer negotiations are concerned, many cases settle for reasons that have nothing to do with moral or legal standards (Menkel-Meadow, 1993a).

The evolving relationship of mediation to the public justice system is one that has always had to be negotiated and clarified. The advent of public funding (legal aid) for family mediation in the late 1990s precipitated an urgent debate on the vexed question of whether or not mediation now constituted a 'legal service'. For example, the Advisory Committee on

Legal Education and Conduct (ACLEC), a government body reviewing the standards, education, training and conduct of family mediators, saw, as one of its first tasks, the need to clarify this issue. The Committee, whilst acknowledging the distinctive role of the mediator, concluded that mediation *was* a legal service because of the several respects in which family mediation involved legal information, knowledge about when referral to lawyers for legal advice and legal review was appropriate, legal aid (in relation to family mediation) and the whole arena of legal services and policy (Lord Chancellor's Advisory Committee on Legal Education and Conduct, ACLEC Report, 1999). Although this view was adopted initially by the Legal Services Commission, it was challenged by all the mediation bodies across fields of practice, and the Bar Council and Law Society. Latest government guidance on this matter, issued in respect of the implications for mediators of the Proceeds of Crime Act 2002, is that mediators do *not* provide legal services, a view supported by mediators and lawyers (Home Office, 2004).

A mediator working in the context of family disputes needs to have an understanding of the substantive law and of the legal procedures relating to family matters, divorce in particular, and how these frame negotiations. Marriage is on one level a legal contract between a man and a woman; divorce defines the process by which the legal obligations and privileges of a man and woman towards one another are changed (Bernard, 1971).

Current law of divorce

Although, as already noted, irretrievable breakdown is the only ground for divorce, three of the five 'facts' by which it is proved are fault-based and derive from the old matrimonial offences of adultery, cruelty and desertion (Cretney et al., 2003). The vast majority (over 75 per cent) of divorce petitions are based on adultery or unreasonable behaviour, less than 20 per cent on two years' separation and fewer than 6 per cent on five years' separation (Population Trends, 2003). The most frequent 'fact' cited by women was the unreasonable behaviour of the husband, while for men, it was two years' separation with consent. Women are the petitioners in most cases – latest figures show that in 2004, 69 per cent of petitions were granted to wives in England and Wales (Walsh, 2006).[2] As the White Paper (1995, para. 2.10) comments: 'not surprisingly, the subtlety that the facts are not grounds for divorce, but merely evidence of breakdown, is seldom grasped by those who

---

2   Increases in divorce rates have been linked to the rise in wives' earning power and a consequent reduction in their dependence on a male bread-winner. Men's declining economic position has also been an important influence on trends in marriage and divorce (McAllister, 1999).

are sued for divorce'. 'Unreasonable behaviour'[3] is most frequently cited as a 'fact' because, as the petition can be issued at an earlier stage (rather than the couple having to be separated for two years to obtain a consensual divorce), it is the quickest way of getting a divorce. It can also cause the most trouble. Research has shown that disputes about children seem to be more common in divorces based on unreasonable behaviour than in others (Green Paper, 1993, para. 5.12). Unless that tactical purpose behind its frequent use is made clear, especially to the respondent, the repercussions can often be serious. Many disputes can be exacerbated by a spouse's outrage at receiving a petition cataloguing a history of 'unreasonable behaviour'. The concern is that animosity is likely to be increased and litigation instigated and protracted if the respondent seeks to defend the petition as a means of refuting these allegations. In the wake of the Woolf Report (1996), however, family lawyers are now enjoined to adopt conciliatory approaches to resolving claims speedily and justly; without costs being unreasonably incurred; with the needs of children addressed and safeguarded and the minimum distress to the parties; and 'in a manner designed to promote as good a continuing relationship between the parties and any children as is possible in the circumstances' (Family Law Protocol of the Law Society, 2002, section 3.1; see also the Code of Practice *Resolution*, formerly the Solicitors Family Law Association, which requires members to 'conduct matters in a constructive and non-confrontational way').

What is more helpful to the parties in these circumstances is that they understand that most allegations about conduct as a spouse do not prejudice the respondent's position, either vis-à-vis the children or vis-à-vis property and financial rights and obligations. Conduct is disregarded by the court unless it would be inequitable to do so, and this occurs only exceptionally. In deciding how to respond to a petition based on unreasonable behaviour, the respondent needs to know too that there is no public hearing if the petition is undefended and that the decree absolute makes no reference to any of the facts required to prove irretrievable breakdown (Grant, 1981). Clarification of these issues by the mediator can help to prevent misunderstanding and the escalation of conflict.

---

3   Matrimonial Causes Act 1973 section 1(2)(b): 'that the respondent has behaved in such a way that the petitioner cannot reasonably be expected to live with the respondent'. The test is objective – the question is not 'has the respondent behaved reasonably?' but, given that the respondent has behaved in a certain way, can the petitioner 'reasonably be expected to live with the respondent' (Cretney et al., 2003).

Matrimonial Causes Act 1973 (section 41) (Children Act 1989, schedule 12, 31)

The policy of protecting the child in matrimonial proceedings is embodied in section 41 of the Matrimonial Causes Act l973, which requires the court to consider the interests of the children before making absolute a decree of divorce, or nullity or before granting a decree of judicial separation. The court has to declare itself satisfied that where there are children of the family, arrangements for the welfare of each child have been made. To enable the court to discharge these duties, the petitioner is required to file with the petition, a 'statement as to the arrangements for children'.

Until amended by the Children Act l989 (schedule l2, 31), section 41 required the court to make a declaration as to whether the arrangements were satisfactory or 'the best that can be devised in the circumstances' (section 41(1)(i)). The Children Act l989 removed this requirement to make a declaration of satisfaction, replacing that with an increased duty on the petitioner to provide more detailed information about arrangements for children.

The Children Act 1989 makes no attempt to influence the nature or content of parental agreements and the court is unlikely to interfere with agreements made by the parties except in exceptional circumstances. However, the increased disclosure requirements of section 41 mean that divorcing parents must provide the court with details of proposed arrangements for their children. This means that although the Children Act removed the requirement for the court to make a judgment as to the adequacy of those arrangements, more is expected of parents in considering carefully and comprehensively the vital arrangements affecting their children.[4] The Children Act 1989 attempts to redress a historical imbalance that has, in the past, favoured the protection and welfare of children over their autonomy and rights. This is a qualified autonomy, however. Children are entitled to participate in the decision-making process but they do not, however, have the final say. The difficult balance has always to be struck, whatever process of decision-making is adopted, between the need to recognize the child as an independent person and the risk of imposing on the child the burden of responsibility for making choices. The important point is that the law upholds the principle that children are persons to whom duties are owed rather than objects of welfare, or possessions over whom power is wielded.

---

4   See Law Society's Family Law Protocol, 2002, section 6, which emphasizes the importance of careful completion of the Statement of Arrangements in order that the court can fulfil its statutory obligations, and of the encouragement of agreement over arrangements for parenting 'where appropriate'.

Civil partnerships

The Civil Partnership Act 2004 came into force in 2005, enabling same-sex couples to obtain legal recognition of their relationship as 'civil partners', and to enjoy equal treatment, with married couples, in a wide range of legal matters, for example tax (including inheritance tax); employment benefits; the right to apply for parental responsibility, and the duty to pay reasonable maintenance, in respect of any child of the family. Where there is a breakdown of a relationship in a civil partnership, this can be terminated by 'dissolution' in a procedure similar to that of divorce. 'Dissolution' can be obtained after one year of civil partnership. The main difference to divorce is that adultery is not one of the five 'facts' or indices for evidencing irretrievable breakdown of the relationship, the sole ground for dissolution, in a petition. Where there are children of the family, a court has to approve a 'statement of arrangements' concerning plans for the children, before dissolution can be finalized, just as in divorce.

Divorce reform

Introduction

Government proposals for divorce law reform were published in April 1995 in a White Paper entitled *Looking to the Future: Mediation and the Ground for Divorce* following an extensive two-year consultation process. The Family Law Bill, announced in the Queen's Speech on 15 November 1995, was enacted in July 1996 with the intention that it be implemented in 1999. Parts I and II of the Bill introduced the government's proposals for reform of the law of divorce, Part III dealt with legal aid for mediation in family matters, and Part IV incorporated an amended version of the Family Homes and Domestic Violence Bill covering the occupation of the family home in cases of domestic violence, the prevention of molestation and other related matters.

Criticisms of the existing divorce law

The White Paper (1995) set out the five objectives that should be fulfilled in a good law of divorce and which the present law, it argued, failed to meet in a number of respects – their emphasis placed on the importance of the consequences of divorce for the parties and especially for their children:

- to support the institution of marriage;
- to include practicable steps to prevent the irretrievable breakdown of marriage;
- to ensure that the parties understood the practical consequences of divorce before taking any irreversible decision;
- where divorce was unavoidable, to minimize the bitterness and hostility between the parties and reduce the trauma for the children;
- to keep to the minimum the cost to the parties and the taxpayer (White Paper, 1995, para. 3.5).

It was argued that not only was the present law not working well but that it failed to meet the above objectives. Some of the main criticisms of the current law, still applicable, are set out briefly below (White Paper, 1995, paras 2.12–2.30):

- The system did nothing to help save saveable marriages. In 75 per cent of cases, the fault facts of unreasonable behaviour and adultery were used to establish irretrievable breakdown in order to obtain a quick and easy divorce, exacerbating hostility. In many cases, the consequences of the dissolution of the marriage – for example, the financial reality and the loss of day-to-day contact with children – were not faced until it was too late. The present system required the parties to take up opposing positions, increasing conflict. Even where solicitors representing the parties adopted conciliatory approaches to negotiation, the divorce process itself required the parties to sue each other and to make allegations. Furthermore, arms' length negotiations and litigation reduced communication between the couple and could increase or create misunderstandings and, therefore, conflict.
- Divorce could be obtained without proper consideration of its consequences and implications.
- The system made things worse for children because of the conflict inherent in the casting of blame necessary in seeking a quick divorce or the prolonged uncertainty involved in waiting two years for a consensual divorce, or worse, five years on the basis of separation.
- The system was unjust, confusing, misleading, open to abuse and discriminatory – the option of a consensual divorce relying on two years' separation available only to those who had the means to separate and arrange separate accommodation before divorce.
- The system distorted the parties' bargaining positions. The party who did not want to divorce would be in a stronger bargaining position because s/he could exact concessions over finance and the children, especially in separation cases, in return for their consent to the divorce.

While the White Paper (1995) focused on the use of family mediation in the context of divorce proceedings, it recognized that the advantages of mediation were not confined to divorce. Mediation could be appropriate for addressing issues relating to children as well as property and finance, in situations other than divorce (White Paper, 1995, para. 8.1).

The Family Law Act 1996

Major reforms, relating to divorce in particular, were introduced by the Family Law Act 1996, the only divorce legislation in the twentieth century to be initiated by a government. Yet the Act was also abandoned by government – Part II on divorce reform, in particular. There were a number of reasons for this abandonment, some disputed – for example: a change of government (from conservative to labour); opposition by powerful lobbying groups; the lack of detailed transitional implementation provision; the limitations of the two research projects set up to monitor the new procedures; concerns (from different political quarters) about costs (of the Information Meeting in particular), about the removal of fault, and about the lengthening of the divorce process (the introduction of 'delaying hurdles' that were seen to constitute a 'road block' rather than a 'motorway'); and fears about 'social engineering' perceived to be involved in seeking to change people's divorcing behaviour (see Roberts, 2001; Freeman, 2006, pp. 120, 121).

The problems associated with divorce law have not gone away and a resurgence of interest in divorce reform and the Family Law Act, in particular, is current, for example:

> One of the areas where the law is ripe for reform is in relation to divorce itself. Surely the time has come when we should be pushing for the introduction of 'no-fault' divorce; if so, we need to consider whether this should be along the lines originally contained in the Family Law Act 1996 – divorce over a process of time. The current requirement to rely on adultery or allegations of unreasonable behaviour to secure a divorce where the parties have been apart for less than two years does not sit comfortably with the laudable principles set out in the Family Law Act 1996 that a marriage which has irretrievably broken down should be brought to an end with minimum distress to the parties and the children. Issues were to be dealt with in a manner designed to promote as good a continuing relationship between the parties and the children as possible, and without due costs being unreasonably incurred. (McCulloch,[5] 2007, p. 381)

Notwithstanding the demise of the Family Law Act 1996, its main principles and features remain relevant, increasingly so, and are therefore set out in outline below.

---

5   National Chair, *Resolution*, formerly the Solicitors Family Law Association.

The general principles underlying the Act (Part I, section l)

The Act set out four main principles to which the court or any person exercising functions under Part II (divorce and separation) and Part III (legal aid for mediation in family matters) should have regard. These were:

(a) that the institution of marriage is to be supported;

(b) that the parties to a marriage which may have broken down are to be encouraged to take all practicable steps, whether by marriage counselling or otherwise, to save the marriage;

(c) that a marriage which has irretrievably broken down and is being brought to an end should be brought to an end –

    (i) with minimum distress to the parties and their children;

    (ii) with questions dealt with in a manner designed to promote as good a continuing relationship between the parties and any children affected as is possible in the circumstances; and

    (iii) without costs being unreasonably incurred in connection with the procedures to be followed in bringing the marriage to an end; and

(d) that any risk to one of the parties to a marriage, and to any children, of violence from the other party should, as far as reasonably practicable, be removed or diminished.' (Family Law Act, Part I, section l).

Marital breakdown (section 5)

Irretrievable breakdown remained the sole ground for divorce (Family Law Act, section 5). What was new was that no facts requiring allegations of fault were necessary to establish irretrievable breakdown. There was, therefore, no legal requirement to prove fault. Irretrievable breakdown was to be established by an objective test of breakdown – the sole fact of the passage of a period of time, a period to be used for the purposes of reflection (on whether the marriage had broken down irretrievably) and consideration (of the consequences of breakdown). The primary purpose of the period was to demonstrate, adequately and with certainty, that the marriage had broken down irretrievably, as well as to make arrangements for the future.

The period for reflection and consideration (section 7)

This demarcated period was 'a period with a purpose', originally one year, later amended to 18 months where there were children of the family (Consultation Paper, 1993, Foreword). During this period, initiated by a statement of marital breakdown (Family Law Act, section 6), the opportunity was created for reflection and consultation with the aim that saveable marriages could be saved and the parties, where they did decide to proceed to divorce, understood the practical consequences for themselves and their children before taking irreversible decisions. It was in considering what arrangements should be made for the future (Family Law Act, section 7(l)(b)), that the main opportunity for mediation was provided and for which, in Part III, legal aid was made available.

The information meeting (section 8)

Those wishing to make a statement of marital breakdown were required *first*, except in prescribed circumstances, to attend an information meeting. Attendance at such a meeting was compulsory for the party making the statement of marital breakdown and must have taken place not less than three months before the making of the statement (Family Law Act, section 8). It was envisaged that meetings would be on a one-to-one basis and not conducted in groups (although a husband and wife might attend together if they chose).

The purpose of the Information Meeting was to ensure not only that information was made available to people (both those whose marriage had not yet reached a crisis point and those who were already contemplating divorce), but also that 'they have assimilated the information as it affects them' (Lord Chancellor, 1995). What was to be made available included information about marriage counselling, mediation and legal advice and representation; child welfare, particularly in the context of marital breakdown; financial services; and protection against violence.

The three months that had to elapse between attendance at the Information Meeting and the making of the Statement of Marital Breakdown was intended to allow the parties time to reflect on their marriage in the light of the information received, and to encourage them to take every opportunity of saving their marriage by seeking appropriate help, as well as to take early advantage of the provision of mediation, where appropriate.

Mediation

Family mediation was introduced as the major element in the development of a more constructive approach to the problems of marital breakdown (as both titles of the Green and White Papers highlighted: *Looking to the Future: Mediation and the Ground for Divorce*). In line with the Children Act 1989, the proposals extended to divorce the principle that primary responsibility for decision-making should lie with the parties themselves. Mediation, premised on presuppositions of party competence and party authority for decision-making, was envisaged as a new part of an integrated divorce process, to be available as a resource, supportive of the parties' own decision-making. Issues to be decided included the primary question of whether or not the marriage was over (with the possibility of reconciliation that this entailed) and the arrangements relating to finance, property and children that were to be settled as a precondition of the granting of the divorce order.

Mediation, it was acknowledged, should not be compulsory – 'compulsory mediation quite simply does not work and is a contradiction in terms' (Lord Chancellor, 1995, p. 704). However, mediation was to be given 'definite encouragement' as the means of providing a 'decent and civil' way of ending the marriage (White Paper, 1995, paras 5.21, 5.22). In this way, it was envisaged that the parties would retain control and responsibility, would deal with fault and other relevant matters themselves in face-to-face discussions, which would encourage direct communication and as a result reduce misunderstanding and conflict. In supporting more direct negotiation between the parties assisted where necessary by mediation, the expectation was that there would be less need for arms-length negotiations *on behalf of clients* by lawyers, with the associated litigation, increased costs and increased conflict.

The Family Law Act created four primary opportunities for mediation to take place:

- following the compulsory Information Meeting (section 8);
- following the Statement of Marital Breakdown; the central purpose of the period for reflection and consideration, once it was decided that there was no hope for the survival of the marriage, was for the parties to make joint decisions about arrangements for the future. This was likely to be the main occasion for resort to mediation (section 7(l)(b));
- following the direction of the court once a statement has been made (section 13);[6]

---

6   The court, on its own initiative or on the application of either of the parties, might give directions with respect to mediation to enable each party to attend a meeting to receive an explanation about facilities for mediation and to have the

- when civil legal aid in respect of legal representation was being determined for financially eligible clients (section 29).[7]

That participation in mediation remained a matter of choice for the parties was significant. In upholding the principle of voluntariness of participation in mediation, the Act recognised the fact that mediation would not be appropriate in all cases, including those involving domestic abuse. In addition to these provisions, the usual routes into mediation remained available – for example, self-referral, referral from other agencies, solicitors, health visitors, and so on.

Public funding for family mediation: Part III legal aid for mediation in family matters

Until the Family Law Act 1996, legal aid in divorce cases has been available only for legal advice and representation. The new proposals introduced public funding for mediation in the form of legal aid, available for the first time. Part III of the Family Law Act 1996 amending the Legal Aid Act 1988, provided for legal aid for mediation in family matters to those financially eligible.[8] Public funding for family mediation was thus made available for the first time. Part III of the Act survived and Family mediation and Help with mediation (legal advice and assistance for those attending family mediation) are among a range of services for which the Community Legal Service provides legal aid.[9]

---

opportunity to agree to participate in mediation (Family Law Act, 1996, section 13(l)(a) and 13(1)(b)). There was no *requirement* to participate in mediation.

7   An applicant for legal aid for legal representation is required to attend a pre-mediation meeting with a recognized mediator, for the purpose of determining *suitability* for mediation in Family Law Act (1996, section 29(3F)(b)). This section survived, incorporated into the Access to Justice Act 1999, section 11.Mediation itself remains voluntary.

8   Part III of the Family Law Act 1996 is now incorporated, under the Access to Justice Act 1999, section 8, in a revised form in the Legal Services Commission Funding Code (procedures C27–C29, guidance regulations, directions and orders).

9   Mediation can be privately or publicly funded. The Legal Services Commission, which funds family mediation, contracts with 215 family mediation services nationally in both the not-for-profit and the private sectors (although current contracting arrangements are under review). Under the Funding Code, services can mediate on a 'family dispute', which is defined as a legal dispute arising out of a family relationship, including disputes concerning the welfare of children or which may give rise to family proceedings. Those applying for legal aid for legal representation are required to meet with a recognized mediator in order to consider whether or not mediation is suitable (in relation to the parties, the dispute and all the circumstances).

Mediators contracted to provide publicly funded mediation needed to comply with a code of practice, which also required the mediator to have arrangements designed to ensure the voluntariness of participation in mediation; the identification of the fear of violence or other harm; the review of the possibility of reconciliation; and that each party was informed about the availability of independent legal advice (Family Law Act, section 27(7)).

Under the code, such arrangements had to ensure too, that the parties were encouraged to consider the welfare, wishes and feelings of each child and that there be opportunities for the consultation of the child in mediation (Family Law Act, section 27(8)).

Pilot projects

The Government proposed testing and monitoring the new arrangements for information and mediation services through a 'major comprehensive pilot project' before full implementation. The broad aim of the family mediation pilot was 'to enable the LAB to ensure that arrangements are in place to meet the demand for mediation services created by the Family Law Act 1996' (Legal Aid Board, 1996, p. 3). The LAB recognized the problems of the then limited provision of family mediation services and the limited number both of fully trained and accredited mediators and of qualified supervisors. The aim would be achieved therefore 'by facilitating the development and expansion of the most effective arrangements to provide publicly funded and quality assured family mediation services for eligible clients throughout England and Wales (Legal Aid Board, 1996, p. 3). This investment in development had to be recognized, notwithstanding the main objective of these proposals, which was to reduce the costs of matrimonial proceedings to the Treasury at that time (legal aid claims totalling £328 million for private law cases in 2005–2006, NAO Report, 2007).

Roberts (2001) has identified problematic aspects that beset the research projects[10] set up to monitor the pilots, in particular the fact that the new procedures (Information Meetings and mediation pilots) were tested under the 'old' adversarial divorce regime, proving too different to be effectively evaluated in that context. In addition, probably the result of the change of government, an alteration in the research objectives, subtle yet critical, occurred. Whereas initially the pilots were intended to ascertain *how* the new arrangements for providing information and mediation could be best delivered, there was a gradual refocusing on *whether* the new arrangements of the Act was such a good idea in the first place (Roberts, 2001).

The big questions became:

---

10   See Walker (2000) and Davis et al. (2000).

- whether the parties could be quickly persuaded to undertake mediation in 'sufficient' numbers;
- whether consumers would view the performance of mediators favourably compared with lawyers;
- whether mediation would prove cheaper than legal representation (Roberts, 2001, pp. 269–70).

It is argued that this shift of understanding about the purpose of the research project, combined with other pressures and interests to reduce the already remote prospect of Part II of the Act being implemented. In the relatively short time-span allotted for the research, it was unlikely that 'entirely reassuring' answers to these questions would emerge (Roberts, 2001, p. 270).

Domestic violence: Part IV of the Family Law Act 1996

This is a version of the Family Homes and Domestic Violence Bill, amended specifically to make a distinction between cohabiting and married victims of domestic violence, which, with Part III, was also implemented. The original Bill was perceived by some Members of Parliament as undermining marriage by according cohabiting couples equal status to married couples in cases of abuse. As it happened, existing law enabled an abusive partner, whether married or cohabiting, to be excluded from the family home. Although unmarried victims of domestic violence would enjoy lesser protection under the Bill than their married counterparts, the quality and quantity of personal and housing protection for adults, married or not, was improved and expanded. For example, occupation orders reduced the threat of homelessness and non-molestation orders could apply to 'associated persons' as well as partners, married or cohabiting. 'Associated persons' could be ex-partners (married or cohabitees), relatives and non-related members of the same household (Family Law Act, section 62(3)). The Act increased powers of arrest attached to injunctions 'unless satisfied that in all the circumstances of the case the applicant or child will be adequately protected without such a power of arrest' (Family Law Act, section 47(2)). The risk of violence to children was reduced and their interests given greater consideration in Magistrates Courts as well as County and High Court proceedings.

Part IV of the Family Law Act 1996 has been amended by the Domestic Violence, Crime and Victims Act 2004. One new provision is that included under the definition of 'associated persons', people who 'have or have had an intimate personal relationship with each other which is or was of significant duration' (section 62(3)) (see also the Protection from Harassment Act 1997, which created two new criminal offences relating to courses of conduct (including speech) amounting to harassment and causing fear of violence).

The Children Act 1989

The main aims of the Children Act were twofold: to have a single body of law relating to the care and upbringing of children; and to provide a consistent set of legal remedies for all courts and in all proceedings.

Principles of the Children Act 1989

The Act sets out the basic principles upon which the courts shall decide issues relating to children, namely parental responsibility, no delay, and minimum intervention. These principles of law are governed by the overarching principle, that the child's welfare must be the court's paramount consideration.

The welfare principle (s.1)

The 'welfare principle' has been described as 'the golden thread which runs through the whole of this court's jurisdiction' (Re D 1977). The child's welfare must be the paramount consideration for any court in deciding any question relating to children. The court makes no distinction between children in private law proceedings, in public law proceedings and children in need – for example, applying the same principle in deciding any question relating to the upbringing of children or the administration of a child's property. The child's welfare is considered 'first, last and all the time' (Re D 1977). This has been the cardinal principle guiding the court in relation to decisions over children since the Guardianship of Minors Act 1971 (re-enacting the Guardianship of Infants Acts of 1886 and 1925). As Walsh (2006, p. 194) highlights, welfare 'is a concept easy to recognise but hard to define'. This is the definition cited by the Law Commission (Working Paper 96):

> Welfare is an all encompassing word. It includes material welfare in the sense of adequacy of resources to provide a pleasant home and a comfortable standard of living and in the sense of adequacy of care to ensure that good health and due personal pride are maintained. However, while material considerations have their place, they are secondary matters. More important are the stability and security, the warm and compassionate relationships, that are essential for the full development of the child's own character, personality and talents. (Quoted in Walsh, 2006, p. 194, section 4.1)

Non-interventionism of the court (section 1(5))

> Where a court[11] is considering whether or not to make one or more orders under the Act with respect to a child, it shall not make the order or any of the orders unless it considers *that doing so would be better for the child than making no order at all.* (Children Act 1989, section 1(5); emphasis added)

This is the second radical new principle of the Act. It reinforces the concept of parental responsibility (see below) in its presumption that there is no need for a court order at all except where an order is the most effective way of safeguarding or promoting the welfare of the child. In other words, the order must positively contribute to the child's welfare, for example, in meeting a need for certainty, security and predictability in situations of domestic abuse. This presumption against the making of court orders is based both on the expectation that the meeting of parental responsibility will lead to a reduced need for court intervention and on the view that the court does not necessarily know what is best. The court does not have the right to impose its own values. The Children Act, in upholding a preference for parents to make their own arrangements about children (as well as property and financial matters) without the necessity for court intervention, has placed a radically new emphasis on the value of private ordering.

In both the private and the public law, the assumption that the court should make an order is removed, although section 1(5) does not create a 'no order' principle either (see above). There is a presumption, therefore, that parents are the best carers of their children (unless there is a risk of harm) and that just because they are separating or divorcing, there is no need to assume that the court should make an order particularly where there is no dispute. The court will make an order if there are circumstances when making an order would be better for the child than making no order.

The same principles apply to matters between non-married parents concerning children. Where they make a parental responsibility agreement under the Children Act 1989 (whereby they both have full parental responsibility for the child) and the agreement contains formalities including lodging the agreement with the court in London (The Principal Registry), this may be done without a court order (Walsh, 2006). Even where there is parental agreement or parental co-operation (with local authorities, for example), there are circumstances where a court order may be beneficial, for example:

---

11   For the purposes of this Act, 'the court' means the High Court, a county court or a magistrates' court (Children Act 1989, section 92 (7)).

- in order to confer some security in a 'door of the court' settlement;
- in order to confer the legal status of parental responsibility on carers who are not parents by means of a residence order;
- where there is a risk of child abduction, a residence order could confer useful security;
- where the lack of an order may result in harm to a child (for example, if a child is removed precipitately from foster carers without a proper assessment of the impact) or where there is concern that parental co-operation may not last (see Walsh, 2006, for more detail).

Delay is bad for children (section 1(2))

> … The court must have regard to the general principle that any delay in determining the question is likely to prejudice the welfare of the child. (s.1(2))

Delay is considered to be bad because it creates uncertainty and harms the relationship between parents and their capacity to co-operate in the future, with the result that the welfare of the child is likely to suffer. This principle embodies the only explicit value judgment in the Act. What this means in practice is that the court will be much more involved in the conduct of each case. It is the court that controls timetabling (not the parties), so that drift, as a result of unnecessary adjournments and/or delay, is prevented. Good case management is intended to minimize expense and delay and procedures in private and public law dictate that the overriding objective is to deal with every children's case 'justly, expeditiously, fairly and with the minimum of delay' (Private Law Programme: Guidance issued by the President of the Family Division, 2004, p. 5).

Notwithstanding concerns about the detrimental effects of delay, good reasons for delay have been endorsed by the courts, such as the advantages of allowing 'things to settle down' (*Re S. (Minors) (Custody)* 1992) and of monitoring a programme for interim contact (*Re B. (A Minor) (Contact) (Interim Order)* 1994). Although the avoidance of delay is a basic tenet of the Children Act 1989, persistent and endemic delay continues to be a cause of concern (Walsh, 2006).

Provisions of the Children Act 1989

Parental responsibility (s.3)

> In this Act 'Parental Responsibility' means all the rights, duties, powers, responsibilities and authority which by law a parent of a child has in relation to the child and his property. (Children Act 1989, section 3(i))

This was a fundamentally new legal concept introduced by the Act. 'Parental responsibility' and the primary status it accords to parenthood, replaced the old concept on which the law was based, namely 'parental rights'. In contrast, parental responsibility gives significance to the everyday practical responsibilities of caring for children – bringing up the child, caring and making decisions.[12] Parental responsibility rests automatically on both parents if they are married when their child is born or if they have been married to one another at any time since the child's conception. It is an enduring status that is not lost on separation or divorce (or when a child is in the care of the local authority) and one that recognizes that parenthood is a responsibility that begins at a child's birth and cannot be surrendered. On divorce, therefore, both parents continue to have parental responsibility, which resides independently in each.

In 2003, the Children Act 1989 was amended by the Adoption and Children Act 2002 to extend the status of parental responsibility to unmarried fathers whose name was registered on the child's birth certificate after 1 December 2003.[13] A further extension of parental responsibility has occurred in relation to step-parents and civil partners, who may now obtain parental responsibility for their partner's child(ren) by agreement or by court order (see Adoption and Children Act 2002 and the Civil Partnership Act 2004). This means that, for the first time, a person other than the biological father may obtain parental responsibility *directly* rather than by having to obtain a shared residence order (Walsh, 2006). Several people therefore can have the status of parental responsibility in relation to the same child(ren). (For more detailed coverage of the scope of parental responsibility recognized by the court, see Walsh, 2006, pp. 210–214.)

The introduction of the legal concept of 'parental responsibility' has the following implications.

- It replaces a 'rights' approach to parenthood, which tends to foster a competitive, adversarial approach.
- A person with parental responsibility does not cease to have it solely because another person has it.
- It preserves the equal status of each parent.

---

12   That there is no statutory list of matters covering parental responsibility is deliberate. Those aspects of parental responsibility decided on by the courts include a child's religion, education, medical treatment, emigration, adoption, name, property, and so on.

13   Because this provision is not retrospective, it can result in the anomalous situation of some fathers having parental responsibility for one child but not another.

- It gives each parent the authority to act independently of the other in relation to the children (unless the court orders otherwise). Therefore parental responsibility can be met alone.
- It is intended to encourage both parents to feel responsible for the welfare of their children and to have a continuing role to play in relation to the children.
- It removes one significant area of dispute during divorce – the issue of legal custody.
- It is intended to reduce conflict and therefore enhance the continuing involvement of both parents in the care and upbringing of their children.
- In promoting agreement, it is intended to advance the welfare of children.
- Parental responsibility may not be surrendered or transferred. Some or all of it may be delegated but it remains intact always (unless removed by adoption). This means that a parent with parental responsibility will be responsible always for ensuring adequate arrangements for the care of the child. If a Care Order is made, the local authority shares parental responsibility with those who already have it.
- Local authorities have a duty to consult parents, the child and non-parents with parental responsibility. There is no equivalent legal duty in the private law for those with parental responsibility to consult each other. The Law Commission (1990) considered this to be both 'unworkable' and 'undesirable', likely to lead to an escalation of disputing.[14]

Section 8 orders

The private law orders available under the Act are available in all 'family proceedings'. Family proceedings include proceedings under the inherent jurisdiction of the High Court and a number of different Acts (Children Act 1989, sections 8(3) and (4)).

Section 8 orders – residence orders, contact orders, specific issue orders and prohibited steps orders – are designed to resolve concrete, practical issues relating to the care and upbringing of children. They are not designed to confer rights. Section 8 orders are not made once a child has reached the age of 16, except in exceptional circumstances.

---

14   The Children (Scotland) Act 1995, section 11, goes further than the Children Act 1989 in introducing a requirement that all those with parental responsibility should have regard, so far as is practicable, to the views of the child if s/he wishes to express them.

These orders incorporate, in one enactment, with one common procedure, a wide variety of different remedies formerly requiring Access Orders, injunctions, custody and custodianship orders and others. The aim is to simplify cases particularly where more than one remedy is sought.

The court is not bound by or confined to what has been asked for. It has the duty to consider all the powers open to it and has the utmost flexibility in exercising its powers. It must choose the most appropriate order in the particular case, not necessarily the order sought (Children Act 1989, section 1(3)(g)). The court may add conditions, give directions and make any other provision it thinks fit. Even if there is no dispute, if a child needs an order for purposes of security or stability, then the court will make an order. In family proceedings therefore, s.8 orders can be made by the court of its own motion even if no other family proceedings are being undertaken.

The object of section 8 orders is to preserve, as much as possible, each person's independence in meeting his/her parental responsibility. The orders are designed to encourage the continuing involvement of both parents in their children's lives. They are not, therefore, the equivalent of a joint custody order, with its right of veto by one parent over important decisions by the parent with care and control. Residence and contact orders are not the same as the old 'Custody' and 'Access' orders. Their aim and purpose is to promote parental responsibility by encouraging parents to try to resolve disputes themselves and not regard custody as a first prize and access as a consolation prize, that is, their aim is to lower the stakes where there is disagreement. In addition, a residence order is different from a custody order, in that it is more flexible (different arrangements are possible) and is separate from parental responsibility. A residence order regulates the practical arrangements relating to where a child lives. It does not transfer or re-allocate parental responsibility, which continues in both parents. If there is agreement, there is no need for a court order.

Residence orders

Residence orders confer parental responsibility and therefore legal security on those who do not already have it, for example, unmarried fathers (including those whose names are not registered on their child's birth certificate after December, 2003), non-parents, or relatives. Residence orders provide a link between the private and public law. They are a means by which, for example, foster parents may acquire parental responsibility and hence legal status in relation to foster children. They are also a means whereby, for example, grandparents can care for a child at risk who might otherwise go into care. A residence order discharges a Care Order, and vice versa.

Once a residence order is in force, the child may not be removed from the UK or have his/her surname changed without the written consent of every person with parental responsibility, or without the leave of the court (Children Act 1989, section 13(1)). While a residence order imposes an automatic restriction on the removal of a child from the country, this does not prevent the removal of a child for a period of less than a month by the person with a residence order. There is no limit on the number of short trips that may be taken, but if there is a fear of abduction a prohibited steps order may be necessary.

Residence orders may be made in favour of two or more persons who do not live together. The order may specify the periods for the different households concerned (Children Act 1989, section 11(4)). The view of the court used to be that shared residence orders were 'non-conventional' orders and should be made only where it can be clearly demonstrated that there is a positive benefit to the child (*A*. v. *A*. 1994). Judicial opinion now is that such an order 'is not necessarily to be considered an exceptional order and should be made if it is in the best interests of the children concerned' (per Wall J. in *A*. v. *A*. *(Shared Residence)* [2004] 1FLR 1195). A harmonious relationship between the parents is also not now a prerequisite to the making of a shared residence order (*D*. v. *D*. *(Shared Residence Order)* [2001] 1 FLR 495; see below for further discussion on shared residence).

Contact orders

Contact orders are intended to be wider than the old Access Orders, also covering arrangements other than physical contact, for example, letters, telephone, or, in some cases, Internet video conferencing. The contact order is also more child-centred in that it allows the *child* to visit or stay or have other contact with the person named in the order rather than the other way round (section 8(1)). Contact with a parent is a fundamental right of a child save in exceptional circumstances (*Re W*. 1994). Yet it is not possible to compel an unwilling parent to have contact and the government has dismissed the suggestion that there should be such a power (Government reply to Report 2005). There may be more than one contact order, made out to anyone, that is anyone with a serious interest in the child.[15]

Recent case decisions confirm the courts' endorsement of the principle that it is important to preserve the child's contact with both parents. This principle of continuing contact is enshrined in Article 9 of the United Nations Convention on the Rights of the Child (*Re R*. 1993).

---

15   The introduction of contact activity directions and conditions, inserted into paragraphs 11A–11G of the Children Act 1989 by the Children and Adoption Act 2006, gives the court powers, when considering making or varying a contact order, to require a party to take part in an activity that promotes contact with the child concerned, for example, advice, guidance or information programmes or classes, counselling, or mediation. There is no power to require a party to mediate.

Specific issue orders and prohibited steps orders

Specific issue orders and prohibited steps orders cover decisions the court would make, for example, over which school a child is to attend, whether or not a child is to undergo an operation, whether a child may be taken abroad, and so on.[16] A prohibited steps order can be made against anyone. That person does not have to be a party to the proceedings (*Re H.* 1995).

The checklist (section 1(3))

The checklist is a checklist of *factors* (not a set of guidelines) relating to the child's needs that the court must have particular regard to in making an order that places the welfare of the child as paramount. The checklist applies only in contested private proceedings under Part II of the Act (Orders With Respect To Children In Family Proceedings) and any proceedings under Part IV of the Act (Care And Supervision).

The factors to be considered are:

- the ascertainable wishes and feelings of the child concerned (considered in the light of his/her age and understanding);
- his/her physical, emotional and educational needs;
- the likely effect on him/her of any change in his/her circumstances;
- his/her age, sex, background and any characteristics of his/hers which the court considers relevant;
- any harm which he/she has suffered or is at risk of suffering;
- how capable each of his/her parents, and any other person in relation to whom the court considers the question to be relevant, is of meeting his/her needs;
- the range of powers available to the court under this Act in the proceedings in question.

In enshrining in law for the first time (other than in adoption proceedings) that in family proceedings the child's wishes and feelings must be ascertained, the perspective of the child assumed a new significance and became the central focus of the Act. Case law has clarified the question of the weight to be attached to this factor and whether the fact that it features first on the checklist gives it a predominance over the other factors.

---

16   'A "specific issues order" means an order giving directions for the purpose of determining a specific question which has arisen, or which may arise, in connection with any aspect of parental responsibility for a child. "A prohibited steps order" means an order that no step which could be taken by a parent in meeting his parental responsibility for a child, and which is of a kind specified in the order, shall be taken by any person without the consent of the court' (Children Act 1989, section 8(1).

The courts, over the last few years, have become increasingly aware of the importance of listening to the views of older children and taking into account what children say, not necessarily agreeing with what they want nor, indeed, doing what they want, but paying proper respect to older children who are of an age and the maturity to make their minds up as to what they think is best for them. (*Re P. (A Minor) (Education)* [1992] 1 FLR 316, 321 BUTLER-SLOSS LJ)

Therefore, important though the child's wishes are when determining what, if any, order ought to be made, they are ultimately but one of the factors that have to be taken into account under the statutory checklist. (See also *Re R.* [1995] 1 FLR 716.) In this case, notwithstanding the expressed wish of the children to stay with their mother in the UK, the court ordered their return to US where custody proceedings were taking place.

The checklist is intended to achieve consistency among courts in their orders relating to children and their welfare. Although limited in its application to contested proceedings, the checklist is useful where out-of-settlements are being negotiated (by solicitors or the parties themselves), bearing in mind what factors the courts will consider in making decisions. The checklist is not an invitation to solicitors, mediators or social workers to apply it themselves in interviewing children or making assessments and so on.

The Lord Chancellor warned of the need for care in the application of the checklist:

> The Act sets out important principles many of which require those applying them to think as carefully about their attitudes and values as about legal concepts. The checklist in section 1 is a prime example: to evaluate a child's physical, emotional and educational needs, the effect on him of change, or any harm he may have suffered or is at risk of suffering – *these are complex questions, as complex as life itself*. No one profession can provide the answers to all of them but by working in partnership a better answer for the child may emerge upon which the court may then act. (Emphasis added)

Since the Children Act 1989's inception, Government inquiries and consultations examining the Act have upheld its principles and affirmed its legislative framework as fundamentally sound. The difficulties that have arisen have been found to lie not in the law but in problems arising from its interpretation, resources and implementation (Walsh, 2006). In respect of public law in particular, important lessons for policy and practice have been incorporated in the Children Act 2004, the Children and Adoption Act 2006, and *Working Together to Safeguard Children* 2006.

The decisions of the court

One important aspect of the legal environment of private decision-making is the kind of decisions that the courts are likely to make in similar circumstances. It would be helpful obviously if there was certainty in the law, or at least if the legal rules involved were reasonably capable of being ascertained. Unfortunately as far as financial and children cases are concerned there is a lamentable uncertainty.

It is however possible, broadly speaking, to discern some of the principles that underlie decisions of the court, and which therefore, should inform the legal backcloth against which solicitors as well as private individuals negotiate. But these 'legal endowments' (Mnookin and Kornhauser, 1979) do not necessarily influence the bargaining positions within these negotiations (Menkel-Meadow, 1993a).

Richards (1981, 1994a) has identified four broad principles influencing the decisions of the court.

The primacy of the welfare of the child

This principle, rarely challenged (although see Guggenheim, 2005), is the standard test for determining disputes concerning children. Richards (1994a, p. 260) proposes that the simple definition be adopted to reduce the scope for argument, that the children should reside with whichever parent is able to convince the court that they are the parent most likely to foster and maintain the children's links with the other parent and the wider family:

> Such a criterion has a long history (Solomon, 1 Kings 3. 16–28) and should ensure that attention is focused on the welfare of the children rather than the supposed moral worth of each parent.

The status quo

As far as decisions over the care and upbringing of children are concerned, it is very unusual for the court to change the child's place of residence. In most cases the court confirms the de facto situation – it accepts the arrangements made by the parties (Eekelaar et al., 1977). The status quo is, therefore, rarely altered, both in uncontested and contested cases, unless it is unsatisfactory. This judicial reluctance to interfere recognizes that what is best for the child is the minimum of disruption of the child's emotional, social and educational life. It is also an acknowledgement of the limited effect of legal proceedings in such complex social and psychological circumstances.

What this highlights for mediators is the fact that the initial arrangements relating to children, made informally after separation, have important long-term legal implications. These arrangements are likely to persist and become the status quo confirmed by the court.

The primary caretaker

The courts do not, on the whole, favour either sex as the more suitable parent (Eekelaar et al., 1977). In pursuit of the objective of minimum disruption to the existing emotional and social ties of the child, the paramountcy of the status quo usually prevails. In many cases, confirming the status quo results in making the parent who provided the bulk of the child care within marriage, the residential parent after divorce. This can resemble the return to the maternal presumption which preceded the welfare principle.

As all decisions are in the discretion of each judge, there are bound to be variations in the significance that is attached to the age or sex of the child or to other considerations. Although, in practice, mothers frequently end up with care of their children following divorce, a preference for maternal care has not been adhered to as a matter of principle (Maidment, 1984). It is because women are, in the main, the chief child-carers in marriage that they are likely to continue being so on divorce. Although a father may intend to press for residence initially, he is often influenced against pursuing his claim in the belief that he is unlikely to succeed. This clearly illustrates the way prevailing court decisions can affect the bargaining positions of the parties.

Shared parenting

The Children Act 1989 aims to promote the involvement of both parents by means of the legal concept of parental responsibility. Within marriage, parents share parental responsibility and have equal rights in relation to them (Children Act 1989, section 3). This situation continues after divorce whether or not a residence or contact order is made. Parental responsibility may not be surrendered or transferred, some or all of it may be delegated but it remains intact always (unless removed by adoption). This means that a parent with parental responsibility will be responsible always for ensuring adequate arrangements for the care of the child. If a Care Order is made, the local authority shares parental responsibility with those who have it already.

Prior to the Children Act 1989, a joint custody order enabled both parties to retain their right to be consulted on major decisions affecting the child's upbringing, while recognizing that the child would live with only one parent (Cretney et al., 2003).

However, the significance of a joint custody order lay, not in conferring any additional legal rights on the absent parent, but in its symbolic value in affirming for that parent a continuing commitment to and involvement in the upbringing of the child. The advantage of a joint custody order was therefore psychological. Neither parent 'won'. The advantage from the child's point of view was the affirmation that both parents stood equally in relation to him/her. One possible legal disadvantage of the joint custody order, particularly for the parent with care and control, was that independent action by either parent was limited to where no disapproval has been signified by the other (Children Act 1975, section 85(3)). In the absence of a joint custody order, however, the rights of each parent were equal and exercisable without the other (Guardianship Act 1973, section 1). This meant that separate equal rights allowed greater freedom of action than a joint custody order (Maidment, 1984). Situations where there was no custody order at all therefore usually proved to be the least problematic, both legally and psychologically. Parental responsibility similarly gives each parent the authority to act independently of the other in relation to the children (unless a court orders otherwise).

Where parents are unmarried, the mother has parental responsibility automatically. The father does not have parental responsibility unless he acquires it either by an agreement with the mother made in a prescribed form ('a parental responsibility agreement'), or by application to court (Children Act 1989, section 4(1)) or on being appointed guardian. However, from 1 December 2003, both parents of a child born to unmarried parents have parental responsibility provided that the father's name is registered on the child's birth certificate. Until then, only the unmarried mother had automatic parental responsibility. An unmarried father whose name is not on the birth certificate can acquire parental responsibility in the usual way (see above). The essence of the grant by the court of a Parental Responsibility Order is the grant of status given to the father by fatherhood (*Re S.* 1995). The court will give express consideration to the father's degree of commitment shown to the child, the degree of attachment existing between father and child and the reasons for the application (*Re H.* 1991). If the father fulfils these requirements, then, *prima facie*, it is in the child's interests that such an order be made (*Re G (a Minor)* 1994).

'Shared parenting' is described as

the concept that, following divorce or separation, mothers and fathers should retain a strong positive parenting role in their children's lives, with the children actually spending substantial amounts of time living with each. There are a wide variety of parenting arrangements to suit a range of situations and these provide for time-splits from 30/70 to 50/50. (Hunt with Roberts, 2004, p. 6)

There has been pressure in the UK (in line with an international shared parenting movement) to replace the concepts of residence and contact with a presumption of shared parenting, which, it is argued, would send a stronger message that both parents are expected to be substantially involved in their children's lives; discourage the restriction of contact by one parent; set the framework for negotiation; and reduce disputes (Hunt with Roberts, 2004).

However, the courts have been reluctant to make joint residence orders. All decisions depend on the individual facts, but a decision of the Court of Appeal indicated that such an order should only be made where it can be clearly demonstrated that there is a positive benefit to the child in making such a 'non-conventional' order (*A. v. A.* 1994, CA). Where there is no order between married parents, the effect equates virtually to that under a shared residence order, with both parents retaining parental responsibility and exercising it independently, subject to their duty to consult and inform one another on the important matters concerning the child (Cretney et al., 2003).

Hunt with Roberts (2004, p. 6) have highlighted the ways in which debates about shared parenting, across jurisdictions, are confused by the 'elision of different concepts': shared responsibility (often referred to as joint legal custody); shared residence (joint physical custody) and equal parenting time (a legal presumption of equal parenting time unusual in the UK). While initial research in the UK was reasonably positive about children's experiences of 50/50 living arrangements, which most regarded as 'normal' (see Smart et al., 2001), the follow-up study found that, from the child's perspective, these arrangements had often become increasingly unsatisfactory and many children found it extremely hard to change the arrangements once they were in place. Even where children thought shared residence a good thing, with their needs prioritised and feeling at home in both households, they looked forward to the time when they could stop 'living like nomads' (Neale et al., 2003, quoted in Hunt with Roberts, 2004). The researchers concluded that: 'Shared residence is not a magic solution to a difficult problem. To some extent it merely stretches an existing problem over years and it can be the children who have to absorb the pressures' (Neale et al., 2003, quoted in Hunt with Roberts, 2004, p. 7).

Contact

Prior to the Children Act 1989

In about one-third to one-half of divorces, no Access Orders were made (Eekelaar et al., 1977). This is because they were not asked for and the courts did not make Access Orders unless requested to. Only rarely was access denied to the then non-custodial parent (as in the case of *Wright* v. *Wright*

1980, where the father would use access visits to indoctrinate the child with Jehovah's Witness beliefs and possibly cause emotional disturbance). Sometimes the court ordered conditions to be attached to access, for example, that it be supervised by friends or unbiased relatives or that the child should not be brought in contact with a named person.

After the Children Act 1989

The principle of continuing contact is generally upheld by the courts. This means that the court regards it as important that the child's contact with both parents is preserved, a principle enshrined not only in the Children Act 1989 but also in the UN Convention on the Rights of the Child (Article 9) (*Re R.* 1993). Contact with a parent is regarded as a fundamental right of the child save in exceptional circumstances (*Re W.* 1994). There must be cogent reasons why a child should be denied contact with both parents (*Re H.* 1992).

Despite the importance that the courts attach to preserving links with the non-resident parent, the legal system can do little if parents fail to exercise their right to contact, or if a parent obstructs contact, psychologically or practically. The courts are reluctant to enforce an order for contact if it has been flouted.

Powerful, occasionally disruptive lobbying campaigns by father's groups (such as Fathers 4 Justice) have drawn attention to the discrimination fathers claim to experience under the family justice system. It is considered likely that this may have resulted in an increase in the number of residence orders in favour of fathers. In two recent cases, the Court of Appeal has upheld judgments moving children from their mother's to their father's home after the mothers flouted orders that allowed the fathers to have regular contact with their children.

Domestic violence

Only recently has domestic violence attracted attention commensurate with its incidence and impact in respect of family breakdown and court decisions (see above Part IV of the Family Law Act 1996; and Chapter 11 for further examination of domestic abuse policy and practice issues in the context of family mediation). The courts were slow to apprehend the serious implications of domestic violence in relation to contact until the late 1990s, when the significance of the problem was acknowledged first, in the CASC Report on *Contact with Violent Parents* (1999) and then in a government consultation paper, *Safety and Justice* (2003). Until then, even proven violence could be treated as less important than contact with the child, and parents who did not agree to arrangements that they regarded as unsafe, could be seen as 'implacably hostile' (Hunt with Roberts, 2004; see also Chapter 10). It was recognized too that contact arrangement could be potentially hazardous (physically and psychologically) for children where the adult carer was the victim of violence, the risks increasing when disputes were litigated (Hunt with Roberts, 2004).

In the landmark decision (*Re L. (Contact: Domestic Violence)* [2000] 2 FLR 334), the Court of Appeal, describing domestic violence as 'a significant failure of parenting', refused direct contact, urged greater awareness of the consequences for children of domestic violence, and issued guidelines in line with the CASC Report (Hunt with Roberts, 2004; Walsh, 2006). The Court of Appeal decided that, while there should not be a presumption against contact where domestic violence was established, it was a 'highly relevant and significant factor which must be taken into account'. The President of the Family Division took the unusual step of seeking the advice of two expert child psychiatrists, whose view it was that there should be no automatic assumption that contact to a previously or currently violent parent was in the child's interests; if anything, the assumption should be in the opposite direction (Sturge and Glaser, 2000). The Adoption and Children Act 2002 (section 120), which came into force in 2005, amended the Children Act 1989 to include, in the definition of harm to a child, impairment (of the child's health or development) resulting from witnessing the ill-treatment of others. As well as physical violence, the definition of harm includes sexual abuse and other forms of abuse, and it operates in all proceedings where the court applies the welfare checklist including section 4 (parental responsibility) and section 8 (residence and contact) orders (Walsh, 2006).

Following a recommendation by Lord Justice Wall in 2006, the Family Justice Council is considering, in a multi-disciplinary context, the approach that should be adopted by the courts to proposed consent orders (where the parties have agreed the terms) in contact cases where domestic violence was in issue (Walsh, 2006).

Finance and property

Ancillary relief

The Children Act 1989 principle, of non-intervention of the court, has also been applied to ancillary relief matters and divorcing couples have been encouraged to reach their own agreements on finance and property rather than resort to legal proceedings. In reaching their own agreement, it has been strongly recommended that couples take independent legal advice in the process and embody their agreement in a court order (Consent

Order). Where couples cannot agree in finance and property cases, or require assistance in reaching agreement, mediation or lawyer negotiation (including new collaborative lawyer approaches) is officially encouraged. It is now the accepted view among family lawyers, and the Legal Services Commission, that a negotiated agreement is better that a court-imposed order (see the Code of Practice of *Resolution*; and the Law Society's Family Law Protocol 2002).

Where the matter does go to court, a FDR (Financial Dispute Resolution) appointment with the judge is now a well-established part of ancillary relief proceedings, in order to explore possibilities of agreement through discussion and negotiation. In addition to facilitating settlements in a more informal setting (compared to that of a final trial), the FDR appointment, is designed to reduce delay, limit costs and provide the court with greater and more effective control over the conduct of the proceedings (see below).

The court has extensive discretionary powers to make financial and property orders ancillary to divorce, nullity or judicial separation (the principal relief) – similar orders also now made ancillary to the dissolution of a civil partnership. All orders can be made in favour of either party to the marriage[17] and the court seeks to realize the objective of the Matrimonial Act 1973, section 25, in achieving certainty and equality in its adjudications.[18] While the court's powers are extremely flexible, certain types of orders have become common.[19] The court applies the yardstick of equal division, which means that the court adopts equal division as a starting point, not as a presumption or principle (Cretney et al., 2003). Equality is to be understood as '… formal equality of division, and not that of substantive equality of outcome' (Cretney et al., 2003, p. 375). Ancillary relief orders fall into two categories – those orders relating to income (periodical payments) and those relating to the transfer of capital assets (Cretney et al., 2003).

In proceedings for divorce or judicial separation, the court has very wide powers to do what it thinks just in relation to the ownership and occupation of the family home (MCA 1973, sections 23–25).[20] This may extend to the

---

17   Although if one party is a respondent and has remarried, s/he may not be able to bring a claim if no application has been made before the remarriage.

18   The statutory guidelines for the exercise of the court's discretion are contained in section 25 of the MCA 1973 as amended by the Matrimonial and Family Proceedings Act 1984.

19   For example, the Mesher order, an order for sale and division postponed during the dependence of children, was very popular at one time since it enabled the court to preserve each party's stake in an (appreciating) capital asset while at the same time preserving a home for the mother (usually) and the children (*Mesher* v. *Mesher* [1980] 1 All ER 126, CA).

20   Although the Matrimonial and Family Proceedings Act 1984 amended the law in accordance with the recommendations of the Law Commission, the statutory guidelines remain substantially unchanged.

transfer of ownership rights from one spouse to the other. It is nearly always a 'purely theoretical exercise' to determine the strict property rights of the spouses in these proceedings, although the court will be reluctant to interfere with joint ownership. The primary objective of the court will be to consider how the asset can best be used as a home. Each case is dealt with on its own facts, which means that the court needs to adopt the greatest flexibility in coming to its decisions.

Before 2000, a divorcing wife would get enough for her reasonable needs but, in that year, the English courts introduced the new principles of fairness and equality, rating the homemaker's contribution as highly as the breadwinner's. Recent decisions of the House of Lords (see *White* v. *White* 2000; *Miller* v. *Miller* and *McFarlane* v. *McFarlane* 2006) provide important guidance on the principles of fairness and equality that underpin the jurisdiction, designed as they are to promote consistency and practicality and to assist in furthering private ordering – as Baroness Hale stated: 'this is not only to secure that so far as possible like cases are treated alike but also to enable and encourage the parties to negotiate their own solutions as quickly and cheaply as possible' (*Miller* v. *Miller* 2006, para. 122). In the *Miller* and *McFarlane* cases (heard together and both involving 'big money'), their Lordships sought to analyse how these principles were to be applied, identifying three 'rationales', 'elements' or 'strands' which should inform judicial discretion and influence the law of ancillary relief: (1) need; (2) equal sharing of 'matrimonial property' and (3) compensation. Now that marriage is defined as an equal partnership with an entitlement to share both assets and income, it was emphasized that the court must not discriminate between husband and wife in their respective roles. The significance of the principle of equality was expressed by Lord Nicholls in this way:

> A third strand is sharing. This 'equal sharing' principle derives from the basic concept of equality permeating a marriage as understood today. Marriage, it is often said, is a partnership of equals. This is now recognised widely, if not universally. The parties commit themselves to sharing their lives. They live and work together. When their partnership ends each is entitled to an equal share of the assets of the partnership, unless there is a good reason to the contrary. Fairness requires no less. But I emphasise the qualifying phrase: 'unless there is good reason to the contrary'. The yardstick of equality is to be applied as an aid, not a rule. (*Miller* v. *Miller* 2006, para. 16)

So the 'ultimate objective', as Baroness Hale articulated it, '... is to give each party an equal start on the road to independent living' (*Miller* v. *Miller* 2006, para. 144). Furthermore, the goal of achieving the chance of a clean break (see MCA 1973, section 25A, and *Minton* v. *Minton* 1978) 'is qualified by the demands of fairness when it requires that the earner compensate the non-earner for marriage-generated economic disadvantage' (Brasse, 2006,

p. 647; see also Bridge, 2006). These cases also confirm that consideration of conduct is irrelevant unless 'gross and obvious' and so marked that it would be 'inequitable to disregard it'.[21]

The principles adumbrated in these exceptional 'big money' cases (for example, *Miller* v. *Miller* and *McFarlane* v. *McFarlane* 2006) have yet to be considered in their application to more usual financial circumstances where family resources are limited. It is recognized that in the vast majority of cases financial needs cannot be met just as other strands of fairness may be irrelevant. As Lord Nicholls stated:

> In most cases, the search for fairness largely begins and ends with needs. In most cases, the available assets are insufficient to provide adequately for the needs of two homes. The court has to stretch modest finite resources as far as possible to meet the parties' needs. (*Miller* v. *Miller* 2006, para. 12)

Baroness Hale (para. 128) identified three statutory 'pointers' towards the correct approach of the court in exercising its jurisdiction under the MCA 1973:

1. Consideration should be given to the welfare, while minors, of the children of the family;
2. Regard must be had to the foreseeable future as well as with the past and the present;
3. A clean break, severing the spouses' continuing financial ties where appropriate, is to be encouraged.

The House of Lords, it is claimed, has attempted 'to put in place a framework within which property and financial disputes on divorce could be disposed of on a fair and principles basis' (Eekelaar, 2006). Yet, it is also argued, much of the judgment focused on general principles, the overarching principle of fairness in particular, and this remains a subjective concept susceptible to varying interpretations depending on the facts. Because this can create difficulties for couples seeking to make their own agreements and for those who advise parties, it is likely to lead to further litigation (Meehan, 2006).

---

21   One of the most difficult aspects of the House of Lords' decision in the Miller and McFarlane cases, relates to the question of what is meant by 'matrimonial' and 'non-matrimonial property' – neither concepts found in the MCA 1973 – and how these are to be treated in the ancillary relief claim (see *Rossi* v. *Rossi* [2006] EWHC 1482 (Fam); and *H.* v. *H.* [2007] EWHC 459 (Fam) in which Charles J. sets out a three-step approach for achieving the flexibility of the statutory provisions and the objective of a fair result in the given case. The 'big money' case of *Charman* v. *Charman* ([2007] EWCA Civ 503) also highlights the way in which, since *White* v. *White* (2000), the shift of focus of the court has been from needs, to the computation of resources. The Court of Appeal in the Charman case has called for a review, by the Law Commission, of the English law of the property consequences of marriage and divorce, and the state of international law in this area.

In addition, with the law of England and Wales seen to be so 'wife-friendly' and London, acknowledged (by Court of Appeal judges) as 'the divorce capital of the world for aspiring wives', an increase in 'forum-shopping' by the wealthy seems inevitable (see *Charman* v. *Charman*, 2007).

Where the parties are not married or where the litigation does not fall within s.26 (1) of the MCA 1973 (petitions for divorce, nullity or judicial separation), the power to vary title is unavailable. The court therefore has to determine the legal and beneficial interests of the parties in accordance with the rules of property law.

As far as the occupation of the home is concerned, consideration should be given to the impact of any injunction that may be in operation. An injunction may either exclude a spouse (whether owner or non-owner) from the family home or part of it or a specified area in which the home is situated or it may require a spouse to allow the other to enter or remain in the home or part of it (an occupation order under Part IV of the Family Law Act 1996). An injunction may also be granted restraining one spouse from molesting the other or any child living with the applicant. The court may also exercise these powers in favour of an unmarried cohabitee.

Physical violence, or the threat of it, eviction (actual, attempted or threatened) and conduct making it impossible or intolerable for a spouse or the children to remain in the home all come within the ambit of Part IV of the Family Law Act 1996, which gives the court the power to suspend or restrict rights of occupancy, usually for a short period.

The disposition of the matrimonial home is a matter of profound practical significance in disputes over children. As it is in the material interests of children that they have accommodation, the issue of residence and the issue of the matrimonial home are inextricably connected. Since 1973, the practice of the courts has been to allow the custodial parent (now 'the parent with residence') the use of the matrimonial home by granting him or her occupation and, where appropriate, ownership rights. This applies whether the home is owner-occupied or is rented privately or from the local authority. In practice, therefore, fairness between the spouses vis-à-vis their property rights may be incompatible with the need to secure a home for the children. This accounts in part for the claim by some men that their lot is worse as a result of divorce than that of their former wives who, as mothers, are the main carers of the children. Economic realities too account for the fact that maintenance orders are mainly made against husbands.

Ancillary relief reform

The unacceptably high cost of ancillary relief applications (enormous even to get to the FDR stage of proceedings) has caused considerable concern among all members of the legal profession. As a result, the Lord Chancellor's

Department set up the Ancillary Relief Working Party which drafted New Rules intended to remedy the problems of expense and waste. Frequently, costs can be out of all proportion to the assets, and settlement, because it so often occurs at the door of the court, increases legal costs and wastes public resources.

The objectives of reform were:

- To achieve more settlements cost-effectively by controlling disclosure and isolating relevant facts.
- To concentrate on costs at the outset of the case and to keep the parties publicly informed at every stage.
- To assist the courts better to control the pace and content of litigation in order to achieve the just resolution of disputes promptly, economically and in accordance with the needs of the clients and their children.
- To ensure uniformity in practice and procedure in courts in different parts of the country.
- 'To interlock effectively' with the [then] new procedures of divorce reform (Lord Chancellor's Department, 1995, p. 2).

One of the means of achieving these objectives was the introduction of the Financial Dispute Resolution (FDR) Appointment (Rule 8), a forum for the District Judge 'to explore, guide and direct the parties and their advisers through discussion of the issues in an informal setting' (Lord Chancellor's Department, 1995, p. 4; see above). It was recognized that this was a new kind of ADR process 'neither arbitration, adjudication nor mediation' for which the District Judges would require special training (Lord Chancellor's Department, 1995, p. 4). The FDR Appointment was not, it was stated, to be a 'head banging' process but 'a genuine opportunity to resolve any contentious issues in an atmosphere conducive to settlement with all the known facts and information available' (Lord Chancellor's Department, 1995, p. 4).

Pensions

Pensions began to assume increasing importance in family law with the introduction of the pension attachment (then called 'earmarking') by The Pensions Act 1995. Until then, statute and regulations had provided no guidance on the question of the valuation of pension rights. The Act amended the Matrimonial Causes Act (MCA) 1973 in four respects:

- There was a specific duty on the court to take into account pension rights when considering financial provision on divorce under section 25 of the MCA 1973.

- The court now had power to direct trustees or managers of a Pension Scheme to make a payment of a deferred lump sum or maintenance order on behalf of the scheme member to the party without pension rights when the appropriate benefits under the scheme become due. The court also had power to order the scheme member to commute all or part of the benefits which s/he had or was likely to have under the scheme within the permitted Inland Revenue rules.
- The powers of the court to make lump sum and deferred lump sum orders were extended to the making of orders relating to lump sums payable on death under a pension scheme including the nomination (where that power exists) of death benefit to the former spouse of the scheme member. In making such an order the court could override the discretion of trustees or managers.
- It removed the reference to 'foreseeable future' in section 25 of the MCA1973 as far as pension benefits were concerned.

The Family Law Act 1996 (section 16) would have amended section 25B of the MCA 1973 (clause 15) providing the court with the power to divide the pension assets on divorce, creating pension rights for the party who lacked them. The Welfare Reform and Pensions Act 1999, again amending the Matrimonial Causes Act 1973, introduced pension sharing, thereby enabling the court to make pension sharing orders in the interests of fairness and equality. The method of valuation of benefits (prescribed under 1996 regulations) was the cash equivalent transfer value (CETV), which remains the method most frequently used by the pensions industry because of its advantages of being low cost and readily accessible. Most recent regulations (2000) retain the valuation methodology of the CETV or in the case of a pension in payment, the cash equivalent benefits (CEB) (as no CETV is available for such pensions). Because the CETV can be unreliable, it is not unusual for pension expert reports to be needed in mediation.

The new pension law was introduced in December 2000, affecting anyone who petitioned for divorce after that date. New pension procedures including the introduction of a new prescribed Form P (Pension Inquiry Form) became effective in 2005. These increase the focus on pension information where one of the parties decides to apply for either a pension sharing or pension attachment order (see Salter, 2006, for more detailed discussion on this subject).

The Child Support Act 1991

The Child Support Act 1991 introduced, for the first time, an administrative formula approach to the calculation of child maintenance instead of relying on the jurisdiction of the courts for determining, varying and enforcing individual settlements. A new government agency, the Child Support Agency (CSA), an executive agency within the Department for Work and Pensions, was set up in 1993 under the Act, with responsibility for assessing, collecting and, where necessary, enforcing child maintenance. There are two broad categories of applicants under the Act: (a) parents with care of their children who claim state benefits (such as income support) who must have their maintenance assessed by the CSA and (b) others who can choose to do so.

The aim of the legislation was to increase the level and reliability of child support payments and thereby reduce the amount of income support and other benefits paid to single parents by the state. In theory, the Act upheld the uncontroversial political principle that parenting is 'for life' and that parents should, as far as possible, take financial responsibility for their dependent children even when they do not live with them. The economic goal, born of the view that lone parents who received regular maintenance payments were more likely to take paid work, was a powerful impetus too behind the Act.

In practice, the application of the Act has been fraught with problems – largely foreseen – the result both of flawed original proposals and incompetent implementation. A number of criticisms were identified, including the following (Utting, 1995).

- The child support formula was over-complicated and draconian in its effects.
- Disincentives to work were created.
- 'Clean break' capital settlements made prior to the Act (for example, giving sole ownership of the family home to the parent with care of the children) were not taken into account when calculating payments.
- The financial commitments of non-resident parents and their new families were inadequately recognized by the formula, creating difficulties and pressures for stepfamilies.
- Because maintenance obtained from the non-resident parent was deducted pound for pound from their benefit, lone parents on income support had little incentive to co-operate with the CSA.
- Long delays in issuing maintenance assessments resulted in demands for the payment of large sums in arrears.
- Errors in calculation of the formula (reckoned to occur in two thirds of cases) and slowness in securing payments created hardship for resident parents.
- Government targets for the number of claims to be processed and the amount of benefit to be saved in the first two years of the Agency were unrealistic.

In 2000, legislation (The Child Support Pensions and Social Security Act 2000) was passed by government introducing a new method of calculating child support, and initiated in 2003 (for a detailed account of how the system works, see Walsh, 2006, p. 180). An operational improvement plan was instigated in 2006, designed to address the many problems associated with the Act and to improve the delivery performance of the CSA over three years. The aim of the plan has been to improve service to clients, increase the amount of money collected,[22] achieve greater compliance with non-resident parents and 'provide a better platform from which to implement evolving policy in the future' (Walsh, 2006, p. 181).[23]

The Child Maintenance and Other Payments Bill, published in June 2007, intends to replace the Child Support Agency with the Child Maintenance and Enforcement Commission (C-MEC) (a smaller body deploying a simpler, more cost-effective method of collecting child maintenance); to increase enforcement powers; to allow parents on low incomes to keep more of the maintenance owed to them; and to encourage more parents to make and maintain their own private maintenance arrangements where possible. Measures included in the Bill are aimed at reducing the financial burden of the child maintenance system on taxpayers and encouraging parents to pay promptly by allowing the C-MEC to operate a charging scheme in respect of non-resident parents who default on payments in order to help recover the costs of enforcement.

Mediation and the Child Support Agency (CSA)

When couples use mediation to sort out finance and property as well as children issues, they must take full note of the impact of the Child Support Act on their negotiations. Mediators have a responsibility therefore to ensure that couples are informed about the possible impact of the CSA formula upon all their arrangements. If either party is already on income support, or as a result of separation or divorce is likely to become dependent on state benefit, they are informed of the way the CSA operates and, in particular, that no calculations can be made without an accurate CSA figure being obtained

22   After years of neglect the Child Support Agency has started, very recently, to devote increased resources to enforcing child support assessments (Wikely, 2006).

23   The former Solicitors Family Law Association (renamed Resolution) has urged reform of the role of the Child Support Agency by proposing that where the court is already dealing with financial matters it should have the power to determine child support liability (in line with the Child Support Agency formula and rules) as part of the ancillary relief package (and retain jurisdiction to deal with any changes in the future) rather than that this single issue be dealt with separately by the Child Support Agency, thereby replicating the court's investigative functions, creating delay and possibly undermining the 'carefully crafted court package by the level of its assessment' (see Pirrie and Fellows, 2006, p. 587).

from the CSA. It is *the parties'* responsibility to obtain this CSA calculation. In all cases, whether or not one or both parties is or is likely to resort to income support, the possibility of the operation of the CSA should always be examined. As a benchmark for negotiations, a 'ballpark' figure for what the CSA calculation might be, based on the couple's existing circumstances, will be used. This ballpark figure may be obtained from a variety of sources, such as the Citizens' Advice Bureaux, solicitors, legal consultants or the mediators, usually calculated outside the session.

The effect of the CSA on mediation practice has been problematic. It can increase anxiety, mistrust and tension and inflame disputes over children. While one advantage of the formula is that it establishes the expectation of realistic financial support for children, as a fixed item in an otherwise negotiable array of items, it can inhibit option development. Its overall impact on mediation is undoubtedly to complicate and possibly prolong negotiations. On the other hand, greater understanding about the CSA and its impact may be achieved in the joint discussions of mediation, leading to a reduction of suspicion and fear.

Cohabitation

There is no legal definition of cohabitation, although it is generally recognized to refer to couples who live together without either being married or in a civil partnership. Although cohabitation has increased greatly in recent years and is accepted as 'normal' (over 2 million heterosexual, unmarried couples in England and Wales in the twenty-first century), the vast majority (90 per cent) take no legal steps before or after starting to cohabit – often in the mistaken belief that they have a 'common-law marriage' that affords them the same rights as married couples – and, in fact, have significantly fewer rights and responsibilities than their married counterparts (see Probert, 2007; Walsh, 2006).

On the breakdown of a relationship, cohabiting couples have none of the protections of matrimonial divorce law and, as far as property is concerned, have to rely on general property law principles. Where children are concerned, however, less of a distinction is drawn between married and unmarried parents (see Children Act 1989, section 15, relating to orders for financial relief with respect to children). The Law Commission, following its consultation paper (2006) that examined options for reform of the law applying to cohabiting couples on separation and death, has now published a report that recommends the introduction of a new legislative scheme of financial remedies for certain cohabiting couples in the event of their separation. The scheme would apply to cohabiting couples who have had children together, or if they do not have children, had lived together for a minimum duration (the suggested minimum being between two and five years) except where they had made a valid opt-out agreement (Law Commission, 2007). Under this recommended scheme, the court would have a 'weaker' discretion than the wide-ranging discretion it can exercise in determining ancillary relief on divorce, but the principles on which the court is to act would be correspondingly stronger, a benefit in terms of the predictability of likely outcome (Bridge, 2007, p. 998). Even if legislation is passed providing cohabiting couples with a remedy on separation in line with the recommendations of the Law Commission, general property law will continue to be determinative should it prove necessary to ascertain the respective interests of the parties if there is a dispute with a third party; or on the death of one of the parties; or if the parties fail to satisfy the eligibility criteria.

A landmark decision of the House of Lords in *Stack* v. *Dowden* (2007) – the first case to focus on the particular circumstances of cohabiting couples to reach this level – establishes that where a cohabiting couple own a property jointly, there is a strong presumption that they also own it beneficially in equal shares. The evidential burden rests on the person seeking to show that the parties intended their beneficial interests to be different from their legal interests and each case turns on its own facts (Burrows and Orr, 2007).

Pre-nuptial (pre-marital) agreements

Spouses and those registered in same-sex civil partnerships are, unlike cohabitants, unable to bind themselves on divorce in contracts made prior to marriage that set out agreements on what should happen to property and finance should the marriage break down. Such pre-nuptial or pre-marital contracts are not enforceable currently in England and Wales because they are seen to be contrary to public policy for two reasons: first, because they may undermine the institution of marriage and second, because they may undermine the discretion of the court to make tailor-made financial decisions for families on marriage breakdown.

Reform is being recommended (for example, Resolution published its arguments for reforming the law on pre-marital agreements in 2004) on the basis that pre-marital agreements would address the current lack of clarity and certainty of outcomes for parties on divorce and promote greater private ordering, thereby avoiding the conflict, stress and expense of litigation (often affecting children) frequently associated with dividing the family's financial and property assets on divorce. The increasing demand for such agreements (particularly since the House of Lords judgments in Miller and McFarlane in 2006; and the Court of Appeal in Charman 2007) is associated with the growing numbers of second and subsequent marriages, later marriages, and a more diverse cultural society as well as the increasing desire of couples to make their own agreements.[24]

Other proceedings

Proceedings of relevance in mediation, other than those related to divorce, which may affect the parties or the children, include, for example, wardship proceedings (where the High Court exercises its inherent jurisdiction with respect to children); injunctive proceedings (for example, occupation and non-molestation orders); applications under the Children Act 1989 in the case of unmarried parents; Hague Convention proceedings in respect of child abduction cases; and TOLATA claims under the Trusts of Land and Appointment of Trustees Act (TOLATA) 1996.

The impact of litigation and adjudication

Although the disadvantages of litigation (cost, delay, further conflict, and so on) must be clearly understood by the parties in assessing their options, these should not be used by mediators to pressure couples into or within the process. It may well be that an adjudicated decision based on a full assessment of all the facts would be the best solution to a genuinely irreconcilable conflict of interest, for example in some disputes over children. If mediation in such a case fails and the parties choose to litigate, this does not necessarily mean they do not have their children's best interests at heart or that they are being 'selfish'. On the contrary their decision to seek an adjudicated decision may be precisely because they do care about the welfare of their children but differ fundamentally as to how to promote this. The benefits of adjudication in appropriate cases include, for example, where an immediate decision is necessary in the interests of either of the parties and their children, where there are serious disparities of power and resources or where an issue of public importance requires an authoritative ruling. The Law Commission (Law Com. 192, 1990, para. 7.24) endorsed mediation as 'an important element in developing a new and more constructive approach to the problems of marital breakdown and divorce' yet it did not fudge the adjudicative responsibility either:

---

24   The existence of a pre-nuptial agreement, if properly executed and made with the benefit of legal advice, has been increasingly influential upon the court (see *M. v. M. (Pre-nuptial Agreement)* [2002] 1FLR 654). The Court of Appeal judgment in *Charman v. Charman* (2007) contains not only what appears to be a strong endorsement of pre-nuptial agreements, but also what appears to be support for a change in the law to make such agreements binding.

There are also dangers in relying too heavily upon conciliation or mediation instead of more traditional methods of negotiation and adjudication. These include exploitation of the weaker partner by the stronger, which requires considerable skill and professionalism for the conciliator to counteract while remaining true to the neutral role required; considerable potential for delay, which is damaging both to the children and often to the interests of one of the adults involved; and the temptation for the court to postpone deciding some very difficult and painful cases which ought to be decided quickly. It is important that, whatever encouragement is given by the system to alternative methods of dispute resolution, the courts are not deterred from performing their function of determining issues which require to be determined. (para. 5.34)

The legal position of parents

Both parents of a legitimate child are treated by law as each having parental responsibility and its accompanying bundle of rights, duties, powers and authority in respect of their child (Children Act 1989, section 3; see above for discussion relating to parental responsibility in respect of unmarried parents). Until legal proceedings are initiated, therefore, parents have considerable power in relation to their children. But once the court is invoked, as in divorce or in proceedings relating to the care and upbringing of a child, then the court has the widest powers to make any order it thinks fit and the welfare of the child becomes the first and paramount consideration (Children Act 1989, section 1). As there is no agreed definition of what constitutes the welfare of the child (or 'best interests of the child' as in the US), the chief value of the welfare principle lies in the moral and social ideal that it represents, that is, that dependent and vulnerable children need to be protected from harm and given every opportunity to become happy and successful adults (King, 1987). Although, in practice, this principle may be used to legitimise the subjective values and prejudices that underlie the decisions of the court, it does at least require that the decision-makers attempt to look at the issues from the child's point of view (Children Act 1989, section 1(3)(a)).

While, in divorce proceedings, the court has the widest powers to make such orders as it thinks fit in respect of any child of the family, it must be recognized that the intervention of the court, however powerful, is a relatively brief affair.

Referrals

Referrals to out-of-court mediation services come from many sources including Citizens' Advice Bureaux, marriage guidance agencies (Relate, for example) and self-referrals. The majority of referrals however, are from legal sources, solicitors, county court judges, the magistrate's courts and CAFCASS. Where referrals are from the court or its welfare service, the mediator has a special responsibility to ensure that the parties know their attendance is a voluntary matter. Although the court has no power to order a person to attend an out-of-court service, a recommendation or strong encouragement may be interpreted as an order (Davis and Roberts, 1988). With voluntariness so essential a principle of mediation, it is important that people are not and do not feel coerced into participation. Research suggests that such pressure reduces the chances of agreement and that those agreements that are reached are unlikely to last (see for example, Davis and Roberts, 1988; Hunt with Roberts, 2005; Genn et al., 2006).

Some American commentators have distinguished between coercion (of a mild kind) into mediation, which, some argue, might be acceptable (as part of the process of educating the parties), and coercion within the process, which they regard as unacceptable (for example, McCrory, 1985). While it is doubtful whether many of those ordered into mediation would experience any lifting of pressure once involved, it can be argued that there are those for whom the compulsory attempt at mediation might prove a valuable face-saving device (for a fuller discussion of this topic see Chapter 11).

The legal status of mediated agreements

While couples are living together there is a presumption that the domestic arrangements they make are not intended to give rise to legally enforceable obligations (*Balfour* v. *Balfour* 1919). No such presumption operates once they have separated or are about to separate (Lowe and Douglas, 2006). In those circumstances, it is their intention to create legal relations that are decisive and that becomes a matter of fact to be inferred from all the evidence (*Merritt* v. *Merritt* 1970).

As far as children are concerned, in one way, the actual intention of the parties is of less importance, as the court always retains an ultimate authority to intervene and with the widest discretion (MCA 1973, section 42 as amended by the Children Act 1989, section 10). Nevertheless, the court will be reluctant to alter the agreed arrangements made by the parties if these are fair and satisfactory (*Beales* v. *Beales* 1972) and the 'no order' principle of the Children Act 1989 operates as an encouragement to parties to reach agreement. An agreement that is written down is not more binding than an oral agreement, although as a record it could be of evidentiary importance. The parties in mediation need to be clear that the court must consider whether or not to exercise its powers regarding the arrangements made for the children before it will grant a decree absolute (Matrimonial Causes Act 1973, section 41 as amended by the Children Act 1989, schedule 12, 31).

As far as privately agreed financial and property arrangements are concerned, the court will usually be prepared to impute to them an intention to create legal relations (Cretney et al., 2003). This applies whether or not the agreement is in writing. Maintenance agreements in writing are legally binding and therefore enforceable. Their legal status is governed by statute (Matrimonial Causes Act 1973, sections 34–36) and the definition of a maintenance agreement is wide, including agreements about the matrimonial home, its contents and the education of the children. The definition of a maintenance agreement also covers separation deeds and separation agreements.[25]

The parties must be aware that they can never achieve finality in their financial arrangements by making a private agreement. This will always be open to review. In the first place it is against public policy for any agreement to fetter or to oust the jurisdiction of the court in matrimonial proceedings relating to financial provision or property adjustment. Any agreement that might restrict the right of either party to apply to court for financial provision is void (*Jessel* v. *Jessel* 1979). Furthermore, either party has the statutory right to apply to court to vary a subsisting maintenance agreement if there has been a change in circumstance or if the agreement does not make proper financial provision for any child of the family (Matrimonial Causes Act 1973, section 35(2)). If these conditions are met, the courts have extensive powers of intervention. There are also other, more rarely, employed means of reviewing private agreements, for example an agreement may be attacked as unconscionable. It should be noted too that once a financial agreement is embodied in a Consent Order, its legal effect derives from the court order and not any more from the agreement.

Notwithstanding these powers, the court is reluctant to interfere with freely negotiated agreements on financial matters made by the parties with full knowledge and proper advice 'unless there are clear and compelling grounds for concluding that an injustice will be done if the parties are held to it' (such as a drastic and unforeseen change of circumstance, duress, failure to disclose, poor legal advice, and so on) (Cretney et al., 2003, p. 325).

At the conclusion of mediation, where a record is drawn up of the outcome, whether a parenting plan, Outcome Statement or a Memorandum of Understanding (following all-issues mediation), this will set out all the

---

25   The choice of whether 'proposals' should be incorporated in to a separation agreement or a Consent Order, depends upon whether divorce or dissolution proceedings are taking place and whether or not a pension sharing order is sought. The court can only make an order in ancillary relief proceedings once there is a decree nisi, and the order takes effect on decree absolute, which is when a pension sharing order can be made. Because it can take at least three months to get to decree nisi stage, it is often useful to encourage clients in mediation, who are intending to divorce, to proceed with divorce alongside mediation.

matters mutually agreed (and, where appropriate, the reasons for decisions reached) accompanied by all the documents required for full disclosure of assets and income. Even where there is no written record, agreement over contact or residence may not easily be separated from agreement over maintenance or the family home. Because the legal implications of these arrangements are far-reaching, mediators need to be vigilant in urging the parties to check the agreements reached in mediation with their legal advisors. These outcome records are made 'without prejudice' until transformed into legally binding contracts or Consent Orders.

The Council of Europe 1998 Recommendation on Family Mediation (Recommendation No R (98)1) recognizes that agreements reached in mediation are not normally legally binding, although highlighting the considerable variation in Europe on this matter (for example, in Germany and Norway such agreements are legally binding though usually not enforceable unless and until endorsed by judicial authority). Judicial enforcement, in endorsing or ratifying agreements, must ensure that such agreements comply with current legislation, do not infringe either party's legitimate interests and, in particular protect the best interests of children (Principle IV, 49). In recommending that member States facilitate the approval of mediated agreements by judicial authorities, and provide mechanisms for the enforcement of such agreements, Recommendation No. R (98) 1 notes that 'the establishment of such mechanisms could contribute significantly to the credibility of and respect for mediation' (Principle IV, 52).

Rule 2.61 Family proceedings rules: Full disclosure

Where the parties make a private agreement that includes any financial or property arrangements, and that private agreement is to be embodied in a Consent Order (under sections 23, 24, 24A and 27 of the Matrimonial Causes Act 1973), the court requires that there be full and frank disclosure (Rule 76A revised by Rule 9 of the Matrimonial Causes (Amendment No.2) Rules 1985). This is an important protection against dishonesty by both parties and non-disclosure by one party and is of particular value where only one party is legally represented. Most practising mediators are required by their Code of Practice to ensure that the parties make their decisions upon sufficient information and knowledge (see the UK College of Family Mediators Code of Practice 2000, 6.5). They must inform each party of the need to give full and frank disclosure of all material relevant to the issues being mediated and assist them, where necessary, in identifying the relevant information and any supporting documentation (Form E can be used for this purpose by both solicitors and mediators, promoting consistency and seamless documentation from one process to another, although some NFM services choose not to use Form E, or have adapted it to be more 'user friendly'). Mediators must make clear that they do not verify the information and that the parties may obtain independent legal advice as to the adequacy of the information disclosed (see the UK College of Family Mediators Code of Practice 2000, 6.8). The open financial summary is used by solicitors and/ or the litigant-in-person to provide the background financial information needed for the Rule 2.61 statement. Research confirms that discovery and disclosure of assets were undertaken carefully in the not-for-profit services offering mediation on all issues (Walker et al., 1994).

Legal advice and legal information

It is contrary to the mediator's role to give legal (or any other) advice (for example, see UK College Code of Practice, section 6.7–6.11). However, a mediator can give legal information. The differences between advice-giving and information-giving are set out below.

Legal advice involves applying the relevant law to the facts of the case and giving a legal opinion on those facts. In other words legal advice involves interpreting the particular circumstances of the case in the light of the relevant law. Legal advice therefore includes evaluation and the recommendation of a particular course (or courses) of action: 'This is what you ought to do'. The giving of legal advice, because it involves a partisan relationship with the client (that is, a relationship of loyalty) is also inseparable from a relationship of representation (Riskin, 1984; Ryan, 1986).

Legal information involves setting out information as a *resource* without recommending which course of action or which option to choose. The information could include statutory definitions, criteria used by the court, court procedures, 'grounds' for divorce, tax consequences, legal rules and legal perspectives. This is more complex than it sounds as subtle judgments are often required to explain the application of the law in general, in setting out options, risks and benefits. A lawyer giving legal information does *not* represent either party and remains impartial.

Informed consent protects the disputants, the lawyers and the mediators. When a lawyer acts as a consultant or as a mediator, it must be made clear to the parties that there is no representation of either party involved. This is important particularly where legal information is given by a lawyer to *both* parties. What is important is the nature of the relationship with the party and the objective of that relationship. This must be clarified explicitly with the parties and their consent obtained, again explicitly (Riskin, 1984). It is also important that the parties' legal interests are being protected – by their own solicitors.

Lawyers

The growing interest in family mediation of lawyers, solicitors initially, came at a time when there was official consensus about its nature and benefits and its relationship to legal process (Conciliation Project Unit 1989; Roberts, 1991, 1993(a)(b); 1995b). The Court of Appeal landmark decision on privilege in family mediation (*Re D.* 1993) was significant too in officially confirming understanding about the institutional location of mediation. Their Lordships stated explicitly that mediation did not form part of the legal process thereby affirming unambiguously the independence of mediation from legal process (the benefits of mediation being seen to lie in the process being a true and viable alternative to the legal system). Concerns have arisen where alternative processes have become adjuncts to an adversarial legal system because they have usually been co-opted to subserve overriding diversionary and cost-saving purposes, often without the protection of due process or a lessening of court control. Other dangers to the mediation process have been seen to lie in attempts by lawyers to regain control over domains of dispute resolution traditionally perceived as theirs. During the early development of family mediation in the UK, The Law Society was instrumental in seeking to confine dispute resolution to the sphere of legal activity and therefore the control of lawyers. This profoundly influenced, and distorted, the terms in which family mediation (or 'conciliation' as it was called) was then perceived – as a form of welfare activity primarily concerned with issues over children. This early way of thinking was reinforced by the professional ideology of the early mediators, many of whom came from professional backgrounds involved with child protection and welfare such as social work, counselling and family therapy.

From the time when the radical reforms embodied in the ill-fated Family Law Act 1996 were first introduced – and witnessed in the US over a decade earlier, when 'legal professionals tumble[d] over each other in their enthusiasm for non-legal dispute resolution alternatives', the dangers of lawyers seeking to dominate the development of alternatives remains current in the UK. 'The relentless force of law in modern American society can be measured by its domination, and virtual annihilation, of alternative forms of dispute settlement' (Auerbach, 1983, pp. 15, 139). Ironically, it was the emergence of lawyers in the late medieval and early modern period, as a specialized service of advisers and champions, parallel to the rising dominance of the courts, that was the reason why 'mediation was elbowed aside and virtually ceased to be a recognized part of the disputing cultures of the West' (Roberts, 2002, pp. 17–18).

Solicitors as mediators

Solicitors have historically claimed for themselves a partisan, advisory and representative role and have come to be associated with it by the public. In acting as a mediator, the solicitor has to adopt a role that is essentially different – that of impartial, non-directive facilitator of other people's own negotiations. As active, dominant, specialist advisers and champions, some solicitors have understandable difficulty in transforming to a role that is completely different.

There is, nevertheless, no reason why, with careful selection for personal aptitude, training and experience, a solicitor should not also act as a mediator bringing valuable legal information into the process. A number of lawyer mediators (barristers and solicitors) already work both in the independent, not-for-profit sector and in the private sector of provision of family mediation. In the latter sector, lawyer mediators have to distinguish their offer of mediation from their legal practice and to make clear to the parties the capacity in which they are acting in accordance with their codes of practice – this applies in respect of any profession of origin (see for example, the UK College Code of Practice, 2000, 4.4.4). However, worrying pressures are being exerted too towards confusing the separate roles and functions of lawyers and mediators, diluting and damaging both. Examples of this trend are set out below.

- Notwithstanding the creation by the main mediation providers of an independent professional body for establishing standards and for monitoring and regulating professional practice (the UK College of Family Mediators), the Law Society of England and Wales (which is not a mediation professional body) has determined its own mediation professional standards and accreditation procedure (The Family Mediation Panel) for solicitors. This could be seen to be damaging to the carefully nurtured development over many years of mediation as a distinct and autonomous professional activity, one requiring its own regulatory body.
- The Law Society has authorized the practice of mediation by solicitors as part of their legal practice provided the parties to the dispute are sufficiently informed as to the solicitor's role (Professional Conduct of Solicitors, Principle 11.01).
- The Law Society has adopted the terminology 'solicitor-mediator'. This linkage of incompatible roles creates confusion, especially for the public, as would such juxtapositions as 'barrister-mediator' or 'judge-mediator'. If, in doing so, the Law Society intended to highlight the value of the kind of substantive knowledge the mediator (who is also qualified as a solicitor) brings to the process, the role neutral term 'lawyer mediator' could usefully serve that purpose.

- The definition of mediation used by the Law Society, while identifying most of the essential features of the process, does not make clear the crucial point that in mediation it is the parties who are the negotiators assisted in their negotiations by the mediator. This is a serious omission in a report for solicitors, given this fundamental departure from traditional practice, under which it is the solicitors themselves who are the negotiators (Brown, 1991).

Some solicitors endorse their practice of what they call 'evaluative' mediation. This is a directive form of intervention, which involves an assessing and evaluative role for the intervener – assessing information about the parties and their quarrel; identifying and evaluating the options available to them; and persuading the parties to adopt a course of action which *the intervener* considers, in the light of his/her professional expertise, to be the best in the circumstances on the basis of an evaluation of the merits of the case and of what the court might decide. In 'evaluative' mediation therefore, the 'mediator' proffers him/herself as an authoritative specialist adviser who determines the outcome on the basis of knowing better than the parties what is best for them. With the advent of public funding for mediation and externally introduced notions of 'success' defined in terms of 'cost effectiveness' that reflect government priorities of reducing legal aid expenditure, especially on family disputes, there is a concern that the more directive, evaluative settlement approaches in mediation, those traditionally practised by lawyers, appear more likely to be rewarded financially (Davis et al., 2000).

Other pressures, such as increased formalization, over-reliance on documentation and the elevation of the importance of legal (compared to mediatory) expertise, can lead to the mediation process becoming an alternative form *of* legal process rather than an alternative *to* legal process (Effron, 1989).

Lawyers as consultants in mediation

Where expertise that is not already within the ken of the parties is required in mediation (such as legal, tax or welfare rights information), this may be introduced into the process in two main ways – either via the mediator him/herself (for example, a lawyer mediator) or via a consultant outside the process, providing the necessary expertise either to the mediator or to the parties. Research endorses the efficacy of both models in the practice of all-issues mediation (mediation on property and financial matters as well as on children) and confirms that the occasional presence of a lawyer causes no difficulty to clients or disrupts the flow of negotiations. Clients appreciated the contribution of this legal expertise (Walker et al., 1994).

Lawyers acting as lawyers (representatives or advocates) within mediation

While it is common ground that parties in mediation should have independent legal advice available to them outside the process, the presence of the parties' own legal advisers during family mediation is not the usual practice in this country nor does it appear to be a popular notion (McCarthy and Walker, 1996a). The situation in commercial mediation is different, where it is routine practice for lawyers to participate in mediation as representative advisers, sometimes termed 'mediation advocates'. Specialist training is available for lawyers acting in such a roles.

Solicitors as advisers

Mediation is not a substitute for legal advice nor is it an alternative to legal representation. Mediators consider it important that the parties have resort, before and during mediation, to their own independent legal advisers, especially where financial and property issues are being decided (McCarthy and Walker, 1996a). Solicitors are also needed after mediation is completed to provide advice on the merits of the agreement and drafting assistance in converting the Memorandum of Understanding (the record of agreed joint decisions reached in mediation) into a legally enforceable agreement or a Consent Order. When the Green Paper on Legal Aid Reform (1995) recommended provision of legal aid for these purposes, it denied the necessity for solicitors or other legal advisers 'to "shadow" the mediation process throughout, or to go over ground already covered or, except in rare cases, to unpick understandings reached in mediation' (Green Paper, 1995, para. 9.13).

Research has shown that the thoroughness of discovery and disclosure of assets in all-issues mediation has made it extremely unlikely that mediated agreements need to be unpicked by solicitors. Findings showed that clients valued the partisan support they received from their solicitors during and after mediation and the reassurance they received about the decisions they were taking, especially the protection against unfavourable settlements (Walker et al., 1994).

It is not uncommon that negotiations between solicitors, and even litigation, over financial and property matters, may be going on in parallel to mediation efforts over children. The attitude of solicitors to mediation, the course of prevailing negotiations between solicitors, the way information is or is not communicated by lawyers to their clients, the imminence of hearing dates: all these legal influences affect the environment within which mediation is taking place.

The expertise and modes of intervention of lawyers and mediators are complementary and the differences between their respective roles and functions need to be understood and respected. Interdisciplinary co-operation, particularly over referrals, is essential if the needs of families are to be met.[26] The parties need to be informed of their legal rights and mediators should urge those who are un-represented to consult solicitors whenever necessary. Similarly, solicitors should refer suitable cases to mediation.[27] The mediator needs to hear what the dispute is about from the parties themselves not from solicitors. The mediator can help the parties to be clear about what has or has not been agreed (in writing where appropriate) so that they can communicate information directly and unambiguously to their own solicitors, who may then translate any agreement reached through mediation into a legally binding agreement such as a formal Consent Order – again if that is preferred by the parties. It is the parties' responsibility, not that of the mediator (unless this is expressly agreed), to inform their solicitors or the court (when un-represented) of the progress or outcome of mediation.

Mediators and court proceedings

In exceptional circumstances, mediators could find themselves caught up in court proceedings involving clients as a result of events occurring (and/or information arising) during pre-mediation or intake meetings or mediation sessions. Examples of the kind of situations that might arise include:

- an act of violence between the parties or on the premises of the mediation service during or after mediation followed by the police issuing proceedings and compelling the mediator to be a witness;
- confidential information given in mediation (or pre-mediation) meetings that one party wishes to be disclosed in subsequent court proceedings (civil or criminal).

26   One research study in the UK has highlighted the fact that 90 per cent of those interviewed, who had attended mediation, had also consulted a solicitor, as well as the fact that 38 per cent of those who had attended mediation, had been referred by their solicitors (Walker et al., 2004; see also Davis, 2001).

27   One of the key findings of the NAO Report (2007) is that legal advisers are not sufficiently fulfilling their duty to inform their legally aided clients of the option of mediation – financial disincentive being one of the reasons – leading to an unacceptably low take-up of mediation, and recommending curtailing contracts as a sanction, where necessary. Genn et al. (2006) confirms this reluctance of legal advisers to refer to mediation in the context of civil mediation, stating it 'a critical policy challenge ... to identify and articulate the incentives for legal advisers to embrace mediation on behalf of their clients.'

Guidance on the principles to be observed in such circumstances recommends that mediators should uphold their Code of Practice at all times, observing the general principles of impartiality, confidentiality and privilege in relation to legal proceedings (UK College of Family Mediators Code of Practice 2000, 4.12–4.14). They should have regard, in particular, to the objectives of minimizing distress to the parties and their children and promoting as good a continuing relationship as possible between the parties and their children so far as is practicable. Furthermore any risk of violence should be removed or diminished.

While confidentiality is the cornerstone of the relationship of trust between the mediator and the parties, in normal circumstances it belongs to the parties, not the mediator, and, except where there is risk of harm, can be breached legally only where a client (for example, in a separate meeting with the mediator) or clients (in joint meetings) waive it and give their consent to disclosure (see Chapter 9 for more detailed discussion on confidentiality and privilege). In exceptional circumstances, the mediator may, through statutory obligation or the order of the court or other competent authority, be compelled to disclose information regardless of the consent of the parties. If a mediator believes that such exceptional circumstances exist, s/he must take appropriate action (including taking appropriate legal or other advice) in order to be satisfied that the duty of confidentiality is, in those exceptional circumstances, overridden by legal obligation.[28]

The Family Justice Council

The Family Justice Council was set up in 2004, following a consultation by the then Lord Chancellor's Department, published in 2002, called 'Promoting Inter-Agency Working in the Family Justice System'. This proposed the establishment of a committee with the purposes of promoting and monitoring interdisciplinary co-operation and best practice, and advising the government on issues affecting the family justice system. The Council is a non-statutory, advisory Non-Departmental Public Body consisting of a representative cross-section of those who work, use or have an interest in the family justice system. Its membership includes therefore, members of

---

28　NFM Notes of Guidance 1999 detail the procedures that mediators should follow in these circumstances – for example, a mediator should only give evidence as a witness where s/he has been subpoenaed to do so and has received a witness summons as this compellability will establish clearly a mediator's independence. Also, where a mediator is compelled to be a witness and is required to disclose information, s/he should (subject to any overriding legal obligations) withhold documented information until subpoenaed to provide it, give factual data only and give information that is as fair to both sides so far as is practicable.

the judiciary, family lawyers (barristers and solicitors), a family mediator, a child mental health specialist, an academic, a director of children's services, a paediatrician, civil servants working in the field of family justice and related areas, a chief constable and consumer representatives (parents and children). The Council meets four times a year, the majority of its work conducted by its committees and working groups, which consist of three main committees addressing these areas:

- Children in Safeguarding Proceedings (public law and adoption);
- Children in Families (private law);
- Money and Property (matrimonial law).

Other committees and groups address specialist matters, for example, the use of experts in the family justice system, domestic violence, contact issues, the voice of the child, transparency (in order to improve openness and public confidence in court proceedings – a particular focus of concern of fathers' pressure groups), and education and training.

The aspirations of the Family Justice Council (and its newly created 41 Local Family Justice Councils) have been high as the then Family Justice Minister, Lord Filkin (2004), stated at the time of its inception:

> The family justice system plays a crucial role in protecting vulnerable people at stressful times. These people might be abuse victims or they might be experiencing a traumatic family breakdown.

> Many children and families come into contact with the family justice system each year. This new Council will play a crucial role in improving the way their cases are handled.

> Many will use their wealth of personal and professional experience to look at the family justice system and identify how it can be improved for the benefit of those who come into contact with it.

> The family justice system cannot work effectively without the contributions of all involved. This new body will guarantee better communication between the different agencies, ensuring a more joined up approach to family justice for the benefit of those who matter – the children and families.

> The Family Justice Council will build on the existing good work of an inter-disciplinary committee, which has been chaired by a senior judge, Lord Justice Thorpe, to improve the way agencies work together and so ensure better delivery of justice.

For details of the terms of reference of the Council and an up-to-date account of how it is going about its primary business of facilitating the delivery of better and quicker outcomes for families and children, see Walsh (2006).

4   Conflict and disputes

Just so, there probably exists no social unit in which convergent and divergent currents among its members are not inseparably interwoven. An absolutely centripetal and harmonious group, a pure 'unification' ('vereinigung'), not only is empirically unreal, it could show no real life process. (Simmel, 1908b, trans. 1971, p. 72)

The primary focus of the mediator is on disputes. These are the specific, identifiable issues that divide the parties and which need to be distinguished from the wider conflict that is also associated with family breakdown. The settlement of a dispute is achieved when the parties find a mutually acceptable basis for disposing of the issues over which they are in disagreement, even against a background of continuing conflict (Cormick, 1982). This may be compared with the resolution of conflict that is achieved when the basic differences of value or fact or inequalities of power that divide the parties are removed.[1] The dispute brought to mediation may be the tip of the iceberg so far as conflict between the parties is concerned.

---

1   In the international context, usage of the term 'conflict resolution' (and 'conflict prevention') meets with criticism because of their implied emphasis on avoiding or ending conflict. The term 'conflict transformation' is a preferred term because it reflects the importance of the need to address underlying structural and cultural violence and to recognize the inevitability of conflict in the process of change (Francis, 2002). 'Conflict transformation' denotes more accurately a whole collection of processes at work and their results – processes aimed at making relationships more just, full and equal participation, protecting dignity, and so on – and the different ways of addressing conflict without violence, possibly resolving it or managing it (by minimizing its destructive effects, for example) – processes for developing a new 'constructive conflict culture' in the interests of contributing to the well-being of a society (Francis, 2002, p. 7).

Conflict

Conflict can be of many kinds, dimensions and levels; it can take many forms and derive from a range of sources – intra-personal, interpersonal, intra-group, inter-group, local and international. Scholars across fields have developed a range of taxonomies for defining conflict (constructive and destructive) in its multiple manifestations in order better to understand and address it (see, for example, Moore, 1996, for his delineation of spheres of conflict, causes and interventions in the context of mediation; see also Menkel-Meadow et al., 2005, for a summary of some of the theoretical underpinnings of conflict and dispute resolution). Conflict is 'after all one of the most vivid interactions which furthermore, cannot possibly be carried on by one individual alone … Conflict is thus designed to resolve divergent dualisms; it is a way of achieving some kind of unity, even if it be through the annihilation of one of the conflicting parties' (Simmel, 1908b, trans. 1971, p. 70).

Broadly speaking conflict in the domain of family break-up can be of three kinds.

Interpersonal conflict usually occurs between the two adults who are separating and is associated with powerful, usually negative, feelings about each other, such as anger, resentment, betrayal and hurt.

> The deepest hatred grows out of broken love … To have to recognize that a deep love – and not only a sexual love – was an error, a failure of intuition [*Instinkt*], so compromises us before ourselves, so splits the security and unity of our self-conception, that we unavoidably make the object of this intolerable feeling pay for it. We cover our secret awareness of our own responsibility for it by hatred which makes it easy for us to pass all responsibility to the other … This particular bitterness … characterizes conflicts within relationships whose nature would seem to entail harmony. (Simmel, 1908b, trans. 1971, p. 93)

Conflict often spreads. Children may take sides in the matrimonial battle, involuntarily or from choice. New partners and grandparents may become embroiled as well. One basic cause of interpersonal conflict (and an inevitable consequence as well) is poor communication between the parties. Misunderstanding, mistrust and hostility are frequent concomitants of broken lines of communication.

A conflict of interest may exist independently of the interpersonal conflict. For example, there may be a genuine conflict of interest over residence or property. On the other hand, lawyers necessarily transform all issues and the objectives of their clients into established categories of legal conflicts of interest, simplifying them in the process, the better to gain control (Mather and Yngvesson, 1981). This and the competitive strategies of an adversarial legal system may exacerbate interpersonal conflict between the parties.

One conflict of interest not easily acknowledged is that between parents (the parties) and their own children. 'Divorce is the archetypal situation in which it is thought that the interests of adults and children conflict' (Bainham, 2000, p. 116). As former partners, both parties may want a 'clean break' and an end to contact with one another so that they may start new lives afresh. This wish will clash in most cases with the preferences and needs of their own children for whom the continuation of a loving relationship with both parents requires their continuing contact (Richards, 1981). The decision of the parties to divorce is itself imposed on the children of the family, regardless of their views or needs (Mitchell, 1985).

Structural conflict – this includes the social-economic conflict of interest that can exist between men and women (Bottomley, 1984). In many cases, family breakdown exposes the structural dependence of women in marriage, as far as work opportunities, wages and the division of labour within the home are concerned. The single-parent household, composed in the main of separated and divorced women caring for children on their own, has borne in full the adverse consequences of women's economic dependence on men within marriage (Smart, 1984). The high number of children living with lone parents, and the low percentage of lone parents who work – although this is increasing (the percentage of lone parents in work having risen from 45 per cent to 56 per cent since 1997) – combine with other factors (such as low relative pay, and the limited extent of redistribution through the tax and benefit system) to create persistent (compared with temporary) poverty in the UK, particularly for children (Joseph Rowntree Foundation, 2006a). Among children in poverty in workless families, two thirds live with one parent (Joseph Rowntree Foundation, 2006b).[2]

Conflict associated with family breakdown is complex, with many causes, some of which have been outlined briefly. Research highlights the diversity of family structures and the many adversities that can affect families and their children, of which separation may be only one – others include poverty, unemployment, poor housing, parental ill-health, family violence, and drug abuse and crime in some cases (Wade and Smart, 2002). In addition, individual shortcomings, difficulties in getting along with others, stress, changes in circumstances, isolation, combative legal advisers and an alienating and expensive legal system may, in the most unfortunate situations, cumulate to place people, and their children especially, under impossible pressures.

Yet it may be helpful to emphasize four general points relating to family conflict. In the first place it would be misleading to associate conflict

---

2   Though there has been a reduction in child poverty owing to the impact of tax credits and out-of-work benefits for families with children, child poverty in the UK remains higher in relative terms than in all but three of the 24 other European Union countries (Joseph Rowntree Foundation, 2006a, 2006b).

exclusively with separating or divorcing families. With little or no research on the subject, practically nothing is known about conflict in intact families. It is usually when families break up that private conflict becomes public, perhaps for the first time, and the stresses and strains, insensitivities and inequalities of ordinary family life become manifest.

Secondly, attitudes to conflict, and the emotional and behavioural cues signalling conflict, differ according to culture and ethnicity. In some cultures, for example, direct confrontation is regarded as the means of exacerbating conflict which is best therefore avoided. In other cultures, on the other hand, confrontation is seen as desirable (Goldstein, 1986).

Thirdly, the positive benefits of conflict must be acknowledged. Conflict can signal constructive ways of bringing about change and of re-ordering lives. At least the potential for positive change is greater where there is anger than where there is the helplessness and hopelessness of depression. Conflict can also energize and vitalize, as has been noted in the context of mediation involving the elderly – 'when you are angry, the hormone of adrenalin is strong ... being angry is a flash of adrenalin. It makes them [older people] feel great. It makes them feel once again on top of the world. Being angry is quite therapeutic for older people' (Craig quoted in Roberts, 2007, p. 79).

Finally, there are limits to the impact of outside intervention of any kind. The healing effect of time itself, plus people's own efforts in overcoming their difficulties, cannot be underestimated.

Disputes

A dispute may be defined as a sense of grievance over a specific issue, which is communicated as a contested claim to the person regarded as responsible or blameworthy (Roberts, 1983b, p. 7). The complex evolutionary processes by which experiences of injustice and conflict become grievances, and grievances become disputes – the 'naming', 'blaming' and 'claiming' stages that characterize the emergence and transformation of disputes – have been identified by Felstiner et al. (1980–1981). Gulliver too illustrates the way in which a disagreement (large or small), when unable or unwilling to be resolved by private problem-solving within a dyadic relationship, can be put into the public domain ('a different frame of reference and action'), with the intent that, by appealing to others, 'something must be done'. In this way a *disagreement* becomes a *dispute* (Gulliver, 1979, pp. 75–6).

Disputes can be about many things (Caplan, 1995):

- material goods – for example, rights to land and property;
- the right to make decisions;
- social relations – for example, marital relations;

- the need to work out 'existential predicaments', such as the meaning of love, beneath the ostensible reasons – for example, land, sexual jealousy (Caplan, 1995, p. 2);
- ways of grouping people together, even in the short term;
- the need to highlight important differences.

Anthropologists have identified the importance of the dimension of time for understanding disputes. That certain structural relations can give rise to 'chronic eruptions' of dispute, even if each episode is settled, reflects the longer history of which each episode is part (Falk Moore, 1995, p. 32). The story goes on in 'the still-to-be experienced futures' of the individual protagonists and the larger social group (Falk Moore, 1995, p. 32).

Family disputes

The focus of family mediation in this country used to be primarily upon issues over children following separation or divorce, residence and contact disputes; for example, which parent is to have the day-to-day care of the child, and how, when and for how long the non-resident parent can have contact with the child. Financial, property as well as children issues are now routinely mediated as well as the first issue that sometimes needs to be decided, namely, whether or not the relationship is over or reconciliation is a possibility.[3] Disputes can also occur over the divorce itself (whether there should be a divorce, who should petition, on what 'grounds' and so on). Since the Children Act 1989, a wider range of family issues have been the subject of mediation, some involving grandparents, step-parents, adult family members, local authorities in public law (child protection) cases, and, more recently, young homeless people and cases involving child abduction. Family disputes generate intense emotional reactions, although disputes of any kind, particularly between individuals, have a high emotional content as well (see Roberts, 2007). While recognizing that those disputes brought to mediation may well have deep and tangled emotional (as well as social and economic) roots, it is not the function of the mediator to reinterpret issues in ways that give underlying conflict a greater significance than the 'surface' disputes defined as problematic by the parties themselves.

---

3   The latest figures give some indication of the volume of family mediations taking place in the UK. In the period October 2004 to March 2006, 29,000 people were funded by legal aid to resolve their disputes through mediation – only some 20 per cent of those funded by legal aid for family breakdown cases (National Audit Office Report, 2007). It is estimated that in the year 2005, between 3,000 and 4,000 privately funded family mediations were completed, constituting about 20 per cent of the total family mediations undertaken that year (UK College of Family Mediators, 2006b).

Disputes over contact with children

In most cases, parents make their own arrangements over the children, contact in particular.[4] This fundamental fact has crucial legal as well as social and psychological implications, and yet there was, until recently, practically no information available about either this process of voluntary negotiation or what factors contribute to the making of such successful arrangements. The only UK study to look in some depth at the question of why some parents do manage to make contact work (rather than just 'happen') and others do not, highlights the complexities of the issue and the wide range of factors (rather than any single individual or ingredient) that influences contact[5] (Trinder et al., 2001).

Child contact, when it does become problematic, can be highly contentious. This can arise, for example, where there is a failure to establish regular contact as a consequence of conflict or parental distress, or where there are serious concerns about a child's safety and well-being (Hunt with Roberts, 2004; Joseph Rowntree Foundation, 2004). Other practical factors also create difficulties in the establishing of successful contact arrangements between children and non-resident parents – housing, distance, financial hardship and working hours, for example, can create barriers for both developing and maintaining contact (Joseph Rowntree Foundation, 2004). Murch (1980) described in the 1980s, how access/contact problems are often symptomatic of a fundamental dilemma that faces divorcing parents – how to disengage from a broken marriage while still being an adequate parent with a part to play in the children's future. Thus, separation of spousal and parenting roles involves the recognition that the kinship relationship between the parties as parents, created by the very existence of their children, can never be sundered (Bohannan, 1971). But although the kinship relationship is not altered, the way that it is carried out is (Simpson, 1994). And this requires the working out of contact arrangements both by the negotiation of the parties (in order that

---

4   See below for more detail on the change of terminology and differences introduced by the Children Act 1989 – in particular, 'contact' replacing 'access', and 'residence' replacing 'custody'.

5   This study found that there were direct *determinants* (commitment to contact, role clarity, quality of relationships, and so on); *challenges* (nature of the separation, new partners, money, logistics, parenting style and quality, safety issues, and so on); and *mediating factors* (beliefs about contact, involvement of the wider family and external agencies, relationship skills, and so on) and all of these interacted over *time*. It was found that making contact work required commitment (in attitudes, actions and interactions) from *all* family members, both adults and children. An important aspect of successful contact was the 'parental bargain' whereby parents with residence positively facilitated, rather than simply allowed, contact while non-resident parents, on their part, accepted their contact status (Trinder et al., 2001).

joint decisions can be made) and by their co-operation, however meagre, over the practical ways and means of carrying out those decisions.

Yet in the aftermath of the breakdown of personal relationships, conditions for direct negotiation could not be more difficult and the potential for conflict is enormous (Kressel, 1985). It is not surprising, therefore, that findings suggested that access generated more contention than custody, largely because access was a continuing source of friction, requiring the parties to collaborate over arrangements for their children over many years (James and Wilson, 1984; Kressel, 1985). It also generates great anxiety, particularly of loss or the threat of loss (Murch, 1980) and it has been found that the course of access reflects most accurately the success or otherwise of the re-organization of the post-separation household and the adjustment of its members, most especially the children (Wallerstein and Kelly, 1980; Murch, 1980; Hunt with Roberts, 2004).

Public policy in the UK encourages the maintenance of contact between children and their non-resident parent because it is perceived to be in the interests both of children and of the wider society. The declared aim of government is 'to enable children to benefit from the stability offered by a loving relationship with both their parents, even if they separate' (Lord Chancellor's Department, 2002). Yet there is a polarization of views over the operation in practice of this policy approach where contact is perceived *not* to be good for children; that is, where there are concerns about their (or the resident parent's) safety and well-being (for example, in situations of domestic violence, child abuse or child abduction). International research tends to show that what is crucial is *the nature and quality of parenting* by the contact parent, rather than contact in itself (Hunt with Roberts, 2004).

Contact and the law

The approach of the law is that contact is a private matter best agreed between parents, without the need for court intervention. Nor does the law, in England and Wales, seek to influence the nature of those agreements (unlike Scotland, there is no requirement for allowing or maintaining contact) (Hunt with Roberts, 2004). Divorcing parents must provide information to the court about the proposed arrangements for the children, although there is little scrutiny of those arrangements. There is no such requirement where parents are not married.

Parents who cannot agree arrangements over contact can apply to the court for a Contact Order. Section 8 of the Children Act 1980 governs the orders that the court may make over contact (see Chapter 3). They are to resolve specific areas of dispute rather than confer rights. A Contact Order 'means an order requiring the person with whom a child lives, or is to live, to allow the child to visit or stay with the person named in the order or for that person and the child otherwise to have contact with each other' (Children Act 1989, section 8(1)). Contact Orders are wider than the former Access Orders and may cover arrangements other than direct physical contact, such as letters, telephone calls or Internet video communication. The emphasis has also shifted from the adult to the child. The Contact Order is more child-centred than an Access Order in that it allows the *child* to visit, stay or have other contact with the person named in the order, rather than the other way round.[6] There may also be more than one contact order made out to any person. The Contact Order is a positive order, *requiring* contact to be allowed.

Another difference of note is the emergence of contact as a legal entity in its own right. Under section 42 of the Matrimonial Causes Act 1973, which used to govern the orders the court made over access, access appeared to be of little juristic importance. It warranted no separate mention, subsumed as it was under the definition of 'custody' (Matrimonial Causes Act 1973, section 52). Judges continue to have the widest possible discretion in the making of Contact Orders, governed by the same welfare principle that formerly informed the making of decisions over custody (Guardianship of Minors Act 1971, section 1) and which now informs any decision relating to the upbringing of children or the administration of a child's property (Children Act 1989, section 1).

In about 45 per cent of divorces the court made no order for access at all, leaving arrangements to the parents themselves (Eekelaar et al., 1977). Where the court did make an Access Order (and there was wide variation between individual courts), 'reasonable' access was the rule rather than the exception. Reasonable access, premised as it was on the principle of parental competence, left to the parents' responsibility for making whatever arrangements were suitable to themselves (Wilkinson, 1981). Where conflict made this co-ordination impossible, access might be defined by the court and conditions and details laid down, such as location, frequency and duration. Occasionally, the court exercised a supervisory function, with access overseen by the court welfare service or, where facilities were more suitable, by a local authority social services department nominated by the court. In addition, a child might be made subject to a Supervision Order where this was thought to be in his/her interests.

---

6   Bainham (2000) has considered the implications of the implementation of the Human Rights Act 1998 on court decisions relating to children, in particular the real shift of emphasis from interests to rights, adults' as well as children's rights. He states: 'In my view, it is a great mistake to describe contact (formerly access) as a "right of the child" if by this is meant that it is *not* a right of the parent' (Bainham, 2000, p. 114). The important and difficult question is how the law can strike a desirable balance between the potentially conflicting interests and rights of children on the one hand, and those of the adults on the other.

Most access disputes that were brought to the attention of the court were 'settled' either by solicitors or court welfare officers. Contested access cases rarely reached the hearing stage and those that did were some of the most difficult to come before the court (Eekelaar et al., 1977). Long delays were common, in some cases a year passing before the hearing (Eekelaar, 1978). Section 1(2) of the Children Act 1989 now states:

> In any proceedings in which any question with respect to the upbringing of a child arises, the court shall have regard to the general principle that any delay in determining the question is likely to prejudice the welfare of the child.

Courts have a proactive duty to ensure that section 1(2) of the Children Act is not contravened (*Re A.B.* 1995).

Whatever the court orders, however, the implementation of contact depends ultimately on the willingness and ability of the parents themselves to make contact work, a fact seldom appreciated by those threatening legal action over contact. In *Re D. (A Minor)* (1993), the Court of Appeal held that 'implacable hostility' may be a cogent reason for departing from the general principle that a child should grow up to know both his/her parents and certainly would be a reason if the mother's implacable hostility put the child at serious risk of harm.

Organizations campaign for the rights of the non-resident parent (particularly fathers' groups such as Fathers 4 Justice) on the basis that the legal system is biased in allowing mothers to marginalize or exclude fathers from their children's lives for no good reason. It is recognized that there is what is described as 'situational power' in that women do typically get residence and are more likely to get legal aid, and that some do exploit their power unreasonably, flouting court orders and sabotaging contact. Yet research findings do not support the perception that courts systematically operate a maternal preference over fathers, although it is also recognized that more research in the UK is needed (Smart et al., 2003; Hunt with Roberts, 2004). Furthermore, there is research evidence in Australia to show that the courts may have been too ready to brand as 'implacably hostile' parents who have sound reasons for opposing contact, such as major concerns about the quality of care of the non-resident parent and about safety; and also that resistance to contact may be a way of coping with high levels of conflict (see Chapter 3, the section on domestic violence; see Hunt with Roberts, 2004).[7]

---

7   Parental Alienation Syndrome (PAS) is a controversial theory that attempts to explain 'implacably hostility' in terms of a parent seeking, sometimes unconsciously, to turn a child against its other parent resulting in the child developing false or distorted perceptions and, as a consequence, rejecting the denigrated parent. While PAS is accepted in some jurisdictions, it is not endorsed by the courts in the UK. PAS has been criticized for its simplistic causal assumptions and for being unscientific (see Hunt with Roberts, 2004).

There is no statutory presumption in favour of contact as the welfare of the child is the paramount consideration of the court. However, the prevailing approach of judges is that in most cases contact between the child and the non-resident parent is desirable both for the child and the parent (Butler-Sloss, 2001). Coincidentally, in line with recent social research findings, contact is believed by the courts to be in the interests of children and will be denied only in exceptional circumstances. This presumption also extended to illegitimate children (*S. v. O.* 1978). An unmarried father does not, however, have parental responsibility automatically, unlike an unmarried mother, unless he acquires it either by an agreement with the mother or by an application to the court, is registered on the birth certificate (since December 2004), or is appointed guardian (Children Act 1989, section 4).

Whether contact is regarded by the court as a basic parental right (as in *S. v. S.* 1962) or as a basic right of the child (as in *Re W.* 1994), the outcome should not be affected as the welfare principle applies, according paramount consideration to the best interests of the child. While the implementation of the Human Rights Act 1998 is unlikely to affect the outcomes of disputes involving children, it does affect the process of reasoning behind the decisions of the court in that the rights of all family members have now to be taken into account and openly acknowledged: '... the process [of reasoning] will be one which abandons the pretence that children disputes are only about children when in reality they are also about adults' (Bainham, 2000, p. 126). In the majority of cases, the arrangements the parents make over contact are accepted by the court at the Children's Appointment (MCA, 1973, section 41). But as the petitioner will want no restriction on obtaining the decree absolute, as the respondent is not required to be present at the Children's Appointment and seldom is, and because of constraints of time and a reluctance by the court to disturb the status quo, difficulties over contact are seldom likely to surface.

Although the court has powers of enforcement, (the imposition of a fine or imprisonment of up to two years for contempt of court) and has threatened an obstructing parent with the removal of residence, in practice little can be done if a parent is determined to thwart a court order and make contact difficult or impossible.[8] While 'enforcement' is therefore a major problem, informed thinking currently recommends that this usage

---

8   Hunt with Roberts (2004) note the bias that is associated with construing the problem about contact and non-compliance almost exclusively in terms of the resident parent denying contact. The problem of the non-resident parent not complying with the terms of a contact order may be as great yet it seldom features in debates on the subject. A key theme in the limited research on non-compliance is that it can arise from a lack of clarity relating to contact orders, often originally consent orders, which may be ambiguous, or poorly framed or understood (Hunt with Roberts, 2004).

itself may be unhelpful suggesting as it does, 'a discrete and drastic act', for example, sending a recalcitrant mother to prison:

> In our view, the reality of successful implementation of court orders is that of a continuing process, involving negotiation, non-punitive options, continuous reconsideration and the continuing promotion of the child's welfare interests. Accordingly, we have concluded that the more neutral terminology 'the management of non-compliance' would be more appropriate. (LCD Facilitation and Enforcement Group Report, 2003, Appendix 7, section 1[9])

Non-compliance may be one element only of a complex of difficult post-separation problems, often involving domestic violence, substance abuse, serious parenting deficits as well as child abuse. Simplistic solutions are therefore unlikely to resolve these problems. The Report highlights the fact that while 'enforcement' proceedings are rare, preventive interventions could further promote 'a culture of compromise and agreement whereby fewer cases ever reach the court system' – *facilitation* being preferable to *enforcement* (LCD Report, 2003, Appendix 7, section 2).

Contact and social research findings

Early research findings have stressed the importance of stability and security through continuity of the child's relationship with both its parents after divorce and of contact as the means of implementing this (Walczak with Burns, 1984; Wallerstein and Kelly, 1980; Benians, 1976, 1980). At the same time, research findings in Britain and the US have revealed that regular contact is actually exercised in a minority of cases and that, within a short time, separation results in the virtual end of the relationship of the child with one of the parents and the wider family, usually the father, with significant effects on the child's social development and capacity to form and sustain relationships with others (Richards, 1994a).

There has been a broad consensus of professional opinion, sociological, psychological and medical, that has emphasized the importance of the

---

9   The Facilitation and Enforcement Group was charged with advancing the recommendations of the Children Act Sub-Committee (CASC) Report to the Lord Chancellor, *Making Contact Work*, 2002. The Group defined its remit as one *'to devise recommendations designed to promote and facilitate **safe and beneficial contact** between children and their non-resident parent and to consider the CASC proposals for the enforcement of contact orders'* (LCD Final Report, 2003, emphasis added). The Group identified a number of important approaches to improvement – for example, judicial continuity; speedy court responses; the presumption of separate representation for the child; observing the UN Convention on the Rights of the Child (Article 3.1) making the best interests of the child the primary consideration in proceedings for non-compliance, and so on (LCD Final Report, 2003).

successful management of contact – 'the single most important factor in reducing to a minimum the emotional upheavals for children' (Benians, 1980, p. 378). This is subject to two caveats. First, the research of psychiatrists has been biased towards the disturbed cases, which were the ones that come to their attention. Second, there are so many variables that affect children on separation, such as the age of the child, experiences before and after separation, the circumstances of separation itself, the quality of relationships, the impact of domestic violence,[10] poverty and class,[11] to mention a few,[12] that in the light of existing knowledge generalized conclusions should be regarded with great caution.

Recent research findings, re-affirming these complexities, provide more detailed understandings of what factors make contact work or not – a lack of parental commitment to contact and parental conflict being the two main reasons why contact has been found not to work (Trinder et al., 2002). Research has also focused, although rarely, on the perspectives of children themselves on family changes following parental separation. This suggests that children, far from being 'passive victims' are, on the contrary, 'active social agents, capable of thinking for themselves' and who act on and influence their circumstances (Wade and Smart, 2002, p. 1). This research challenges the prevailing emphasis of family policy and legislation on continuing contact with both parents as a 'right' to which children are entitled, on the basis that it assumes that all children have two equally committed, caring, loving parents when not all children are so fortunate and where the value of contact, in those circumstances, may be questionable[13] (Wade and Smart, 2002). In some cases, they suggest that 'children may find it easier to live without a parent (even if temporarily) than to repeatedly

---

10   In situations of domestic violence, findings have shown that the welfare of children may not be best served by children having *direct* contact with fathers who continue to behave abusively towards their ex-partners and/or their children (Hester and Radford, 1996).

11   Simpson (1994) has highlighted the relationship between the level of contact and class. The maintenance of continuing ties after divorce depends on resources – the support of family and friends and crucially, material resources (for example, money for maintenance, travel, gifts, socializing, and so on).

12   Research, for example, also indicates that, for parents, contact and child support are interrelated matters and that where the obligation to maintain is fulfilled, contact is more likely to take place (Hunt with Roberts, 2004). The law, however, treats contact and financial support as two separate issues despite suggestions that this should change (CASC Report, 2002). Yet this has been rejected by government on the grounds that 'contact is not a commodity to be bartered for money' (LCD, 2002).

13   Wade and Smart (2002) cite examples where the simple presence of a parent may be insufficient to communicate commitment; where a parent–child relationship may never have been established; or where that relationship may be damaged or compromised and a parent may be unable to sustain the necessary commitment to restore that relationship.

face the failure of their hopes and legitimate expectations … [and] that the absence of a genetic parent from children's lives does not invariably spell harm' (Wade and Smart, 2002, p. 16). Their research highlights, again, the complexity of contact decisions. These require that the risks and benefits be individually assessed in each situation. What does matter is the quality of children's relationships rather than biological connection *per se*.

> Children can feel confident in themselves and their family relationships whether they have two committed parents or one; equally, the care shown by social parents can be no less valuable than that of genetic kin. We would therefore argue that, while the promotion of contact has undoubtedly done much to ensure that children's family relationships transcend divorce, this policy needs to be balanced by support for the relationships which children have and which work for them, whether based in blood or social ties. (Wade and Smart, 2002, p. 17)

Contact and parents

It is incumbent on mediators not to presume that the parties know they can and may make their own decisions over contact. In spite of the fact that in the majority of cases contact arrangements are left to parents to sort out for themselves, it is not uncommon for them to express surprise on two counts:

- that they are in fact 'allowed' to make their own arrangements (rather than that these be determined for them by solicitors or courts);
- that these arrangements do not have to conform to some fixed standard pattern of what contact ought to be like, but may vary in accordance with the wishes and particular circumstances of the family.

One of the advantages of mediation is the scope that it provides for educating the parties in their rights and powers of self-determination. Although in respect of matters of contact, the parents are usually the most informed about the possibilities for addressing the problem, it is not uncommon for one or both parties to try to cast the mediator in the role of arbitrator or adviser. However helpless or confused the parties may feel, and however intractable the problem may appear, their active participation is essential to its resolution.

Contact and mediators

Until the late 1980s, the bulk of the work of British mediators concerned disputes over children; mainly contact, but also residence, disputes. As already noted, the limitations of the legal process for tackling the complex personal, economic and social facets that often complicate any dispute over contact, plus the fact that ultimately the parents themselves have got to work together if contact is to take place, make mediation a particularly suitable method of dispute settlement for contact disputes.

It would be fair to say that most mediators share the pro-contact presumption of the court where that is consonant with the child's welfare and happiness. Most parents too, in voluntarily resorting to mediation, establish their own concern over the issue of contact. It is not the mediator's task to reinterpret a quarrel over children as a quarrel about finance or vice versa, or as an excuse to act out interpersonal or emotional issues. As one mother frankly put it, 'We are using the children to fight about the children'. This is not to deny the intermeshing of issues or the fact that the settlement of one dispute, say over contact, may lead to co-operation over other issues such as maintenance or the family home. One study in the UK showed that those couples who mediated on all issues (finance, property and children) were more likely to reach agreement than those who used mediation only for sorting out children issues (McCarthy and Walker, 1996b). In the latter cases, there was more likely to be continuing disagreement over contact arrangements and other issues relating to children, such as religious upbringing, education and health care. More recent research reflects a more complicated picture in finding that agreement was slightly *more likely* in disputes about contact and residence of children only (61 per cent) than where property and finance issues were the subject of mediation (56 per cent) as these issues require more technical legal advice to settle and the parties may be less willing to compromise (NAO Report, 2007). An Australian study into the issue of family violence and the practice of mediation highlights another important dimension in finding that, particularly where there is a history of abuse, mediation on property and finance, and mediation on child matters may need to be completely separate processes. Women informants reported that they understated their claims on property for fear that their ex-partners would attempt to gain access and some therefore proceeded with mediation constantly concerned about their children's safety (Keys Young Report, 1996).

Mediators may be tempted to refer to social research findings on divorce and its consequences for children, both to endorse their concern about the damage that might be inflicted on children by parental conflict, and to back up suggestions they might make as to how to mitigate this. Great caution needs to be exercised, however. In the first place it is not the function of the mediator to give advice. Second, offering expertise in matters of childcare is problematic. As has long been acknowledged, research findings can be inconclusive, changing and conflicting (for example, Goldstein et al., 1973, on the central right of the custodial parent to determine access). Then there are the difficulties of extrapolating from general findings to the particular case. There are also dangers that research findings may be used (intentionally or otherwise) to pressurize parents psychologically. For example, parents could be made to feel guilt or fear if told that unless certain courses of action are or are not followed, they may be putting their children 'at risk' (of emotional disturbance, delinquency, or whatever).

The information that the mediator can usefully proffer for consideration to people working out their own arrangements, should be of a neutral kind and related to their particular circumstances: for example, where a couple, who have a relationship fraught with conflict, want a flexible arrangement that requires continuous negotiation over every contact visit, the potential disadvantages of this could be pointed out and compared with the advantages of a predetermined, predictable arrangement, which limits occasions for possible confrontation. For a co-operative couple, on the other hand, such flexibility may be less of a problem.

Contact disputes may erupt at any time, even many years after divorce or separation. However, the sooner a satisfactory regime of contact with the non-resident parent is established, the better, both because the arrangements (or absence of arrangements) set up are the ones most likely to continue, and because at least one of the harmful effects of separation may be mitigated – the loss of contact between children and one of their parents. The longer the delay the more difficult it is to renew a broken relationship (Mitchell, 1985).

Typical contact disputes

Some examples of the kinds of disputes that can arise over children, typically over contact, are set out below, but it should always be remembered that, although there are recurring patterns, no two families are the same and the unique and special circumstances of each predicament should always be considered. On the other hand, parents also take comfort in knowing that they are not alone and that their disputes and difficulties are commonly experienced by others who are separating or divorcing.

- The resident parent reports that the child does not want to see the non-resident parent who is demanding contact. The resident parent may or may not agree with the child's stand. Either way the resident parent says he or she is not prepared to force the child into contact against its will. The non-resident parent blames the other parent for 'brainwashing' the child and for not sufficiently encouraging the child to keep contact.

- The resident parent opposes contact, not in principle, but because of the failure of the non-resident parent to abide by certain conditions, such as reliability or punctuality. Contact involving overnight stays ('staying contact') may be opposed because the resident parent does not want the child exposed to 'immorality', namely the presence of a new partner in the non-resident parent's home or bed.
- The resident mother believes the father is using contact as a means of 'getting at' her. The demand for contact is viewed as an interference or an attempt to control, preventing her from leading her own life. Years of past neglect or lack of involvement with the children is cited as proof that the father does not really care about the children. The father may admit taking his children for granted in the past but is now seeking to remedy that situation.
- Contact may be denied in retaliation for the non-payment of maintenance. It may be claimed that if the non-resident parent really cared about his children he would contribute more to their material well-being. A demand for more overnight contact may be perceived as a ruse to avoid or reduce having to make maintenance payments for the children.
- The resident parent wants to decrease or discontinue contact because the children are disturbed or distressed before and/or after contact visits.
- Disputes over 'shared parenting' frequently reveal the entanglement of separate issues – for example, what may be important to a parent is what an arrangement is called (for example, 'shared parenting' may designate equal parental commitment even if the preferred contact may be much more limited), rather than any demand for 50/50 shared care of the children. Hunt with Roberts (2004) have pointed to the way in which debates on shared parenting are confused by the elision of different concepts, such as joint legal custody, shared residence, equal parenting time and shared responsibility (see Chapter 3, section on decisions of the court). Parties too can conflate these different issues, resulting in misunderstanding and unnecessary conflict.
- In many child abduction cases involving children removed or retained by the primary carer, the central issue for the 'left behind' parent may well be that of adequate contact, even though an application under the Hague Convention for the pre-emptory return of the child, appears to be the only available option to secure that contact (see Chapter 10, section on child abduction and mediation; see *reunite* Report, 2006).

While, in many cases, the resident parent is the mother, it would be wrong to regard disputes over contact only in terms of mothers exploiting their powerful position as parents with the care of children in order to obstruct the father's contact to their children. Most resident parents accept that contact is desirable but there are frequently valid obstacles and genuine differences of view about terms and conditions that get in the way of unproblematic contact regardless of the gender of the resident parent. Some resident parents are anxious to improve the quality and circumstances of contact and to effect an *increase* in contact between child and non-resident parent, both for the child's sake and to gain some respite from the unrelieved grind of child care. A sharing of discipline may be positively welcomed, particularly as children get older.

Emotional tensions surrounding contact visits may also aggravate disputes. The contact visit may provide the only opportunity former spouses have of pursuing private quarrels. The presence of an ex-partner on the doorstep may trigger a row. For children, contact may be the equivalent of moving from one hostile camp to the other. The conflict of the adults and the conflict of loyalties that this imposes on the children may make contact a dreaded rather than a happy event. Contact may be a reminder to children of their divided family, so that transitions to and from visits may be painful and the cause of distress, rather than the visits themselves.

Another issue that frequently emerges in negotiations over contact relates to the social and economic context of the specific dispute. Until reckoned with, it may constitute a major obstacle to agreement (Davis and Roberts, 1988). Many women bringing up children on their own demand recognition from the fathers of the important job they are doing and of its difficulties. What is wanted is an explicit acknowledgement from the father of the mother's part in bringing up their children alone in tough, often unremitting circumstances. It is a task not to be taken for granted by the father, associated as he often is with good times, holidays and treats. This recognition must not be confused with a demand for pity or sympathy, or necessarily with a demand for more material support.

Similarly, non-resident fathers often need explicit reassurance from mothers that they will not lose their children, or that nothing will be done to jeopardize their relationship with them. This anxiety is particularly acute when stepfathers are in daily contact with their children, where children may refer to a step-father as 'dad', or there is talk of changing surnames or even adoption. The strength of feeling on this issue is expressed in the words of one non-resident custodial father following a mediation session at which he agreed not to see one of his children:

> I think the biggest thing that came across, other than the two main agreements, was that she [the resident mother] was made to be aware of the fact that I am the children's father and nothing she or anybody else can do, can change that and she shouldn't try to.

5   Negotiation and mediation

Unless the investigator has some theories about the agreement process in negotiation, about why and in what ways the parties do (or do not) reach agreement, it is difficult to see how he can analyze the contribution of the mediator to the resolution of conflict. (Stevens, 1963, p. 123)

The process of negotiation

In negotiation there are two distinct though interconnected processes going on simultaneously: a repetitive, cyclical one and a developmental one. A simple analogy is a moving automobile. There is the cyclical turning of the wheels ... that enables the vehicle to move and there is the actual movement of the vehicle from one place to another. (Gulliver, 1979, p. 82)

Negotiation has been described as 'a distinctive social process of decision-making' (Gulliver, 1979, p. xvii). When two parties negotiate, they engage in a problem-solving process in which they attempt to reach a joint decision on matters of common concern over which they are in conflict, disagreement or dispute (Gulliver, 1979). There is no third-party decision-maker – that absence constituting 'the fundamental characteristic of negotiation' (Gulliver, 1979, p. 3). The nature of the negotiation process, as essentially a process of communication and learning through a series of exchanges of information, has already been outlined (see Chapter 1). This process is not in itself either haphazard or chaotic. If it were, negotiations would be doomed to failure. Whatever the differences in the society, the kind or complexity of the dispute, the length of time needed to reach a settlement, or the framework, the process itself generates an internal structure of its own, a 'succession of stages' that are common to all negotiations, even though no two instances are the same (Stevens, 1963, p. 10). This intrinsic structure emerges from and is shaped by the process of negotiation itself. It also manifests in the rules the parties themselves create, and in the mutual understanding that is a product of the process. The process must be experienced by the parties themselves, as negotiators, participating in a dynamic process of exploration and learning, personally experiencing the 'search process' (Gulliver, 1979; Stenelo, 1972, p. 192). The role of the mediator is understandable only as part of this process.

An invaluable processual analysis of negotiation and mediation, derived from empirical research in the sphere of labour relations in the US and in dispute resolution processes in East Africa respectively, is described in the work of Stevens (1963) and of Gulliver (1977, 1979). This analysis has particular relevance to mediation in family disputes as well. Gulliver (1977, 1979) highlights two concepts that are fundamental to an understanding of mediation and the role of the mediator:

- mediation serves a negotiation process,
- the role of the mediator is understandable only within an understanding of that process.

Gulliver (1977) has described the negotiation process realized through mediation as the gradual creation of order and of co-ordination between the parties. The mediator orchestrates a process in which the parties begin with a degree of assumed knowledge but also, both consciously and unconsciously, with a considerable degree of uncertainty and downright ignorance. That knowledge is tested and altered and refined in the process of interaction. Exchanges of this kind proceed through a series of 'overlapping phases' by means of which progressive and orderly movement towards settlement becomes possible. Each party is engaged in learning – about the other, about him or herself, about the children and about the possibilities and impossibilities of their common situation and possible outcomes. By a process of improved communication and understanding, the parties have the opportunity to learn not only more about all the circumstances, pressures, feelings, perceptions, attitudes and needs that attend the particular dispute, but also how to negotiate. This involves learning how to listen and understand more fully the other's perceptions and interests, how to act rationally and communicate effectively and how to be open to persuasion rather than coercion or bullying. The wheels of information exchange and learning that the mediator activates, motivate the negotiation process through its developmental progress towards settlement.

These interlocking developmental and cyclical processes reflect the reality of 'a general overall trend from relative ignorance, uncertainty and antagonism towards increased understanding, greater certainty and co-ordination' (Gulliver, 1979, p. 173). What propels this whole process is the basic contradiction between the parties' antagonism (that is, the dispute itself) and their simultaneous need for joint action.

The model of the cyclical process of negotiation

The two processes of negotiation, the cyclical and the developmental, are interconnected intimately, yet there is a logical appropriateness in discussing the cyclical process first. 'Thus, one might say, the wheels turn and the vehicle moves' (Gulliver, 1979, p. 83). The information exchanges between the parties result in more than mere communication as cognition and learning follow. In turn, shifts in attitudes, demands, preferences and expectations and in strategies and tactics, may be induced.

> Thus there is and has to be exchange of information, or more accurately, of messages. Strictly speaking, information is not exchanged but shared since the giver himself retains that which is given, in contrast with economic exchange of goods. A party must respond and wishes to respond to the receipt of messages by giving his own in return.[1] As in other kinds of social reciprocity, a party offers messages in order to obtain a response and to be able to claim a response, or at least some kind of reaction that carries a message. Refusal to exchange messages may, in the short run, draw further messages from the opponent and may be intended to do so. Continued refusal – or what is effectively the same thing, mere repetition of previous messages – leads to impasse and the possible breakdown of negotiations. (Gulliver, 1979, pp. 84–5)

The model of the developmental process of negotiation

The staged process outlined below follows Gulliver (1977, 1979) closely. When a disagreement in a relationship cannot and/or will not be tolerated further, a crisis occurs, precipitating the disagreement into a dispute. One party, or perhaps both, now seek(s) to gain the involvement of others, and the issue then enters the public or semi-public domain (Gulliver, 1977). Gulliver (1979) identifies the six overlapping phases of the process that follows:

1. searching for an arena;
2. defining the agenda;
3. exploring the field;
4. narrowing differences;
5. bargaining;
6. ritualizing the outcome.

---

1   Gulliver (1979) highlights the particular significance of silence in different societies, cultures and contexts – for example, unequivocal agreement with the last message received or, in contrast, non-acceptance of a message or an expression of frustration or of mistrust.

Research data establishes the 'one conclusion' that exemplifies this process – that 'movement, orderly and progressive in nature, stands out as a staid property ... which terminates in agreement' (Douglas, 1957, p. 70). These phases are briefly expanded on below.

Searching for an arena

The arena must be acceptable to both parties, although one may be resistant initially. The arena covers not only the geographical or social location but also who is involved – for example, parties with decision-making authority, and other participants such as partisan representatives or support persons (Roberts, 2003). Ideally, the arena should provide a calm, safe and neutral forum for negotiation – free of coercion, free of stigma, and free of confusion with other interventions. Screening for unsuitability, including domestic abuse, if it has not already occurred, needs to be included at this stage. This is when the communication arrangements, the role of the mediator, structural and procedural safeguards, and the principles and ground rules of engagement need to be clarified and agreed. All these requirements need to be in place if the parties are to be enabled to communicate in a way that is not possible on their own.

Defining the agenda

The search for an arena is also part of the attempt to define the dispute. One party may not know what it is that is in dispute or the issue may have to be clarified and distinguished from other issues or emotional implications. In composing the agenda therefore, the negotiable issues need to be defined and distinguished from those issues, however important to the parties, that cannot be negotiated, such as facts, the past, and values. This is precisely the phase when the parties have the opportunity to be heard, for there to be the expression of anger and fault, and for historical context of the dispute to be taken in account (see Grillo, 1991). Depending on the context and culture, some structural and procedural arrangements may be better than others if the process is to progress with optimum efficacy from both a negotiation and a psychological perspective; for example, in structuring for separate time with each party at this phase (Roberts, 2005a).

Exploring the field

In this relatively early phase, the preliminary emphasis will be on the differences between the parties. The messages passing between them are intended not to influence or shift the other but to explore the dimensions of the field within which further negotiations are to occur. Initial maximal claims and demands are likely to be set and extreme assertions expressed. The atmosphere is likely to be one of competition, even hostility. As noted in the context of industrial peace-making, the 'vivid monologues' that characterize this phase establish the 'outer limits' of the negotiating range within which the parties must do business, and have an important utility in the overall process (Douglas, 1957, p. 73).

Narrowing differences

There is a progressive shift in orientation from difference and animosity towards co-ordination and even co-operation. This may be accomplished by resort to one or more of several strategies; for example, by dealing with the less difficult issues first or dealing with each issue separately. If this phase goes well, there should be a resolution of some items and the clarification and isolation of any remaining differences. As has been observed in the context of industrial negotiations, this phase can provide the parties with the opportunity for exhausting the possibilities of difference, so that there is no alternative but to move towards consensus and co-operation:

> the parties also need the opportunity to experience exhaustion of their demands before they can be satisfied that they have drained what was there to be had. Premature movement robs them of this experience … and when a negotiator is at last convinced that 'This is all' means just that, it will not be because the opponent has told him so but because he has personally experienced the futility of seeking more … the exhaustion of topics offers one of the most useful criteria for measuring the timeliness of movement. (Douglas, 1962, p. 42)

Bargaining

Bargaining may follow on those items that have been most difficult to resolve, although they may not be the most important objectively. This is when 'I give in on this if you give in on that' may occur. The bargaining phase can be seen, therefore, as a mopping up operation, when differences are split and losses pooled – a phase that does not begin until the parties have reached agreement on the crucial negotiating issues (Douglas, 1962). Sometimes an outcome is reached with an unexpected and arbitrary suddenness when 'agreement *per se* has become more important than the particular point of agreement' (Gulliver, 1979, p. 168).

Ritualizing the outcome

If all goes well and agreement is reached there is a ritualization of that agreement. This means that the outcome is marked in some way, according to culture – for example, breaking bread, shaking hands or drawing up and signing a document. 'The negotiations have been concluded and there may be a good deal of amity. On the other hand, a persisting antagonism and a number of disagreements may remain; the parties may be bitter rivals still. For the moment, however, there is agreement, whether limited or broad, and a mutuality in the achievement of an outcome …' (Gulliver, 1979, p. 169).

The process of mediation

The stages of mediation follow these stages of the negotiation process – a process of discovery and clarification, the essence of which is learning through a series of exchanges of information. The process has to be experienced by the parties themselves as negotiators, participating in a dynamic process of exploration, of each other and themselves. This leads finally to the convergence of a joint decision acceptable to both parties, the end of the dispute and the end of negotiations. It is the task of the mediator to understand and manage this negotiation process between the parties. A greater understanding and experience of the processual nature of mediated negotiations can consolidate a mediator's trust *in the process* with a consequent increase of calm and optimism. This itself can inspire, in the parties, a corresponding trust *in the mediator*.

The phases outlined in Gulliver's model have a psychological and social as well as a logical coherence. For example, at an early phase when maximum claims and demands are likely to be made and antagonism will be greatest, the parties are furthest apart in every sense. Intense emotion and harsh language will characterize this distance, for anxiety and insecurity are acute. With the articulation of resentment, the exchange of information and the increase of learning, stress diminishes. Yet this distance between the parties is necessary if subsequent movement is to be apparent.

Real-life mediated negotiations are often more complex and variable than is suggested by these analytically distinct phases. Breakdown can occur at any stage. But without a regular pattern of expectations, adjustments and behaviour, negotiations would fail. Without an understanding of this pattern by the mediator, negotiations could be prolonged or damaged if through ignorance, hurry or inexperience, short cuts were attempted. Conceptual clarity, including that of an analytically distinct and regular pattern of expectations, is of particular importance given the dynamic reality and powerful emotions that characterize family disputes.

One feature of the mediation process unavailable to judges is its 'procedural flexibility' (McCrory, 1981, p. 56). This enables the parties themselves to determine the parameters of their exchanges, freeing them from legal formalities or prohibitions so that they may include those aspects of the dispute that they deem to be pertinent – for example, the emotional ramifications of the dispute and private ethical attitudes to fault and fairness.

The procedural flexibility of mediation also allows the requirements of full and accurate disclosure necessary for the mediation of financial and property matters to be accommodated. Procedural steps can be inserted at every stage of the process for dealing with the income (gathering, verifying, displaying and sharing), the assets (identifying, understanding, valuing), the options (collating, identifying gaps, dividing and so on) and the outcome (integrating the package, drawing up a Memorandum of Understanding).

The framework of mediation

> For of Mediation one is tempted to say that it is all process and no structure.
> (Fuller, 1971, p. 307)

What this observation serves to highlight is the difference between the processes involved in mediation and those involved in adjudication. The latter is characterized by institutional rules, formal procedures and clearly demarcated roles and authority (judges, barristers, clerks, and so on). It is within this formal pattern of due process that any dispute is dealt with.

As described above, no such institutional framework occurs in negotiation processes. The parties seek to sort out their dispute by voluntary exchanges, negotiation and decision-making. But where the parties cannot manage this on their own and so resort to mediation, some structural changes are inevitable.

First, a simple bilateral process is transformed into one involving a third party. Second, the very presence of this third party imposes the rudiments of a framework upon the encounter – for example, who is to participate and where, the time to be made available, and so on. Mediated negotiations require this minimum of rules at least, although, cross-culturally, mediation processes differ greatly in the way they are organized, the degree of formality (a lack of formality by no means indicating a lack of control), the rigidity of the framework and the number of rules imposed upon the disputants (Roberts, 1983b).

This framework within which mediatory processes occur serves two main purposes.

- It enables the parties to negotiate together in a way that would not have been possible on their own. Ground rules – for example, the right of the mediator to intervene if exchanges cease to be constructive – embody the values that underpin mediation (such as mutual respect and equity of exchange) and establish the potential for rational communication.
- The framework is designed to secure fairness. Rules of procedure make possible equal opportunities for full and confidential expression – for example, the separate meeting with the mediator within the session, and the guarantee that both parties will be able to state their views and objectives without interruption (see Roberts, 2005a, for more detailed exploration of the function of the separate meeting).

The interwoven nature of structure and process is a conspicuous characteristic of mediation – the structure encompassing the process and the process itself informing the structure.

Models of mediation: Structural variations of mediation sessions

I shall try to persuade you that fairness in procedures for resolving conflicts is the fundamental kind of fairness and that is acknowledged as a value in most cultures, places and times: fairness in procedure is an invariable value, a constant in human nature. (Hampshire, 2000, p. 4)

Models of practice embody structural features that frame the mediation process. The rationale of an effective model of practice is that it promotes the realisation of a fair and constructive process. Factors that have an impact on the kind of model that is adopted include the number, role and status (individuals or representatives) of the parties; their personalities, needs and behaviour; the kinds of issues to be negotiated; the cultural, physical and institutional context; and the gender of the mediators. There are a variety of structural arrangements or models that can be used in mediation, some of which could be deployed in order to address specific complexities concurrently, for example in the international field of mediation (workshops, fact-finding exercises, co-mediation, and so on). No single field of practice appears to be associated with any particular preferred model of practice – indeed, major differences in practice models are notable *within* the same context of practice – that of the family and of the commercial context – rather than between different mediation fields (Roberts, 2007). Some examples of models are set out below:

- pre-mediation/preparation or intake sessions,
- plenary or joint meetings,
- separate meetings,
- shuttle mediation,
- caucus,
- co-mediation,
- single or plural meetings,
- conferences,
- combinations of any of the above.

In addition, practical arrangements can contribute to the effectiveness of the model – for example, separate waiting rooms for the parties to ensure safety and avoid heightening conflict; seating arrangements that limit confrontation and encourage relaxed and open exchange; and plentiful, suitable refreshments to ease tension and reflect an attitude of consideration (Coogler, 1978; Haynes, 1981; Folberg and Taylor, 1984).

Some models of practice are discussed in more detail in the context of family mediation.

Single or plural meetings

Some family mediation services (such as the pioneering out-of-court South East London Family Mediation Bureau) offer mediation on children issues in a single one-off session. The intention is to focus effort on reaching an agreement on at least one issue in a single negotiating session lasting up to three hours. A second or even third session could be organized should the parties wish to renegotiate an agreement or when warranted by the circumstances, for example when some trial arrangement is being tested out and needs reviewing, when there were several issues in dispute, or when very entrenched parties needed more time to make the movement necessary for an agreement to be reached. On the whole, however, the parties start out knowing there are clearly defined time constraints and that they were not embarking on a protracted series of counselling-type sessions. This single meeting is particularly suitable for the single-issue dispute, such as contact or residence when the limitation of time and the concentration of focus combine to direct energies and attention on to the settlement of immediate and specific issues. Research has shown that the outcome of the first meeting is usually replicated on subsequent meetings (Davies and Roberts, 1988).

It can be argued that the single mediation session places the parties under too much pressure and that agreements so reached will be superficial and unlikely to be adhered to. There is no evidence to support this criticism in relation to out-of-court mediation, although research findings suggest that, in respect of in-court conciliation, there are significant pressures associated with the coercive court context, the focus on settlement and the rapid processing of cases, all of which undermine the parties' authority and exclude children from the process (Davis and Bader, 1985; Trinder et al., 2006; see also Chapter 2).

The plenary or joint session

A joint session involves the presence of all disputants at the mediation meeting. This may be compared to a meeting involving the mediator and one party only, known as a separate session, which may take place as an early phase within a longer joint session (see for example, the Bromley model).

There are powerful arguments why family mediation is best conducted in the presence of all parties. Joint meetings enable the mediator 'to observe the parties in their direct relationships with each other' and thereby to gain a clearer understanding of the issues in dispute (ACAS, n.d., paras 38, 39). One of the main advantages of mediation in disputes involving children is the opportunity it provides to increase mutual understanding and to facilitate communication and continuing negotiation between the parties. The couple will have to manage the many adjustments that are inevitably part of the process of maintaining contact through their children over the years. They will have to be able to negotiate together. If they will not agree even to be in the room together doubt could be cast on the appropriateness of mediation in those circumstances.

Within the joint session, the parties must have an opportunity to express their viewpoint to the mediator in the absence of their former partner. This vital protection should be available not only at the first meeting but at the outset of any subsequent session. It gives the mediator a fuller understanding of the situation and how each party sees it, and gives the couple the safety and freedom to state their views and feelings fully. This separate time with each party within the session is an additional safeguard to that of pre-mediation screening for unsuitability for mediation. Through this separate time with each party, the mediator is able to monitor circumstances, particularly in providing further occasion for continuing screening for domestic abuse throughout mediation – necessary, for example, where threatening behaviour might emerge for the first time or for the monitoring of current or past abusive behaviour.

Shuttle mediation

Shuttle mediation refers to the way the mediator may function as a go-between, shuttling between the two parties who remain physically (and possibly temporarily) apart. The mediator may act as a simple conduit, passing messages back and forth, or may actively negotiate on behalf of the disputants who obviously cannot negotiate directly. Shuttle mediation is commonly used in international disputes and, on occasion, in community, commercial, family, environmental and labour relations disputes.

There are three main purposes behind the use of shuttle mediation.

- It aims to avoid confrontation, both for the parties and for the mediator, where the level of conflict is high.
- It allows the parties to disclose confidential information to the mediator that they do not want revealed to one another (see Chapter 9).
- It gives the mediator the opportunity to discuss matters that would be uncomfortable to raise if parties were together (Folberg and Taylor, 1984).

In disputes following family breakdown, the disadvantages of shuttle mediation outweigh the advantages, except in special circumstances such as illness, extreme stress, or fear of intimidation, where it could (although not necessarily) be of value as a prelude to joint negotiation. A vulnerable party may feel safer initially communicating at a distance, but it is fair to say that if the level of conflict, anxiety or fear is that high, mediation is probably not appropriate anyway.

Some disadvantages of shuttle mediation are set out below.

- The mediator lays him/herself open to charges of partiality. Alliances may more easily arise or be perceived to arise between the mediator and one party. The mediator is placed in the well-nigh impossible position of having to act as spokesperson for each party and yet not to take sides. In the absence of both parties the mediator cannot demonstrate the impartiality that is central to the mediatory role.
- The mediator does all the negotiating. The parties are not only denied the information derived from direct experience of each other but they do not learn how to negotiate together.
- The added time it takes.
- The power of the mediator and possibilities of manipulating the mediation process are increased. The mediator may find it tempting to exceed the messenger role, especially when negotiations are going badly, as may be likely when the parties cannot or will not meet directly together in the first place. The mediator's total control over communication gives opportunities to control the substance of that communication, for example by changing an emphasis, omitting or reframing statements. Misunderstandings, many of which cause or exacerbate conflict, are often compounded or created in communications between third parties (solicitors' letters, for example).

While the role of a mediator in shuttle mediation differs from that of a solicitor who represents the interests of one party only, the problems arising from third-party communications remain the same. Unless everything is out in the open, and seen to be so, the task of the mediator in improving communication is seriously hampered.

- The protection of confidential information is problematic. Disputants have no means of knowing whether private information imparted in confidence to the mediator remains protected, especially if the subject crops up spontaneously anyway, such as the intention to move house, change job, end the relationship with a new partner, and so on. This could lead to a loss of trust in the mediator and so undermine his or her efforts.

The caucus

The caucus, a North American term, involves the mediator meeting individually with one side or a subset of a participant group (for example, lawyers only or clients only). The primary purpose of the caucus is to enable the mediator to gain access to information and insights that cannot be obtained in the joint meeting (Stulberg, 1987). The caucus can be used effectively for purposes of breaking an impasse in negotiations, for educating a party in their negotiation style, and for exploring possibilities for compromise. In family disputes, the caucus allows the parties to reveal information to the mediator that they do not wish to disclose to the other party, to explore personal feelings about the issues, and discuss matters too uncomfortable or risky to raise in the joint meeting (Folberg and Milne, 1988). Confidential exchanges, whilst one of the main advantages of the caucus, are also fraught with difficulty, requiring considerable skill on the part of the mediator in keeping track of what is known, how that knowledge was obtained and from whom, and any constraints attaching to it (Menkel-Meadow et al., 2005). Disputants for example, have no means of knowing whether confidentiality has been breached, if that topic crops up spontaneously anyway (see shuttle mediation above).

Three dominant approaches, depending on mediator philosophy, have been identified in relation to the use of the caucus: never caucus; the selective use of the caucus; and always or mostly caucus (Menkel-Meadow et al., 2005). The literature confirms the usefulness of the caucus – in generating confidence, intimacy and encouragement in the negotiations. It is also found to be of pragmatic value in enabling commercial mediators to work effectively with teams and for continuing screening for domestic abuse in family mediation (Roberts, 2007).

The co-mediation model

This occurs when two mediators, ideally one male and one female, mediate together in a particular case. Co-mediation by two members of the same sex should be avoided wherever possible because of the risk of perceived bias, and of one of the parties being outnumbered three to one by the opposite sex. Although it may appear to be more expensive and requires careful planning and time for preparation, there are distinct advantages in using two mediators in certain cases – for example, where there are a number of parties, where additional or complementary expertise may be needed, where there is high conflict or there are particularly difficult circumstances.

The advantages of co-mediation are as follows.

- Impartiality is enhanced if neither male nor female viewpoint prevails or is perceived to prevail.
- Co-mediators can set an example to the disputants of how to negotiate. Of particular value to the disputants is the way the mediators overcome their own (occasional) disagreements. Courteous and considerate behaviour by the mediators can set the tone for relations between the parties.
- Co-mediators can share the demanding task of mediating, especially in the longer single sessions. They can monitor each other's contributions, offsetting weaknesses, reinforcing messages and providing complementary skills, information and approaches, particularly if they have different professional backgrounds, for example law and psychology.

In addition to gender bias and imbalance, the disadvantages of co-mediation include the following.

- Problems of authority, status, control and territory can arise between the two mediators, particularly when they have different professional backgrounds.
- Conflicting styles and approaches can result in confusion over strategies, timing and the division of labour, or a power struggle between the mediators.
- An increase in the risks of exerting pressure on the parties for or against certain options and outcomes can occur.
- One mediator may dominate, setting a bad example to the parties.

Many mediators use a mix of models, most involving a combination of plenary and caucus sessions devised to meet the requirements of the particular situation and the parties' needs and objectives.

6   The mediator

... the primary function of the mediator ... is not to propose rules to the parties and to secure their acceptance of them, but to induce the mutual trust and understanding that will enable the parties to work out their own rules. The creation of rules is a process that cannot itself be rule-bound; it must be guided by a sense of shared responsibility and a realization that the adversary aspects of the operation are part of a larger collaborative undertaking. (Fuller, 1971, p. 326)

The values of mediation have exemplified, above all, a fundamental ethic of respect, for the parties' autonomy and for their authority to make their own decisions. The professional skill of the mediator has been seen to lie, ideally, in acting in a manner that reflects an understanding of what has been described as 'the subtleties' of respect – 'acts of recognition and regard that orchestrate the experience of respect' (Sennett, 2003, p. 149). Expectations such as these can be seen to be of most value precisely because of the recognition that the circumstances necessitating mediation, of political, social and personal conflict and dispute, and of stress, distress, and suffering, could be bringing out the 'worst' in people. In pursuit of the objective of autonomy and respect therefore, the intervention of the mediator, however varied and powerful its impact, is different from that of the usual role of the professional, that of the dominant expert.

It is well recognized too, that the minimal numerical transformation that occurs in mediation, of the dyad into the triad, can have radical, complex and paradoxical effects – intellectual, social, psychological and negotiation effects. The presence of the third party qualitatively transforms the interaction. On the one hand, merely by being there, the mediator alters the relationship between the parties and exerts influence – 'I contributed nothing but my presence' (Meyer, 1950, p. 6).

On the other hand, the third party in any dispute resolution process, not only mediation, transforms the interaction in another important respect, by embodying the principle of objectivity and reasonableness in decision-making – 'the non-partisan tempers the passion of the others' (Simmel, 1908a, p. 152). In representing the principle of objectivity and reasonableness, the mediator transforms the interaction in this way:

> The diminution of this personal tone is the condition under which the understanding and reconciliation of the adversaries can be attained, particularly because it is only under this condition that each of the two parties actually realizes what the other must insist upon. To put it psychologically, antagonism of the will is reduced to intellectual antagonism ... no matter in what form the conflict enters from one side, it is transmitted to the other only in an objective form. (Simmel, 1908a, p. 148)

With aspirations as ambitious as these and in circumstances as difficult, the scale of the task requires the mediator to adopt a modest approach, with full awareness of the limits and obstacles. In many instances, mediators can do no more than provide disputing parties with a calm, safe forum for reasonable exchange, and the opportunity to have a conversation that they may not be able to have on their own.

In this chapter the role and functions, the attributes and the ethical responsibilities of the mediator are outlined. Some of the inherent tensions in the mediatory role are also pointed out.

The role and functions of the mediator

The main functions of the mediator are those of catalyst and facilitator. A large body of work exists to illustrate the complex and subtle ways in which the mediator, notwithstanding these minimal functions, is acknowledged to exercise influence within the process (Deutsch, 1973; Rubin and Brown, 1975; Gulliver, 1979; Pruitt, 1981; Stulberg, 1981; for further discussion on this subject, see Roberts, 1992b, 1994).

The mediator as catalyst

> Succinctly stated, the mediator's presence affects how the parties interact. His presence should lend constructive posture to the discussions rather than cause further misunderstanding and polarization, although there are no guarantees that the latter will not result. (Stulberg, 1981, p. 94)

As already noted, the mere presence of the mediator alters the relationship between the disputing parties and exerts an influence. This happens in the following ways:

- The mediator brings about an interaction that would not have been possible otherwise.
- The presence of the mediator is a reminder that the issues in dispute are there to be confronted. In identifying these, the parties may find it necessary to justify and explain their respective positions and demands and therefore have to think them through.
- The mere presence of the mediator generates pressures towards co-ordination, even co-operation. Schelling gives two vivid examples of this aspect of the mediator's role:

The bystander who jumps into an intersection and begins to direct traffic at an impromptu traffic jam is conceded the power to discriminate among cars by being able to offer a sufficient increase in efficiency to benefit even the cars most discriminated against; his directions have only the power of suggestion, but co-ordination requires the common acceptance of some source of suggestion. Similarly the participant of a square dance may all be thoroughly dissatisfied with the particular dances being called, but as long as the caller has the microphone, nobody can dance anything else. (Schelling, 1960, p. 144)

Expectations of reasonableness, open communication and mutual respect can actually bring these about. People want to look good in the eyes of third parties and so behave towards each other with restraint and minimal courtesy (Rubin and Brown, 1975; Pruitt, 1981). In setting up norms of 'rational interaction' the mediator fulfils an important function. At the very least, with fair rules the parties in conflict are helped 'to fight fairly' (Deutsch, 1973).

The mediator as facilitator

The mediator's main function is to facilitate the negotiating process between the parties. The more relevant and accurate the information that passes between them, the greater will be their understanding of the facts, feelings, expectations and values that give rise to and colour the issues that divide them. This shared knowledge of the pressures that affect both parties, and of the implications both of reaching and of not reaching an agreement, may lead to a modification of preferences and goals. This improved understanding is produced by the process of negotiation itself (Fuller, 1971). But the mediator contributes to this process by facilitating the parties' communication, learning and decision-making. Stulberg (1981) analyses the main facilitator functions in the following terms:

- educator – the mediator explains and informs, about aspirations, reasons, constraints, meanings, and so on;

- translator – the mediator conveys each party's proposals 'in a language that is both faithful to the desired objectives of the party and formulated to insure the highest degree of receptivity by the listener' (Stulberg, 1981, p. 94);
- 'agent of reality' – the mediator points out the feasibilities, practicalities and, crucially, the possible consequences of proposals.

These main functions are supplemented by many others (see Chapter 7). There are specific attributes required of the mediator in order that he/she may fulfil these functions most effectively.

The attributes of the mediator

The attributes of the good mediator, both personal qualities and qualifications, have long been recognized, as elucidated in Goethe's description of his character Mittler, in his evolutionary progress as a mediator:

> This singular gentleman was in earlier years a minister of religion. Unflagging in his office, he had distinguished himself by his capacity for settling and silencing all disputes, domestic and communal, first between individual people, then between landowners, and then between whole parishes. There were no divorces and the local judiciary was not pestered by a single suit or contention during the whole period of his incumbency. He recognized early on how essential a knowledge of law was to him, he threw himself into a study of this science, and he soon felt a match for the best lawyers. The sphere of his activities expanded wondrously and he was on the point of being called to the Residenz so that he might complete from on high what he had begun among the lowly when he won a big prize in a lottery. He bought. a modest estate, farmed it out and made it into the central point of his life, with the firm intention, or rather according to his fixed habit and inclination, never to enter any house where there was not a dispute to settle or difficulties to put right. People superstitious about the significance of names say it was the name Mittler, which means mediator, which compelled him to adopt this oddest of vocations.[1]

Of great importance are Mittler's knowledge relating to the matter in dispute, his skills in analysis and problem-solving, his awareness of the moral dimension to the problem, and his wisdom and compassion in his relations with people.

Very little has in fact been written about the qualities of the mediator. One reason for this is the weight that has long been attached to the personal

---

1　Extract from J.W. von Goethe (1809) *Elective Affinities*, translated by R.J. Hollingdale (Harmondsworth: Penguin Classics, 1971), copyright R.J. Hollingdale, 1971, pp. 31–4. Reproduced by permission of Penguin Books Ltd.

rather than the processual aspects of the role. Personal qualities, often elusive and idiosyncratic, are not easily susceptible to analysis. So the catalogues of qualities that have been devised are anecdotal rather than scientific. The most useful approach to an understanding of what qualities make up the 'good' mediator has been to adopt the perspectives of the parties to the dispute. In such studies (for example, Landsberger, 1956; Stulberg, 1981; Raiffa, 1982) a list of preferred qualities was identified, for example:

- originality of ideas,
- sense of appropriate humour,
- ability to act unobtrusively,
- the mediator as 'one of us',
- the mediator as respected authority (that is, personal prestige),
- ability to understand quickly the complexities of a dispute,
- accumulated knowledge,
- control over feelings,
- attitudes towards and persistence and patient effort invested in the work of mediator,
- faith in voluntarism (in contrast to dictation),
- physical endurance,
- the hide of a rhinoceros,
- the wisdom of Solomon,
- the patience of Job,
- the capacity to appreciate the dynamics of the environment in which the dispute is occurring,
- intelligence (both 'process' skills and 'content' knowledge – knowledge that equips the mediator to ask penetrating questions, to be aware of subtle nuances and when artificial constraints are being erected. Such knowledge should not be used, however, 'for the purpose of serving as an expert who advises the parties as the 'right answers') (Stulberg, 1981, p. 96).

What emerged from such a catalogue approach was a consensus about a combination of attributes, intellectual, moral and personal, that goes towards the making of the ideal mediator.[2]

---

2   In the 1990s, National Family Mediation devised a selection procedure (in collaboration with a leading occupational psychologist) for all its trainee mediators, centred not on the prior professional qualifications of the candidate, but on the primary requirement of *aptitude* for mediation. Based on a specification of identified essential and desirable personal attributes (intellectual, interpersonal, ethical, and personal and motivational) relevant to the effective practice of mediation, the selection procedure was designed to elicit a range of personal attributes resulting in the creation of a profile of each candidate's strengths and weaknesses. Mediators selected by this approach represented a range of professional backgrounds, one of the objectives of the exercise. Regrettably this procedure proved to be too expensive and was discontinued.

More recently, attempts have been made to explore 'some deeper and more fundamental quality that the most effective mediators have – a quality that may include such attributes as patience, wisdom or wit, but which involves other attributes that are not on the [above] lists' (Bowling and Hoffman, 2000, p. 9). It is contended that where empirical studies of mediation show favourable results, including high levels of party satisfaction, these occur regardless of the individual style or philosophical or professional orientation of the mediator, or whatever practice skills or models are adopted (Bowling and Hoffman, 2000). It is asserted too that it is 'a mediator's "presence" – more a function of who the mediator is than what he or she does – [that] has a profound impact on the mediation process' (Bowling and Hoffman, 2000, p. 5).

Mediators, irrespective of their field of mediation practice, professional background or gender, have similar views about qualities that are essential for effective practice – few referring to those traditionally catalogued, with the exception of patience (see below) – and these include intellectual capacities (analytic and creative) and the capacity to listen attentively (Roberts, 2007). Additional attributes are also highlighted by mediators – in particular, a genuine interest in, liking and concern for people (recognized to be hugely demanding in practice as this must apply to all the parties who, in all likelihood in the circumstances, are in conflict with one another); personal warmth and approachability; toughness in the face of conflict; and self-knowledge of one's own failings. A distinguished mediator working in the international field exemplifies the conjunction of these attributes:

> … When anybody does work in relation to something, you, they, have to ask yourself why are they drawn to that. I do care very passionately about people. I think I am a very compassionate person and therefore the desire for violence and cruelty not to happen is a very strong desire I have. So that's a strong motivator. But I also think that – well I know – I'm quite an aggressive person by nature, particularly when I view myself from a gender perspective, I know I was always too rough to be a 'proper little girl'. And that probably makes me see myself as more aggressive than I would if I were male. But, I think the plus of that is that I am not uncomfortable with conflict. And I think one of the things you have to learn to do as a mediator, and which some people will find more difficult than others, is at some level not to mind that the micro-conflict that is taking place within the mediation *is* taking place. *That you are there for it to be able to take place.* And I think I am relatively not phased by hot interpersonal exchanges. I think that's useful.

> And I think the other reason why I am comfortable in the facilitator role is because I always have a sense of taking up too much space in the world, in terms of sound time or, even more, in terms of energy, of being too liable to be dominant. And if I am in a mediator/facilitator role I have a framework, in which I feel both that I do contain myself in a very conscious way and as a matter of

habit now. Because I know that my job is not endlessly to be coming up with or holding forth opinions, but is to create space for other people to think and express themselves. So that gives me a kind of sense of OK-ness in that role.

I actually think I've developed good listening skills, anybody could, and I'm very interested in levels of awareness of what's going on, both in myself and in other people. And I can be assertive when assertiveness is needed – and it certainly is if people are going to feel safe. Then they need to know that the room is being held and I'm confident at doing this 'aggressive' bit. It comes out as assertive and it's useful. I'm full of angst. I can be very nervous but in the moment I'm not going to find it impossible to do what has to be done. (Diana Francis quoted in Roberts, 2007, pp. 47–8)

The reflections of mediators also provide fresh insight into the nature and function of that long recognized attribute of the mediator – patience – and the relationship of patience to the purpose of mediation – for example, in the comparison between the 'outcome-driven' and the 'process-driven' approaches in international mediation, and the patience necessary for the latter. If the primary objective of the mediator is perceived to be that of enabling *the parties themselves* to reach their own agreed outcomes, a high degree of patience is also recognized to be a concomitant requirement. Patience is, therefore, not only an attribute of the mediator, but also a function of the process. As a renowned labour mediator expressed it as early as 1950:

The final demand is still for patience and endurance. Be patient, be patient and evermore be patient. Be not too patient! Never tire, but watch for the gathering signs of fatigue in others. Then push over the pins that are already trembling. How? I cannot tell you. A sudden change in attitude, a deepening of the voice, a strident, unexpected urgency … but no two cases are alike and even if they were, no two mediators would attack them on parallel lines. (A.S. Meyer quoted in Douglas, 1962, p. 108)

The well-recognized requirement of 'personal authority' perhaps sums up that *combination* of attributes – individual qualities (intellectual, moral and personal), professional experience (analytic, substantive and practice knowledge and skills) and ability (capacity for critical and creative thinking, understanding and engagement) – that make the practice of mediation a demanding and creative task.

The impartiality of the mediator

The white line down the center of the road is a mediator and very likely it can err substantially towards one side or the other before the disadvantaged side finds advantage in denying its authority. (Schelling, 1960, p. 144)

Maintaining an intermediate position between the disputants is one of the most essential of the attributes of the mediator. The mediator must prevent head-on collision between forces advancing in opposite directions in an unobtrusive, minimal yet authoritative way, providing protection and/or support to one or the other party whenever necessary. This 'non-partisanship' required of the mediation can manifest itself, according to Simmel, when the mediator either

> ... stands above contrasting interests and opinions and is actually not concerned with them, or if he is equally concerned with both ... The idea is that the non-partisan is not attached by personal interest to the objective aspects of either party position. Rather, both come to be weighed by him as by a pure, impersonal intellect; without touching the subjective sphere. But the mediator must be subjectively interested in the persons or groups themselves who exemplify the contents of the quarrel which to him are merely theoretical, since otherwise he would not take over his function. It is, therefore, as if subjective interest set in motion a purely objective mechanism. It is the fusion of personal distance from the objective significance of the quarrel with personal interest in its subjective significance which characterizes the non-partisan position. This position is the more perfect, the more distinctly each of these two elements is developed and the more harmoniously, in its very differentiation, each cooperates with the other. (Simmel, 1908a, p. 149)

The difficulty of achieving this complicated stance is clear, as is the recognition that the mediator has always to be above suspicion that he or she is biased for or against one or other party. Impartiality is therefore essential to the achievement of the trust that the parties must have in the mediator if that intervention is to be effective. This depends on skill and knowledge as well as on the personal integrity and commitment of the mediator (ACAS, n.d., para. 15). Impartiality constitutes, therefore, a fundamental principle of practice, an essential attribute of the mediator, a duty and a skill. The credibility of the mediator depends not only on being impartial, but on being perceived to be so.

Impartiality and neutrality

Impartiality vis-à-vis the parties must be distinguished from the separate issue of neutrality (McCrory, 1985). There are three main problems in confusing neutrality with impartiality. The first is one of accuracy. The mediator is not neutral, inevitably having his or her own views, values and interests. Second, claims to mediator neutrality overstate what is possible, laying mediators open to legitimate challenge. Third, claims to neutrality could be dangerous if neutrality is asserted in situations of inequality (Haynes, 1980).

The impartiality of the mediator may be protected in the following ways:

- The mediator must make absolutely clear at the outset, his/her commitment to impartiality in the decision-making process.
- The mediator must give due weight to each party's point of view. This is best secured by giving each party a separate opportunity at an early stage in the session to express their perspective in the absence of the other and by making sure in the subsequent joint gathering that each point of view is heard and understood by both. The right of each party to hold a different, even conflicting, position on the issue may often have to be affirmed. At the same time the mediator needs to recognize and challenge self-righteous claims about motives and behaviour based on biased perceptions of benevolence and legitimacy – 'I am right/good; you are wrong/bad' (Deutsch, 1973).
- The mediator should avoid pronouncing on the merits of either party's position or expressing a preference for any given outcome. Where it may be appropriate to voice an opinion, to proffer guidance or to make a suggestion, this must be done tentatively and openly so that the risk of imposing views or insinuating assumptions is avoided. Another risk, damaging to impartiality, arises where the mediator's own views may be seen to coincide with those of one of the parties – for example, on the need for stability for children in relation to contact with a parent, or in favour of contact with a non-resident parent.
- An even-handed approach is not incompatible with the mediator pointing to the consequences on each other and their children, of the parties' respective behaviour, especially to the negative effects. It is the way this is done that is important. However, the making of judgements, moral or psychological, is incompatible with the mediator's task of managing the quarrel impartially. The mediator has to accept the validity of a variety of child-rearing practices, religious, cultural and moral beliefs, practices and lifestyles, and not allow private attitudes or feelings to intrude, for example by disapproving or approving of lax or authoritarian approaches to child-rearing.[3]

---

3   On the limits of tolerating behaviour that may test a mediator's understanding and practice, see National Family Mediation's *Cross-cultural Mediation Policy and Practice Guidelines* (1998, section 2 in particular):

The mediator's responsibility involves an acute sensitivity to established cultural norms without falling prey to the danger of tolerating behaviour which is clearly unacceptable to one or both of the parties. In any instance where the boundaries are not clear, the mediator should consult the parties and if necessary terminate the session and seek appropriate advice.

- An impartial stance does not mean that the mediator cannot give support to either party at different moments in the negotiation process. Whatever the objective facts, each party is likely to perceive themselves as the more vulnerable one. The purpose of the mediator's understanding of these feelings is to enhance reciprocal understanding in the parties themselves.
- The use of co-workers of different genders is one way of safeguarding impartiality. This prevents any one perspective predominating or of being perceived as such, or of alliances being formed along or across gender lines (see Chapters 7 and 8).
- The structural framework governing the mediation session may enhance or diminish the protection of impartiality, for example joint meetings. Where the parties are not expected to meet together but negotiate separately through the mediator shuttling in between, impartiality cannot easily be seen to operate and the mediator may lay him/herself open to charges of partiality (see above). The structural arrangements play a vital part in preventing the occurrence of 'negative positioning' of one party, as identified in North American research (Cobb and Rifkin, 1990, 1991).

Whatever form of 'non-partisanship' is adopted, consisting in equal distance or equal closeness, the achievement of impartiality imposes the greatest challenge to the effective practice of mediation, requiring thought, care and attention, experience over time, and skill.

Ethical responsibilities

There are major ethical responsibilities that the mediator carries. These are more likely to be fulfilled if mediators bear constantly in mind the nature of their intervention – as 'outsiders involving themselves in the affairs of others' (Cormick, 1982, p. 264). These responsibilities can only be fulfilled too if the mediator earns trust by practising with integrity and competence (Davis and Gadlin, 1988).

The mediator's first responsibility is to protect the right of the parties to be the architects of their own agreement. The mediator has a responsibility therefore, to ensure that the parties' participation in the negotiation process is fair and equal and that the outcome is one that is mutually agreed. Imbalances in bargaining power must be recognized. Where duress occurs, mediation should cease. (See Chapters 7 and 9 for a fuller discussion of this topic.)

The mediator has a responsibility to those who, although not parties to mediation (that is, decision makers), are affected by any agreement reached there, whether or not they are present at the negotiating table. Children are the obvious example in family mediation. They could, in addition, be participants with an independent interest in the subject matter, such as new partners or grandparents, or representatives with a separate and independent interest; for example, a social worker representing the state's interest in protecting a child.[4] 'The greater the impact of the issues in dispute on parties not at the table, the more critical the responsibility of the mediator' (Cormick, 1977). This does not amount to the mediator representing the interests of those not at the table. However, the mediator must ensure not only that the parties consider the impact on others of any agreement they make but also the impact of others on the agreement.

A premise underpinning mediation in family disputes is that parents love their children and are best able to make decisions for them (Folberg, 1984). The mediator can act neither as the advocate of the child nor as the social worker for the child. In private law disputes where the competency of parents is not challenged, it is the parents' role to protect the interests of their child (Folberg, 1984). The task of the mediator is to assist the parents in fulfilling that role, and to ensure that in making joint decisions they consult and give due weight to their children's views wherever possible and consider all the likely consequences of alternative arrangements, especially on their children. While most mediators will be very concerned about the needs of children, affected by the separation and divorce of the adults, they must be careful in expressing their concern, not thereby to imply a lesser concern in the parents themselves. The mediator therefore has a responsibility to assist the parties to protect the interests of their children (see also Chapter 10 on children in the mediation process).

Mediators have a responsibility to ensure that they understand and respond appropriately to the impact of cultural difference on mediation. One approach to this emphasizes the need for mediators to share the cultural and ethical norms of the disputants, and therefore to come from the same cultural background and community, exploring and adapting indigenous forms of mediation where appropriate. Another approach argues that with training, a single group of mediators can work with a variety of cultural groups. A third approach recommends the combination of the two, recognizing that further research is necessary (for discussion on the subject, see Goldstein, 1986; Gale, 1994; Shah-Kazemi, 1996, 2000).

---

4   Roberts (2003) analyses the roles, functions and status of third persons in family mediation (other than that of the mediator and the child) and proposes a typology that divides participants into four main groups: partisan persons present to support each party (official, such as a lawyer, and unofficial, such as a friend or family member)); participants with an independent interest in the subject matter of mediation (such as step-parents or grandparents); participants representing an interest in ensuring accessibility to and the effectiveness of the mediation process (such as translators); and representatives with a separate and independent interest (such as a social worker representing the child's interests).

Mediators have a responsibility to understand the nature of their authority and power (see Chapter 11 for a discussion on the safeguards necessary to minimize the potential for the abuse of power by the mediator). They need to recognize their potential to influence or manipulate the course of the negotiation process as well as the substantive issues in discussion (see for example Dingwall, 1988; for a debate on this research, see Roberts, 1992b, 1994; Dingwall and Greatbatch, 1993, 1995). This means that they need to acknowledge their own interests and values, however altruistic (for example, in protecting children or the weaker party), and the ways in which these might be insinuated, for example by emphasizing some issues or in rephrasing or ignoring others. The giving of information by the mediator, which is acceptable, must be distinguished from the giving of advice. The latter involves recommending strategic courses of action or the making of tactical suggestions in the light of the law, decisions of the court and the particular circumstances. The giving of information, on the other hand, aims to be neutral, involving an explanation or clarification only of rights, resources, terms, and so on (see Chapter 3).

Central tensions in the mediator's role

> The process of mediation and the role of the mediator in particular is shaped by the strategies adopted to cope with this tension between the need to settle and the lack of power to do so. (Silbey and Merry, 1986, p. 7)

This tension between the need to settle and the lack of power to do so is what Silbey and Merry (1986, p. 7) call 'the mediator's dilemma' – the dilemma of how to settle a case without imposing a decision. The closer the link with the court where pressures towards settlement are greatest, the greater the tension (see, for example Davis and Bader, 1985; Trinder et al., 2006). Although only one of the three agencies studied by Silbey and Merry was officially affiliated to the court, the other two were court-linked. A repertoire of strategies was employed by the mediators in their attempt to resolve this tension, for example in the way the mediators presented themselves and their programme (for instance, laying claim to power based on expert knowledge or legal authority) and in their control over the mediation process.

Kressel (1985, p. 203) highlights the inherent tension of the mediator's role, which derives from three principal and interrelated sources. He describes these as:

- the 'lofty and at times contradictory and ambiguous demands of the role itself';
- the intermediate position the mediator occupies between the two parties;
- the objectively difficult circumstances in which the negotiations typically occur.

The mediator is expected to maintain a calm, disinterested, creative and rational presence – where 'reason is everywhere the principle of understanding' – in the midst of the parties' stress and distress (Simmel, 1908a, trans. 1955, p. 148). At the same time, the mediator is also exposed to great stress, arising from a complexity of sources depending on the field of mediation.[5] Saposnek (1983) gives a number of examples of situations that impose emotionally demanding pressures on the mediator. These are inevitable when the work involves couples in open conflict, but even apparently co-operative couples need to be approached with scepticism precisely because of their resort to mediation. Working with limited information under time constraints can be, for example, like 'stepping lightly across a minefield. If [the mediator] accidentally steps in the wrong place the entire process can blow up in his face' (Saposnek, 1983, p. 27).

Finally, there exists a fundamental tension between the directive control the mediator may need to exert to prevent destructive emotional exchanges overwhelming rational discussion, and the party control that is the chief objective of the mediation process. This ideally requires of the mediator an unobtrusive and minimal style of intervention. Managing this tension effectively and creatively presents mediators with one of their central challenges.

---

5   See Roberts (2007, pp. 183–93) for the reflections of mediators, representing at least nine different fields of mediation practice, on the nature and impact of stress in their context of work and on their approaches to its management.

7   The session and the strategies

The range of settings reminds us, too, that negotiations take place not only in the most intimate of settings but also in the largest and across maximum geographic spaces; they also may be of the briefest duration or take place over long periods of time, and, of course, they may be 'over' the merest trifles or the most momentous of issues. (Strauss, 1978, p. 25)

The conduct of the session

All negotiation interactions are influenced by the structural conditions (implied and overt) that bear on them (Strauss, 1978). There can be a variety of organizational arrangements within which the mediation session may be contained and, as already noted (see Chapter 5), no one model is best for all purposes. Yet there are some features that are essential if the framework is to fulfil its core purpose and address, through the structure of the session, the central issues of party authority for decision-making, mediator power and bias, and the protection of a fair process. In family mediation these typically include:

- gathering individual pre-mediation intake information and screening for unsuitability;
- an introductory joint meeting;
- an opportunity (however brief) for each party to see the mediator on their own;
- the summing up by the mediator of the issues as propounded by the parties.

These are vital preliminaries to the direct negotiation of the parties, which normally constitutes the major content of the session. The separate opportunity for each party to talk alone to the mediators at an early stage of *every* session is one important structural safeguard that ideally should not be dispensed with if full and free expression is to be protected. Its significance and value depends on an understanding of its location both within the overall framework of the session as well as in relation to the general shape of the process of mediated negotiation (see Chapter 5). The inter-relationship of the process and the structure within which it is contained, is set out below in an outline of the phases of the process of mediation linked to the stages of a typical family mediation session.

Stage I   *Establish the arena*: The first joint session

This first mediation session should ideally start with a joint meeting between both parties and the mediator. There are three main reasons why it is desirable for both parties to attend together. First, the mediator needs to establish an even-handed relationship with both parties from the start. Furthermore, he or she must be seen to do so. Initial separate meetings could lay the mediator open to charges of bias or prior recruitment. Second, if the mediator's main objective is to launch the parties on a joint enterprise of negotiation and decision-making, they ought to begin the way they wish to continue, in direct contact, if not yet in direct communication. Third, a joint meeting can be the best means of explaining and clarifying the fundamentals of participation as well as achieving a clear understanding of the issues in dispute (ACAS, n.d., para. 38; Roberts, 2005a).

As mediation is a relatively new and probably unfamiliar process to many resorting to it, it is crucial that, at this stage, mediators give adequate time to describing its characteristics carefully and unambiguously so that the parties understand what they are embarking upon, making their consent to participate fully informed. Initially therefore, the mediator needs to explain or clarify the purpose of the meeting, the structural arrangements to be deployed to best achieve this (for example, the organization of the session, the number of sessions if more than one, and so on), and the terms of engagement – for example, the fundamental principles underpinning participation (for example voluntariness, confidentiality and its exceptions, in particular regarding child protection) and the ground rules including expectations for ensuring a calm and safe forum for reasonable exchanges.

At this stage, mediators needs to elicit, in advance, the permission of the parties to intervene if exchanges become destructive. This request constitutes:

- explicit recognition by the mediator of the existence of the powerful underlying feelings (usually of hostility, bitterness, anger or hurt) that might attend the dispute;
- legitimization of their possible eruption;
- authorization to curb them.

This request for *permission* to step in and stop possibly destructive exchanges is a way of acknowledging, right at the start, that authority lies with the parties (and, therefore, the mediator cannot impose restrictions on the parties without their explicit consent), as well as establishing the expectation for a calm and safe forum for exchange.

Stage II   *Define and clarify the issues*: The separate interviews

This is a vital second stage when each party has separate time with the mediator. These separate interviews with each party can occur as a second early stage of the initial session following the introductory joint meeting, or can be held at another time. The purpose of these interviews is to give each party a crucial opportunity to state to the mediator, on their own, their views and perceptions, their objectives, any apprehensions they may have in coming to mediation, and whatever background history may be relevant to an understanding of why they are there and what they want. It also gives the mediator an opportunity to gain a clearer understanding of any existing or future fears about safety issues and the issues in dispute.

The order in which the parties are seen can be left to them to decide upon, although the mediator should make it clear that it does not matter who is first. This does not usually create any difficulty or raise any concern about fairness, although both need to have a roughly similar amount of time with the mediator.

At the end of the separate time the mediator asks expressly if there is anything stated that each party does *not* want repeated back in the feedback summary to follow. The mediator needs to respect this request where it is not incompatible with the mediation proceeding fully and frankly (for a discussion on the implications and dilemmas of this approach to confidentiality, see Chapter 9).

Research confirms the importance for each of the parties of separate time with the mediator (Davis and Roberts, 1988; Walker et al., 1994; Keyes Young, 1996).

Stage III   *Explore the issues*: Return to the joint meeting

After seeing each party separately, the mediator briefly sums up the issues, objectives and feelings of each party to both of them. The way that this is done can vary but it is necessary to avoid giving any impression that a mediator is acting as an advocate or representative of either party, particularly where co-mediators are involved.

The purpose of each summary is to ensure that each party's point of view and experience is clearly and accurately expressed and understood to their satisfaction. It makes sense, therefore, to address the summary to the *same* person whose account it is. In this way, the validity of each person's viewpoint is affirmed, whatever their differences. What the separate time with each party is also intended to impart, is a particular quality of attention. This requires the mediator to attend extremely carefully as well as to remember what has been conveyed in order to report back accurately. It is each party's perceptions and meanings that are relevant rather than any interpretations of the mediator.

On completion of the summaries, the parties are invited to respond, if they wish, to what they have heard. It may be that new information emerges, that differences are fewer than anticipated, that the parties have heard it all before, or, more usually, that they wish to refute or challenge some or all of what they have heard. This introduces, therefore, in a managed and structured way, the most difficult, contentious and potentially acrimonious phase in the mediation process, the exploration of difference.

Stage IV   *Development of options* and
Stage V   *Securing agreement*

These second of phases is the one towards which the earlier phases progress if negotiations proceed successfully, and so lead to the ending of the dispute, if not the conflict. This may all be concluded in a single session or over several sessions.

The rationale for structuring for separate time

The structural model described above is one that enables the mediation process to proceed with maximum efficacy from both a negotiation and a psychological perspective. It is the start of a process that is itself the gradual creation of order and co-ordination between the parties (Gulliver, 1979). The intended objectives of structuring for separate time are summarized below:

- It is the time in the mediation session expressly allotted for each party to be heard. Each party can have their own say free from fear of interruption or contradiction.
- The mediator has the opportunity to gain a clear understanding – from each party's perspective – of the issues in dispute, ethical and emotional aspects, the historical context of the dispute, and any current or future fears about safety or other relevant matters.

- It is the occasion when the mediator, in attending to the perceptions and meanings of each party, whatever their differences, can give worth to each perspective.
- This is the opportunity for the expression, at the appropriate time, of strongly felt emotional and ethical concerns, for example, personal feelings of fault, hurt, betrayal, hostility and anger and any grievances about unfairness (relating to the past, present and or the future). The opportunity to have these intense experiences and feelings aired, listened to, and acknowledged, can lead to a palpable reduction in tension and anxiety even at this early phase. Grillo (1991), goes further, not only challenging the traditional refusal of mediator to allow a focus on the past in mediation, but also highlighting the value of this opportunity for the exploration of the historical context as a path to clarity, strength and energy, for women in particular.
- In addition, these potentially disruptive powerful issues or strong feelings, once aired, heard and acknowledged, are then much less likely to erupt to sabotage negotiations at a later stage in the process.
- It is the common experience of mediators that a version of the issues with which both parties apparently agree in the introductory joint session often turns out to be perceived quite differently by one party when interviewed alone. That is why this structural safeguard is never dispensed with even though (or precisely because) parties might occasionally argue that this stage is unnecessary when the structure is first explained in the introductory stage.
- Screening for domestic abuse must take place routinely before mediation. The separate time provides further occasion for continuing screening throughout mediation – necessary, for example, where threatening behaviour might emerge for the first time or for the monitoring of current or past abusive behaviour.
- Separate time is also the only opportunity during mediation for specific safeguards to be agreed in advance between the mediator and a vulnerable party in order to address threatening behaviour that might manifest itself during the session. For example, pre-determined signals can be agreed between the mediator and the vulnerable party (for example, placing a handbag on a lap) to signify apprehension or the urgent need for a break. Such a safeguard cannot, of course, be set in place in the presence of both parties.

The rationale for the summing up stage following separate time

There are several objectives that may be achieved by means of the structured summaries following separate time with each party.

- The mediator is able to report the substance of the dispute/issue and the accompanying strength of feeling (that the party feels strongly, how strongly they feel, and what they feel strongly about) but free of the angry tone, aggravating facial expressions and acrimonious language that can so easily trigger emotional recriminations and escalate the conflict.[1]

The non-partisan shows each party the claims and arguments of the other; they thus lose the tone of subjective passion which usually provokes the same tone on the part of the adversary. (Simmel, 1908, trans. 1955a, pp. 146–7)

- Both parties are more likely to listen calmly to the mediator than to each other at this stage.
- Misunderstandings can be sorted out as early as possible. Where communication has been difficult or non-existent, or has taken place through lawyers or other third persons, the potential for misunderstanding is enormous. It is not uncommon for parties to discover that much less divides them than they had imagined once clear lines of communication are opened.
- Acknowledgment of the validity of different perspectives can be demonstrated in the equal worth the mediator accords to each person's viewpoint, feelings and objectives.
- Giving due weight to each person's views and objectives in this way also demonstrates the impartiality of the mediator. The structural arrangements can therefore enhance impartiality in enabling it to be seen to operate.
- The mediator explicitly acknowledges the likelihood of disagreement, thereby legitimizing its expression both in an established calm and safe environment and at the appropriate stage.
- Analytically, two distinct phases may be discerned emerging from Stages II and III. The first is the identification of the issues that are important to the parties, ethical and emotional as well as practical and legal. The second phase is the creation of the agenda for mediation, that is, the clarification of the items that must constitute the joint agenda for mediation. These can only be the negotiable issues, the issues about

---

1   Fuller (1971, p. 321) alerts us to the difficulty of effecting this separation, 'especially since the depth with which a party feels about an issues is something that enters into the valuations that shape the final adjustment of diverse interests'.

which joint decisions can be made. These two phases highlight that matters may need to be aired and addressed that are not confined to any narrow definition of an issue. The summing up of these issues by the mediator thus facilitates the process of agenda formation.

- The structure facilitates the management by the mediator of two of the more difficult transitions in the mediation process, from defining and clarifying the issues to exploring those issues – from examining difference therefore, to the next more constructive phase of developing options. Distance is necessary if subsequent movement is to become apparent. If all goes well, parallel psychological transitions are effected in conjunction with the negotiation transitions – insecurity, anxiety, hostility, uncertainty, fear and ignorance are lessened as the wheels of communication exchange generate greater learning, improved understanding, and therefore the reduction of uncertainty, fear and competition and the progressive modification of expectations and behaviour (Gulliver, 1979).

Practical considerations

Attention to certain practical details can contribute substantially to easing the tense atmosphere in which the parties are likely to meet.

Separate waiting rooms

It is more than likely that the atmosphere between the parties will be strained at best and hostile at worst. They need to be assured in advance that they will be meeting each other in a safe arena and only in the presence of the mediator. The provision of separate waiting rooms is a requirement if protection is to be ensured prior to the meeting. New partners and children will also be able to wait in peace.

Seating arrangements

As many practitioners have pointed out, the seating arrangements are important (Coogler, 1978; Haynes, 1981; Folberg and Taylor, 1984). These should encourage relaxed, informal and open exchanges. A good example is a circular arrangement around a low coffee table with the mediator facing both parties. The mediator should not be distanced in status or place by sitting behind a high desk or table or on a raised dais. The parties should not be placed opposite one another or in any way that would increase confrontation between them. If seated at right angles to one another they can choose then to face each other if they so wish.

Refreshments

A plentiful supply of tea, coffee and soft drink/water can help to ease tension. Anger may diminish if people pause, refresh themselves and feel they have been treated considerately.

The Coogler ('Bromley') Model

This is an example of one long-established model of mediation practice in the field of family disputes in the UK. The way mediation is structured at the South East London Family Mediation Bureau (situated in Bromley, hence the epithet) is based on the Coogler Model of Structured Mediation.[2] The significance of the Coogler Model is twofold. First, central issues of party autonomy, mediator authority and power and the protection of a fair process are specifically and explicitly addressed by means of structure. Second, the way in which these issues are addressed in practice is important; namely, the focus on the 'modest' profile of the mediator, advance agreement on the rules of procedure and the guidelines to be followed.

Coogler emphasized the importance of a clear structure, composed of the integration of three structural components designed to protect the parties procedurally, ethically and psychologically:

- the procedural structure is designed to ensure an orderly process. There is advance agreement upon the 'rules' of procedure and the guidelines to be followed by the parties and the mediator;
- the value structure is designed to secure a fair process and ethical standards of exchange so that the outcome is fair and is perceived as fair by the parties.
- the psychological structure is designed to secure physical and emotional safety. This framework includes:
  - joint sessions only (although with separate time for each party included);[3]
  - direct negotiation between the parties;

---

2   O.J. Coogler, a North American lawyer and psychotherapist and one of the founding fathers of family mediation in the US, pioneered this model (Coogler, 1978). It was first introduced into the UK by Mr Fred Gibbons when he established the South East London Family Mediation Bureau in 1979. It has now been adopted and adapted by a number of independent family mediation services.

3   This may be contrasted with the model of practice of another distinguished North American mediator and teacher, the late Dr John Haynes, who trained many British mediators during the 1990s. One of the central tenets of the Haynes approach is that the mediator meets with the parties jointly only, never separately. Neither is

  – limiting the issues to those for which decisions are needed for settlement to be reached – these include the marriage, property, finance and children;

- dealing with one item at a time;
- using procedural methods for collecting and examining factual information;
- each party having their separate lawyer as adviser outside the process.

The structural arrangements described above illustrate one long-established model of mediation practice in the field of family disputes in the UK. It exemplifies an explicit, theoretically-based approach to achieving procedural fairness and meeting the needs of the parties ethically and emotionally. It is an approach that is designed to make optimal use of session time, in ensuring both purposive structuring and that the session length is sufficient for the negotiation process to be realized. The session is therefore unlikely to end at that stage in the process when conflict is at its most expressed.

In this way the negotiation process is given the maximum chance to achieve its most constructive realization in mediation. The mediator, working within a structured environment, can fulfil their difficult role, in their own unique style, orchestrating the mediation process effectively, flexibly and creatively. Clarity and confidence in an established model of practice are of most value, particularly where the dynamic reality is one of stress, complexity and unpredictability, which characterizes most situations of family breakdown. Above all, the parties have a real opportunity to try to reach consensual, fair and mutually satisfactory decisions and, in addition, to maximize for themselves and especially for their children, the process benefits of mediation – better understanding; a lessening of conflict and an improved capacity to negotiate together in the future.

The strategies of the mediator

The strategies of family mediators are bound to reflect their assumptions about:

- the nature and goals of the process in which they are engaged (see Chapter 5);
- the qualities of the 'ideal' mediator (see Chapter 6);

---

direct communication between the parties encouraged, rather the mediator acts as the primary conduit of communication between the parties.

- the nature and function of conflict in family breakdown – whether conflict is regarded as a pathological phenomenon or as a normal, even constructive, response to the need to re-order relationships (see Chapter 4).

In order to understand what is happening in mediation, there is need to understand the complex inter-relationship of the developmental stages of the process with the cyclical exchanges of information that propel those stages forward towards an outcome. The kind of information exchanged is related to the stage in the negotiation process. The same message may carry different information at a different stage.

Different strategies will be required at different stages. The intervention of the mediator is most needed (and most problematic) at the moments of transition in the negotiation process. For example, at an early stage when uncertainty, insecurity, ignorance and hostility are at their most intense and when the shift of attitude required of the parties is greatest, a greater strength of intervention may be necessary from the mediator than at other, less critical stages in the process. Here, as already mentioned, lies one of the central challenges to the role of the mediator – how to control potentially destructive conflict effectively, and at the same time remain impartial and non-directive. The interventions of the mediator have to be understood therefore not only in terms of *what* they contain but *how* and *when* they take place.

Given that the strategy deployed by the mediator is highly dependent on its timing within the process, what may be appropriate at an early stage may be inappropriate at a later stage, and vice versa. An understanding of the meaning of the strategy can only occur within an understanding of the context of the process it serves.

Nor, of course, are the parties passive recipients of the mediator's interventions. The strategies of the parties themselves combine with those of the mediator in a dynamic and fluid situation of 'reciprocal influence' (Kressel and Pruitt, 1985, p. 196). Whatever repertoire of strategies may be available to the mediator, he/she must recognize that their use will depend both on what the disputants will require or tolerate and on what strategies they will seek to promote themselves – for example, in order to use the mediator as a scapegoat or to win him/her over to the justice of their own cause (Gulliver, 1977).

For these reasons, there should obviously, therefore, be consonance between the strategies a mediator seeks to deploy and the phase that negotiation has reached. This means that the timing as well as the degree of intervention is crucial. For example, for the mediator to emphasize common interests at a stage when the parties have not yet fully explored the extent of their differences could be useless or even harmful. Similarly, where the parties have begun to communicate together directly and constructively, this could be prejudiced were the mediator to adopt strongly interventionist strategies rather than minimal ones. The skill and judgment required for the effective deployment of strategies are best developed through the experience of the process itself (ACAS, n.d., para. 16).

The main constellations of strategies available to the mediator are explored below. These overlap however, and are not so clearly distinguished in practice. Within the dynamics of the mediation session many things are going on, often at the same time. Each interaction is unique and often unpredictable. This unpredictability has in fact been described as one of the most challenging aspects of the entire mediation process (Saposnek, 1983).

Whatever strategies are employed by the mediator it is important to remember that they are operating in two directions:

- to facilitate communication and learning between the parties (the more they understand of each other's predicament the better their chances of co-ordination and agreement);
- to instruct the parties in the norms and methods of negotiation.

As already mentioned, mediation involves adherence to certain key values – mutual respect, shared responsibility and equity of exchange. The dignity and consideration the parties are shown by the mediator sets an example and the tone for communication. Thereafter, in learning how to negotiate, the parties learn to talk to one another again if there has been a breakdown in communication. Communication between them is necessary if they are to work together as parents. Changes of mind and of circumstances over time require that they themselves must be able to renegotiate and modify their agreements. The strategies demonstrated by the mediator could therefore become the present and the future strategies of the parties.

The main strategies

Identifying the issues

One of the mediator's first tasks is to understand what the issues in dispute (or potential dispute) are about. This may be a relatively simple matter or, especially in the early stages of separation, more complex with many interrelated issues over, for example, the matrimonial home, residence, maintenance and contact.

The mediator needs to understand the issues as the parties see them. 'To understand disputes … it is necessary to attend to the categories of meaning by which participants themselves comprehend their experience and orient themselves toward one another in their everyday lives' (Caplan, 1995a, p. 156, quoting Rosen, 1989, p. xiv). This will involve seeing each party on their own at an early stage within a joint negotiating session, so that they can feel free to describe matters in their own way. The mediator needs to listen carefully, asking pertinent questions where necessary. The mediator has no permission to delve into the past history of the couple's relationship or into the details of the interpersonal relationships of the family. What is necessary is for the mediator to understand clearly how each party sees the dispute, bearing in mind that 'a significant portion of any dispute exists only in the minds of the disputants' (Felstiner et al., 1980–1981). The mediator needs to understand the parties' respective objectives and perspectives, the environment of the dispute (its relevant history, the pressures, others involved or affected, and the constraints that impinge on any settlement) and what they hope to achieve by resorting to mediation.

The mediator assists the parties to agree an agenda. It may make sense to postpone the sticky or more contentious issues until later and to tackle the relatively less significant differences first. Single issue disputes – for example over contact – are by no means the simplest to agree, nor are the more obdurate issues necessarily the more important (Gulliver, 1979). 'Graduality' or the detailed step-by-step progression on issues was one of the secrets of success in the Norwegian mediation of the disputes between the Israelis and the Palestinians (Corbin, 1994).

Facilitating communication

Poor communication and mistrust characterize the relationship of many who turn to mediation. Perhaps that is why they look for help to the mediator. Stress and inadequate information impair their ability to see beyond their own hurt or anger or to place themselves in another's shoes (Deutsch, 1973). Mediation can provide the opportunity to open up channels of communication and to improve both the quantity and quality of the information exchanged. The mediator's control over the communications structure is one of the most important aspects of the mediation process (Stevens, 1963; Coogler, 1978). The mediator may act as a translator, stimulating communication and explaining the context and framework that give meaning to communication (Deutsch, 1973; Stulberg, 1981). Furthermore, mistrust may be diminished when two parties who have lost trust in each other find, in the impartiality and integrity of the mediator, someone they both can trust.

As already noted, the mediator needs to have a clear understanding of the dispute, including the respective attitudes, priorities and objectives of the parties, and the pressures each is under (ACAS, n.d., para. 14). This understanding has to be translated to each party if their mutual understanding of one another's position is to be improved. Only then will movement from these positions be possible.

The effective facilitation of communication by the mediator involves not only increasing the flow of information between the parties, but also the careful monitoring of the accuracy and 'non-belligerence' of that information (Kressel, 1985). Too much information (in volume and complexity) may be as problematic as too little or conflicting information. For example, the parties' versions of the past are bound to differ. The mediator can discourage, therefore, the unproductive raking over of past quarrels and should avoid being drawn into any arbitrating role over differences of fact or the merits of an issue. Instead, the validity of different, even conflicting, perceptions can be affirmed – each party's explicit acknowledgement of the other's perspective, however different or conflicting, may itself be significant. It may be appropriate too, for the parties to be encouraged to focus on the present and future implications of their dispute – in a paraphrase of Haynes (1993), 'The past is where the problem lies; the future is where the solution lies' (but see also Grillo, 1991).

One device for ending the futile exchange of accusations, usually about the other party's unreasonable or vindictive acts, is to get that party to rephrase an accusation as a question. Questions invite answers. Direct communication may be initiated. Alternatively, the mediator may encourage the parties to communicate through him or her, where direct exchanges are proving unproductive.

Haynes (1993) advocates the use of questions as the main form of intervention of the mediator. In this way the parties 'own' the answers. Questions can promote a number of objectives in mediation. They can facilitate good information exchange (as above), provide clarification and insight, focus on core issues, encourage explanation, explore alternatives, stimulate new thinking, improve the climate of communication and offset power imbalances. Silence too, as well as conveying certain messages, varying cross-culturally,[4] can be used as a powerful questioning technique.

Where information is inadequate or conflicting, the mediator may ask one or other party to restate their particular demand or point of view and to provide further information to support it. Alternatively the mediator could attempt a restatement. For example: 'Am I right in saying that your view is such and such?' or 'If I understand you correctly, you are saying such and such?'

Restatement may be used to clarify as well as to emphasize important points and positive features, especially those relating to areas of interest

---

4   The particular significance of silence varies in some societies. Among the Arusha peoples of East Africa, for example, it unequivocally conveys agreement with the last message received since it is assumed that a party would otherwise express his/her disagreement. In other contexts, silence can mean refusal of a message, expression of frustration or of mistrust, acceptance of inferiority, non-compliance, uncertainty, unwilling acquiescence, and so on (see Gulliver, 1979).

shared by the couple. This does not mean that the differences between the parties should be underplayed or glossed over. Rather the mediator must be alert to opportunities to draw attention to and encourage gestures of goodwill or offers of co-operation (Coogler, 1978). These might arise, for example, when one party is not listening, or not comprehending the significance of what is being said by the other party, intentionally or otherwise. The other party may then be urged to repeat what he or she has just said so that its import can be fully appreciated. The parties can be halted in what might be a fruitless argument at cross-purposes and forced to listen to what is being said. They can then be re-routed into the same channel of communication and more appropriate reactions thereby stimulated.

A neutral forum free of stigma or coercion, the control and skill of the impartial mediator and the non-threatening framework of the session, all make it possible for issues too highly charged for the parties to discuss on their own, to be brought out into the open and talked about.

Opening up new perspectives

It is recognized that common as well as conflicting interests characterize the relationship between adversaries (Schelling, 1960). One important way a mediator may contribute to settlement is to point out how the parties' own best interests may be served by getting them 'to consider their common interests as more essential than they did previously or their competing interests as less essential' (Eckhoff, 1969, p. 171).

In disputes following family break-up, parents do not usually disagree with the mediator who stresses that certain interests – the interests of the children – are more important than who is right and who is wrong (Davis and Roberts, 1988). In most cases the parents themselves affirm this. Whatever they may think of each other, parents are presumed to be united in a shared love of their children. It is this intertwining of interests that constitutes the most powerful pressure towards collaboration in the mediation effort (Fuller, 1971).

However, a shared concern for the children does not eliminate differences of view over how the child's welfare may best be safeguarded. What the mediator can usefully point to is the dispute as a problem common to both parties. Together, they share a joint interest in reaching a mutually satisfactory agreement. Furthermore, by focusing their attention on their child's perspective, the mediator can enable the parties to move away from their interpersonal quarrelling. The mediator can thereby ensure that the parents themselves fully consider and protect the interests of their own children (see Chapter 10).

One of the creative possibilities of mediation is 'the art of proposing the alternate solution' (Stevens, 1963, p. 146). A fresh view from the mediator may reveal new perspectives and possibilities for solution inherent in the situation, which neither party has perceived. This requires inventiveness, imagination and ingenuity as well as experience. Often the parties have lost perspective, particularly over time. Bogged down and embattled in conflict, they can experience their predicament as hopeless and endless. For example, they are often surprised to realize that it is for only five or so years that contact over children will be a problem for them (depending, of course, on the age of their children). They can begin to realize too that they have a choice as to whether to continue in conflict or try to reach some sort of accommodation, and can examine the consequences of this choice for their children and themselves.

One way of promoting new ideas for possible solutions is by orienting the parties to consider these themselves – for example, the mediator may ask questions that indicate fresh and practicable lines of thinking and acting. Each party could be invited to make their own suggestions including what each thinks the other could do to help the situation.

Contact arrangements may take many forms tailored to each family. There is no prototype of what contact should be like. Permutations are legion. As already noted, a flexible arrangement is more likely to work where there is a co-operative relationship between the parties. The necessary adjustments will need to be constantly negotiated, difficult or impossible where there is a strained or acrimonious relationship. In these circumstances, a predetermined arrangement will be preferable as negotiation, and therefore the potential for conflict between the parties, is kept to the minimum. The mediator may need to point out the possibilities and pitfalls of the parties making their own arrangements, as well as the consequences of court-imposed orders. As far as court-defined orders are concerned, the parties need to be aware that ultimately they still have to co-operate together if contact is to work.

Schelling (1960, p. 144) has highlighted the mediator's power to make a dramatic suggestion, especially where there is no apparent focal point for agreement. This may arise where the parties are so entrenched that they may be genuinely unable to see where common ground might lie or even how to proceed at all (Gulliver, 1977). A suggestion coming from a disinterested third party might be more acceptable than if made by one of the parties, when it may be interpreted as a sign of weakness. The mediator may make it possible therefore for concessions to be offered without loss of face. This opportunity for graceful retreat and face-saving is one of the most useful functions a mediator is able to provide (Rubin and Brown, 1975).

Another opportunity available to the mediator is to explain or interpret statements, feelings or acts positively but without misrepresentation. For example, a parent may cite past lack of interest in the child as a reason for now questioning or opposing contact demands from the non-resident parent. It could be explained that this parent may well have come to realize that s/he had taken their children too much for granted in the past, or was working long hours, and is seeking now to remedy this. The separation itself may have brought about a genuine shift in their appreciation of the significance of their relationship with their child. Unexpected changes in the pattern of relationships between parents and children following separation or divorce are not uncommon, highlighting the fact that the quality of contact visits following divorce may be independent of the quality of relationships in the intact family prior to divorce (Wallerstein and Kelly, 1980, pp. 104–105).

Controlling destructive exchanges

If the mediator's primary objective is to facilitate communication between the parties so that they may negotiate their own agreement, aggressive, irrational and excessively emotional exchanges cannot be allowed if the session is not to end in failure – that is, the parties going away worse off than when they arrived. Presumably, the parties resort to mediation in the first place in order to avoid just such rows.

Some relatively brief opportunity to let off steam and express anger, hurt, or bitterness can obviously be necessary and helpful, especially for those who have had no previous chance to 'get things off their chest'. For others, on the other hand, the mediation session could be yet another occasion for personal recrimination, which may therefore be totally unproductive. In any event, prolonged or too powerful an outpouring of emotion is not likely to be conducive to rational exchange.

The mediator needs to convey to the parties his/her recognition of the fraught climate in which they meet and his/her understanding and acceptance that stress is a normal (and temporary) response to circumstances of extreme emotional and physical upheaval. If the control of the mediator is clear and firm the parties will feel safe to explore some of their potentially explosive differences. Yet the best control in these circumstances is that which is least noticeable (Coogler, 1978). If discussion of a particular topic is not only making no progress but leading to an escalation of hostility, the mediator should stop, temporarily if necessary, any further discussion of that topic. In the last resort, the mediation session itself may be suspended if emotions threaten to get out of hand. As mentioned earlier, the parties will have given advance permission for the mediator to intervene in the event of this being necessary. They should never leave the session worse off than when they arrived. That, rather than not reaching agreement, is failure in mediation.

Focusing on the relevant

In situations of high emotion, it is clear that the mediator needs to direct the parties away from potentially destructive exchanges. These are usually provoked by differences of view over past facts. As already observed, it is important for the parties to realize that there is nothing in the past over which to negotiate. The mediator needs to keep the parties' discussion focused on relevant and constructive issues – the specific dispute, priorities for the future, alternatives and options. The available alternative options must be examined dispassionately, their various merits assessed and their consequences compared and considered. By focusing attention on the immediate, the concrete and the practical, the parties can concentrate on what is feasible and so begin to gain control. Furthermore, the children, as well as being the focus of dispute, provide – currently and for the future – the central reason for the exploration of collaborative rather than competitive stratagems.

The need to concentrate on what is relevant may arise in situations when the information circulating is excessive or confusing. The mediator must ensure that the parties are talking about the same thing at the same time. It is very easy for them to become bogged down or side-tracked by petty yet disruptive red herrings, often without realizing it – for example, who said what, when; whether a coat was sent with a child or not; and so on.

Balancing inequalities of bargaining power

One of the mediator's first tasks in setting out what mediation involves is to make clear the equal and joint efforts that are required of both parties. This recognition by each party of the right of the other to participate equally in the decision-making process is fundamental to participation in the process.

It is the responsibility of the mediator to ensure that this principle is realized in practice. In the first place the parties should start off from positions of relative equality but, as Cormick (1982) emphasizes, the less equal the relative power of the parties, the greater the ethical responsibility of the mediator. If imbalances are gross, approaches other than mediation should be adopted – for example, legal representation, advice, guidance and support, counselling or treatment (see also Chapter 11).

Some of the ways in which the mediator goes about offsetting inequalities between the parties are described below.

First, the mediator needs to ensure that inequalities are recognized by the parties themselves (Folberg, 1983). Rarely is this a simple matter, even in the least complicated contact dispute, given the special vulnerabilities arising in family disputes. Research highlights the two central disparities inherent in situations of family dissolution – emotional inequality (who took the decision to separate, and to what extent the decision was accepted) and where the children are living (Chin-A-Fat and Steketee, 2001). For example, on the face of it, the non-resident parent (usually the father) could be in the weaker bargaining position, presuming that is, that he wants to increase his contact with his children. He has less contact with and therefore less influence over the children and less power to determine the terms of contact. He may feel that he has lost everything – his marriage, his home and his children. The mother with care of the children may suffer equal but different disadvantages, carrying the burden of responsibility for looking after the children single-handed, making ends meet and trying to carve out some independent life for herself free of the emotional stress that contact with her former spouse brings. Where there is a history of abuse, mediation on property and financial matters and mediation on issues relating to children may need to be completely separate processes (Keys Young, 1996).

Second, the mediator must ensure that all the relevant information is in the hands of both parties. This means that information about the mediation process (including the limits of the mediator's role and the ultimate right of the parties not to participate if they so wish) and the dispute and its ramifications must be available to the parties as well as understood by them.

Third, the mediator must see to it that both parties participate freely and fairly in the negotiations. There must therefore be equal opportunity for such participation. The mediator must prevent one party interrupting the other, one party talking for the other, or one party dominating discussion by force of personality, knowledge, greater articulacy or the exercise of moral or psychological pressure. This means that the mediator has to be aware when and why one party is not speaking up and when acquiescence does not signify genuine consent. The mediator must be alert to attempts at bullying (emotional and physical), threats or intimidatory tactics or body language, and must stop these at once, bringing the meeting to an end, as the last resort, if necessary.

Finally, if it turns out that an outcome is being consented to that is patently unjust, the mediator must say so and recommend the party in the more vulnerable position not to agree without taking legal advice or further consideration.

The balance of power between the parties is affected by the mediation process itself, first in the expectations of equality of exchange, equity and mutual responsibility that it engenders; and, second, in the improved capacity of the parties, as a result of mediation, to deal with one another on an equal (or more equal) basis in the future. The mediator too has an impact on the balance of bargaining power. Skill and integrity have to be exercised in ensuring that differences of 'endowment' or ability in negotiation do not result in overreaching or duress.

Towards an agreement

The outcome of mediation should be the result of the parties' own and equal efforts at negotiation and be regarded by them as fair (as is practicable in all the circumstances) and in their children's interests. It is they who have to live with their agreement.

The agreement need not derive from any compromise, although many do. It may follow from the creation of an entirely new option or (more rarely) one party may move to the position of the other. A process of pay-offs may take place – for example, one party may give what is less valuable to them but more valuable to the receiver, and receive what they value but which is less valuable to the giver (Fuller, 1971).

Agreement may consist of deciding jointly that the continuance of the status quo is preferable to anything else that appears possible, or of being prepared to continue talking together in the future.

The mediator must ensure that when agreement appears to be reached, its details are examined carefully and comprehensively. Lack of clarity about wording and the practicalities of implementation may tip an agreement in principle into the immediate danger of disagreement over detail. Relief at attaining consensus should not inhibit the mediator from pointing out possible pitfalls or from slowing down finalization in order to check and clarify. A stable agreement must be fully informed and accurate and founded on mutual satisfaction and mutual understanding.

Where the agreement is drafted in writing, such as in a Memorandum of Understanding[5] or formal Outcome Statement, it must be expressed simply, clearly and unambiguously. On the balance to be struck between clarity and simplicity on the one hand, and comprehensiveness on the other, Fuller (1971, p. 230) writes:

> Now the forms of language, like rivers, have a certain inertia of their own; they cannot always be readily bent to accommodate every nuance of thought and a clause overloaded with qualifications may forfeit its meaning as a clear guidepost for human interaction. In the drafting of any complex agreement there is often an inescapable compromise between what can be simply expressed and what might be abstractly desirable. The mediational process plainly has a place in dealing with such problems.

The words chosen by the parties must be meaningful, not only to themselves but also to third persons. Reasons for decisions can be explained, especially where these are unconventional or appear unfair. The mediator can provide that 'third party perspective' (Fuller, 1971, p. 320). This can avoid future disagreement over what was agreed.

---

5   For a detailed discussion on the requirements of the Memorandum of Understanding in all-issues mediation, see Haynes (1993, Chapter 7).

Special problems of strategy arising in mediation sessions

Overcoming transitions

Mediators have a part to play in all the different phases of negotiation. Throughout, they maintain the momentum for negotiation by their trust in the process and by inspiring a belief in the possibility of agreement (Pruitt, 1981; Davis and Gadlin, 1988; see also Chapter 6).

But mediators are most needed – though their intervention is most problematic – where transitions between phases of negotiation have to be effected (Gulliver, 1977). As already mentioned, one of the most conspicuous of these transitions is from the phase of entrenched opposition, even hostility, to the phases when differences are narrowed and mistrust lessened. This is where the shift of attitude demanded of the parties is greatest, and is what Gulliver (1977, p. 25) describes as 'the principal watershed in the whole process'. Here the stronger, more interventionist strategies of the mediator may be justified (for example, the making of direct suggestions orienting the parties' attention and efforts towards a common goal) and may be more acceptable to, even welcomed by, the parties. But such strategies remain problematic because, in these circumstances, the power of the mediator to influence the course of proceedings is greatest.

Deadlock

In certain circumstances a state of deadlock may develop in the negotiations. This may be a prelude to their breakdown and a return to the status quo before mediation or the dispute may be pursued in other ways, such as litigation. In other circumstances, however, an impasse may be viewed positively as an indication of equality of power and could, for that reason, produce movement towards a settlement (Pruitt, 1981). This is likely to arise in situations where the costs of disagreement (emotional as well as legal and financial) are so high as to be intolerable to all concerned and where the continuing relationship between the parties is important and/or unavoidable to both. In such a case, any change is probably for the better, with some settlement being of value, rather than nothing. In these circumstances, a strategy of minimal intervention by the mediator will be most efficacious as the impetus for co-operation will be greatest.

Manipulation in mediation

Mediators need to face squarely the potential they have to affect the substance of communication by their control over the process of that communication (Silbey and Merry, 1986). Possibilities exist at every level of intervention (from the most minimal to the strongest) for the mediator to exert influence – in reformulating or rephrasing, in editing, in the kind of information and the way in which it is elicited, in stressing some matters and ignoring or obstructing others, and especially in the making of new suggestions. While this potentially presents the most creative of opportunities for the mediator, there are also serious risks. It is because the issue of party authority is central to mediation that the dangers of manipulation need to be recognized and restricted. Some of these are set out below.

Dangers of the mediator adopting a dominant role

A variety of strategies will be used by the mediator in any single negotiating session, depending on the stage reached, as well as on the needs of the parties. As already noted, more positive intervention may be necessary during transitional phases when such interventions will also be more tolerable to the parties. Intervention strategies can range from the most tentative, indirect and unobtrusive to the most directive and dominating. The risks of manipulation of the negotiation process by the mediator increase along the same continuum. The greater the strength and scope of intervention the greater the opportunity for manipulation by the mediator and for exceeding their proper role.

Mediators in different fields do adopt what they may, themselves, call a 'directive' style or approach where appropriate, that is, they may be ready to assert a greater strength of intervention where necessary (Roberts, 2007). This may be associated with a range of purposes and meanings – for example, managing difficult transitions; adopting a business-like or assertive stance; contributing ideas about options; engaging in 'reality testing'; and reminding the parties of their responsibility for making decisions (Roberts, 2007).[6] This form of 'directive style' need not imply, therefore, any departure from good practice principles, such as pressurization, manipulation or coercion of the parties (Roberts, 2007).

---

6   Roberts' interviews with mediators from different mediation fields found that an unobtrusive style, on the other hand, termed variously, facilitative, elicitive or 'laid back', can convey different forms of mediator behaviour as well – for example, a quiet and considered demeanour; a calmness of manner; and an 'abstinence' (Roberts, 2007). This study found that some mediators adopt both styles, directive and unobtrusive, and other possible styles, sometimes in the same session (Roberts, 2007).

Mediators are not neutral (see Chapter 6). They have their own values and attitudes, inevitably. Influenced by prevailing research findings, they may adopt certain child policy approaches, a pro-contact stance for example, in the belief that it is better on the whole for children to have a continuing relationship with both parents after separation and divorce where that is beneficial and safe. In most cases, these values are likely to be shared by parents themselves. However, mediators should not brow-beat parents with research evidence or with warnings of emotional damage, or of the harmful effects of litigation, especially on their children. This exertion of overt influence is incompatible with the facilitating role of the mediator.

Dangers in the adoption by the mediator of family therapy techniques

Family therapy, from its earliest development in the 1950s to its most recent phase in the 1990s influenced by the rise in the ideas of social constructivist theory, is acknowledged to be a manipulative approach (Walrond-Skinner, 1976; Dallos and Draper, 2000). Where family therapy approaches are adopted in mediation practice, there is a danger that covert attempts to manipulate the perceptions and preferences of the parties will occur. In reaching assessments, devising systemic hypotheses, or making judgments – for example, that the parties do not always know what they want because they are too distressed, self-preoccupied or conflict-ridden to make rational judgments – the mediator is using private and subjective interpretations to define issues in his/her terms. The mediator's meanings then predominate and in this way control may be insidiously removed from where it rightfully belongs – with the parties. Even where the therapist disclaims diagnostic expertise and grants validity to each client's point of view,[7] as Nichols (1989, p. 423) observes '[D]uring therapy, however, the therapist's point of view is – to quote Orwell – "more equal"'. The greatest dangers of manipulation, and therefore of distortion to the mediation process, exist where family therapy techniques are used in the course of in-court conciliation. This can result in the parties being subjected, unknowingly and involuntarily, both to the coercive pressures of the court and to the covert controls of 'treatment'. (For detailed exchanges on this subject, see M. Roberts, 1992a; Haynes, 1992; Amundson and Fong, 1993.)

---

7   For example, the dialogical constructivist theoretical position has been adopted to counter ethical concerns about coercive and pathologizing clinical practice carried out under the guise of systemic 'neutrality' (Epstein and Loos, 1989).

Manipulation by the parties

It has already be mentioned that the parties are by no mean passive recipients of the mediator's interventions. The parties;

> bring with them to the table, not only perceptible bodies and cognisable personalities, but freely moving unbounded, infinite potentialities for interchange of energies which are not contained, much less molded by any conceptions which start with conventional 'space' and 'time' as features of the universe of thought to be employed. (Douglas, 1962, p. 160)

For mediation to be effective, importance attaches to the parties' commitment to and good faith in participating, precisely because of the absence of direct or official compulsion to mediate. Three problematic aspects can be discerned – a party's reluctance or unwillingness to participate; a party's capacity to participate; and, of particular relevance here, a party's exploitation or manipulation of the process (Roberts, 2007). So just as the mediator needs to be aware of the considerable opportunities he/she has for manipulating the course and content of communication, so too must he/she be aware of the possibilities of manipulation by the parties themselves (Gulliver, 1977). For example, one party, seeing the inevitability of giving way to the demands of the other, may, by accepting mediation, use the mediator as a scapegoat, a useful way of blaming someone else for the turn of events.

Mediation may also be used by one or both parties in pending proceedings, not in any genuine collaborative effort to sort the problem, but in order to make a good impression in court, that is, to give the appearance that they had tried to mediate but had failed. Research highlights the ways in which an 'instrumentalist' approach to mediation, more likely to occur where mediation is mandatory and court-connected, can exploit mediation as a game or a tool to advance adversarial goals, regarding, for example, mediation as 'a fishing expedition' to obtain early discovery (Macfarlane, 2002, p. 8).

8   When to mediate

Mediation is an educational device even more than it is a problem-solving device. Sure, it helps resolve problems but even when it fails to do that it can help, so long as it is done right, by assisting people to reach, to illuminate what is at issue, and to highlight underlying interests. (Patrick Phear, quoted by A. Sarat in D.M. Kolb et al. (eds) (1994), *When Talk Works: Profiles of Mediators*, p. 198)

Success in mediation

There is no absolute measure of success in mediation. An agreement that endures to the satisfaction of both parties and their children, as well as an improved capacity to negotiate together in the future, are recognized indices of success. Thoennes and Pearson (1985) described success in mediation as a function of the pre-existing characteristics of the dispute and the disputants as well as the degree to which the disputants perceive the mediators to have accomplished the primary tasks of mediation. For mediation to be successful, therefore, certain goals (identified by Thoennes and Pearson, 1985) must be accomplished:

- providing information about mediation;
- establishing ground rules;
- gaining an informed commitment from the parties;
- focusing on the full range of issues;
- maintaining control of pace;
- balancing power;
- opening communication;
- reducing tension and anger;
- ensuring that the parties feel responsible for and happy with the outcome.

Other researchers (Pruitt and Carnevale, 1993) have cited the importance of rapport with and trust in the mediator as a significant predictor of agreement. Genn et al. (2007), evaluating two civil mediation programmes (one quasi-compulsory involving automatic court referral to mediation (ARM); the other, voluntary and court linked), found that, in respect of both schemes, the motivation and willingness of the parties to negotiate and compromise is critical to the success of mediation. In the ARM pilot (with a downward settlement rate reaching a low of 38 per cent of cases), explanations for failure focused on the intransigence of opponents and unwillingness to compromise; poor mediator skills; and time pressures. Where cases were settled at mediation, explanations for the outcome focused on the skill of the mediator, the opportunity to exchange views and to reassess one's own position, and the willingness of opponents to negotiate and compromise. Mediators thought that the key factors contributing to ARM settlement were the willingness of the parties to negotiate and compromise, the contribution of legal representatives, their own skill as mediators and administrative support from the court. 'The significance of the parties' willingness to negotiate and compromise as an explanation both for success and for failure in mediation sits uncomfortably with evident support shown by some mediation organizations for experimenting with compulsory mediation' (Genn et al., 2007, Executive summary).

In the voluntary scheme (where the parties and lawyers were generally positive about their mediation experience) the parties valued the informality of the process, the skill of the mediator, and the opportunity to be fully involved in the settlement of the dispute. Rushed mediation, facilities at court, failure to settle, and the poor skills of the mediator were the users' most common complaints (Genn et al., 2007).

What is achievable therefore depends on a variety of factors. In respect of family mediation, what is also significant is the level of conflict characterizing the state of the relationship between the former couple when mediation is initiated. The worse the state of the parties' relationship with one another, the dimmer the prospects of success. This is likely to be the case where there has been prior litigation, allegations of abuse including physical violence, a wide range of disputed issues, especially over children, and post separation battles. Mediation is also unlikely to succeed where the motivation of one or both parties is low, where there is a refusal to accept the separation or divorce, where there is a high level of continuing psychological attachment and a grave scarcity of financial resources – all these are 'situational determinants' of a poor prognosis of success (Kressel and Pruitt, 1985).

Even if mediation fails to secure either an agreement or an improvement in communication, the parties may have lost nothing by resorting to it. But mediation can be regarded as having failed if the parties emerge from it worse off in terms of conflict, mistrust and misunderstanding, and their emotional well-being, than when they started.

Mediation is more likely to succeed if both parties have reached a minimum 'threshold of trust' at the point of entry into mediation (Davis and Gadlin, 1988, p. 55). These experienced practitioners have identified the interrelatedness of 'gaining entry' and building trust, which has four dimensions:

1. trust in the mediator;
2. trust in the mediation process;
3. trust in one's own ability to negotiate;
4. trust in the other party.

As mediation progresses, there is an expectation that trust will grow, particularly trust in the process and in each party's competence as a negotiator. At the intake stage, however, mediators have to *earn* trust, from the start, by making no presumption that everyone understands what a mediator does, by recognizing the 'legitimacy of scepticism' about mediation, and by addressing, openly and frankly, any reservations about suitability or readiness for mediation (Davis and Gadlin, 1988, p. 57).

It is also clear that mediation is more likely to succeed when there is some specific issue in dispute over which a decision has to be made. Where there is generalized conflict or a range of problems as above, it is likely to prove an unsuitable mode of intervention. Other circumstances may also render it inappropriate.

The introduction, in the 1990s, of public funding for family mediation has brought new pressure to accept an externally introduced notion of success, defined in terms only of cost-effectiveness, that is, a measurable, quantifiable outcome, which reflects government priorities of reducing legal aid expenditure, particularly on family disputes (Roberts, 2005b). The current Legal Services Commission definition of a successful mediation is one where the clients who participate in mediation do not subsequently apply for legal representation, and there is, therefore, diversion from contested legal proceedings. This measure – acknowledged to be a relatively crude one – is, however, the only one by which 'success' in mediation is rewarded. It is acknowledged too that this definition does not take into account those cases referred to mediation which resolve some disputes through mediation – for example, contact and residence issues – but which subsequently involve an application for legal aid to resolve other issues – for example, financial issues. Nor does it take into account more elusive but no less important indices of success in mediation, such as improved understanding and communication between the parties; their enhanced capacity to negotiate together in the future; and the reduction of conflict – all outcomes with concomitant benefits particularly for the children of the family. It is these very 'process' advantages that distinguish mediation from other settlement-directed interventions such as bi-lateral negotiations between lawyers. There is a concern too that more directive, evaluative, settlement approaches, such as those traditionally practised by lawyers, are more likely to be rewarded financially, in the context of mediation, according to standards invented by and accepted by lawyers (Davis et al., 2000). As the Davis Report highlights, if mediation is not to be judged only by its capacity to reduce the demand for lawyer services, or the cost of those services, then the question that ought to be asked is: 'to what extent are things better now?' While there is a growing literature about evaluation methodologies, there is still a question about how to measure the usefulness of the mediation process, as exemplified in the experience of this international mediator:[1]

> And because you're often working at the level of relationships, ideas, concepts, perceptions, it's actually very difficult to measure this. I remember after one of the first workshops we did in Moldova, we went back and we had a communication with the then Head of the OSC (Organisation for Security and Co-operation in Europe) saying: 'I don't know what you did with these guys but you completely rearranged their mental furniture. They are now talking with each other in a different way and are using a different kind of language.' But you can't measure that. (Mark Hoffman, quoted in Roberts, 2007, 172)

When mediation is unlikely to succeed

Unsuitability of referral

There must be an actual or anticipated dispute between the parties that cannot be reconciled by the normal (that is, everyday) processes of decision-making, if referral is to be appropriate. Other problems, for example in inter-personal relationships, or over social and economic difficulties, should be referred elsewhere for help.

Unsuitability of the dispute

The dispute must be capable of being negotiated. If the dispute consists of a fundamental divergence over facts or moral or legal norms, then other processes of dispute resolution may be more suitable. Family disputes are, in most cases, suitable for mediation because they involve the making of decisions relating to the future by two people bound together by an enduring common interest – their children.

---

1   Funding pressures similarly affect the international field in the way that outcomes are determined and success defined. Here too, measurable indices of success displace the significance of other, more intangible, values (Roberts, 2007).

Serious imbalances of bargaining power

There must be no substantial impairment of mental or physical capacity to negotiate, or other inequality between the parties that would render an unfair outcome unavoidable – for example, in situations of domestic abuse; in cases where one party may feel so guilty or defeated or so anxious to be free of the relationship that they may be prepared either to compromise their own interests or acquiesce in ways that they may later come to regret; and in cases where cultural norms deny women any decision-making authority.

Involuntary participation

Neither party must feel that they are participating in mediation against their will (see M. Roberts, 2006; and Genn et al., 2007, on the importance of motivation and a willingness to negotiate as critical to the success of mediation).

Criminal/child protection implications

Mediation in the private law is likely to be inappropriate where the issues to be decided are complicated by these factors.

Extreme conflict

Where conflict between the parties is so intense that co-operation, however minimal, is out of the question, mediation will not succeed. There has to be some willingness, not necessarily to end conflict, but to set it momentarily aside, for any agreement on the specific interim or immediate issue to be possible.

Non-acceptance of the end of the relationship

Where one party uses mediation to try to cling on to the marriage or relationship, they will in all probability sabotage decision-making relating to its dissolution. (See also 'Abuse of Mediation' below.)

Referral that is too early or too late

When emotions are intense and raw, as in the early stage of relationship breakdown, or when a commitment to litigating the dispute is already established (for example, when mediation is attempted within days of a court hearing), mediation is unlikely to be effective.

An unfavourable environment

Powerful third parties, such as combative lawyers unsympathetic to mediation or unco-operative new partners, may fuel hostilities and jeopardize agreements.

Abuse of mediation

One or both of the parties may seek to use mediation for a variety of purposes that have nothing to do with its proper purpose of consensual, joint decision-making. They may, for example, participate in the belief that some strategic advantage may be obtained in subsequent litigation (see Macfarlane, 2002, on the adverse impact of mandated mediation in this respect), or to have a 'go' at the other party, or to exert some ulterior pressure (for example, to use mediation to have personal contact or to impose one's own wishes). Where either party demonstrates a lack of commitment – for example, by failing to keep appointments, produce the necessary information or abide by interim agreements – mediation may be found to be unsuitable.

Lack of clarity and competence

Where a mediator fails to clarify the nature and purpose of mediation with the parties, mistaken expectations may arise – for example, the mediator may be perceived as an arbitrator whose function is to make a decision for the parties, or as an adviser evaluating and predicting possible outcomes, or as a counsellor or therapist who will be dealing with underlying relationship problems. The mediator may actually create misunderstanding and confusion, if he/she uses contradictory terminology such as 'solicitor mediator'; or offers mediation as part of another activity such as legal practice; or, more damagingly, attempts to combine, in the same case, the mediatory function with other forms of intervention, such as therapy or the giving of expert advice.[2] 'Evaluative' mediation, in confusing a mediatory with an advisory role for the intervener, runs these risks (see Chapter 3).

A failure to manage destructive exchanges, so that the meeting ends in an emotional shambles, a lack of innovative thinking, or a lack of intelligent understanding of what is going on, would demonstrate further, a lack of competence on the part of the mediator.

---

2   The Code of Practice of the UK College of Family Mediators (2000a, section 4.4.4) stipulates: 'Mediators must distinguish their roles as mediators from any other professional role in which they may act and must make sure they make this clear to the parties.'

At what stage mediation?

It is generally assumed that the earlier mediation is resorted to, the better the prospects of success, for relationships will not yet be worsened by litigation (*Practice Direction* [1982] 3 All ER 988, para. 2; Booth Committee, 1985, para. 3. 12).

In 1995 Lord Woolf, in his Interim Report on *Access to Justice*, denounced the practice of late settlement that characterized litigation in the civil courts.[3] His proposals for the reform of the civil justice system (endorsing the local initiatives of family court judges in the 1980s (see Chapter 3)) – for intensive 'case management' and the encouragement of early resort to mediation – have resulted in a dramatic change in legal culture (see Roberts and Palmer, 2005). It is the courts' active sponsorship of settlement at the pre-trial stage (rather than any impetus from disenchanted clients or the new professional mediators) that has challenged the lawyers' traditional management of disputing (Roberts and Palmer, 2005).

Advantages of early mediation

Mediation, occurring soon after, or even before, a dispute manifests (for example, when a couple are planning to part or have only recently parted), can contain conflict or limit its damaging effects. The dispute will not yet have had time to develop a past, with its own history and associated pattern of behaviour (Felstiner and Williams, 1985). The parties need not be adversaries. At this early stage, the first question – whether the relationship is in fact at an end – is more likely to be resolved in favour of an attempt at reconciliation, with a referral therefore to the appropriate counselling agency.[4] If they both decide they want a divorce with the minimum of antagonism in sorting out their affairs, they share the same legal interests (Wishik, 1984). The potential for co-operation and agreement can be thwarted by the initiation of legal proceedings – for example, a divorce petition citing

---

3   The Report highlights the many disadvantages for the parties that delay causes – distressing to those who have already suffered damage, deleterious to personal and business relationships, increasing the difficulties of establishing facts, increasing costs – and the reasons for delay in the majority of cases – failures in efficiency, excessive discovery, time-wasting on peripheral issues, or 'procedural skirmishing to wear down an opponent or to excuse failure to get on with a case' (Woolf, 1995, section 36).

4   National Family Mediation (NFM) statistics in the 1990s, showed a higher rate of reconciliation where the couples who came to mediation were not yet separated compared to when they were separated. Of those still living together, about 25 per cent decided to reconsider or reconcile. At the time, however, 82 per cent of mediating couples were already separated, with one or both cohabiting in 42 per cent of cases (NFM, 1994).

unreasonable behaviour, or by communication through lawyers' letters. Early on, there will be a wider choice of options – both short- and longer-term – and before entrenched positions are adopted, a greater willingness to consider them. Furthermore decision-making control can be consolidated and preserved at a time when stress could lead to its abandonment.

Agreement on specific and immediate issues can defuse tension and prevent escalation of animosity. If, through early mediation, the parties acquire a better understanding of each other's perspectives and demands, as well as an improved capacity to negotiate, then future conflict could be reduced or aborted.

Disadvantages of early mediation

Decisions made early on have far-reaching consequences for all concerned – for example, where and with whom the children will live. The obstacles to calm, co-operative and reasoned exchanges cannot be underestimated. In the first place, many interrelated issues will be unresolved – the relationship, the children's future, the home, finances, the division of the property, and so on. At the same time the emotional, social and economic conditions will be fraught. Heightened feelings of anger, hurt and grief as well as physical exhaustion resulting from changes and worry, all increase the difficulties of decision-making.

Research has shown that couples referred to mediation after the granting of the decree absolute achieved higher agreement rates than were obtained by those resorting to mediation before divorce (Davis, 1981; Davis and Roberts, 1988). This is not surprising when a single issue only (contact) was disputed in most cases, and with the passage of time the emotional temperature between the disputants was lowered.

9   Confidentiality

> ... it is plain that the parties will not make admissions or conciliatory gestures, or dilute their claims, or venture out of their entrenched positions unless they can be confident that their concessions and admissions cannot be used as weapons against them if conciliation fails and full-blooded litigation follows. (Sir Thomas Bingham *Re D. (Minors) (Conciliation: Privilege)* [1993] 1 FLR 934 CA)

Confidentiality is integral to the relationship between the mediator and the parties and, as noted in Chapter 1, is one of the four fundamental and universal characteristics of mediation (McCrory, 1981). It is the cornerstone of the relationship of trust that must exist between the mediator and the parties and of the free and frank disclosure that is necessary if obstacles to settlement are to be overcome. It is crucial to the voluntariness of participation of the parties and to the impartiality of the mediator. The parties must not feel that they might be disadvantaged by any disclosure that may be used in legal proceedings, or in any other way. They need to know they have nothing to lose by resorting to mediation.[1]

Confidentiality between the mediator and the parties

Mediators have a duty to make clear to the parties at the outset that communications between them and the mediator are made in confidence, and that the mediator must not disclose any information about, or obtained in the course of mediation to anyone, including the court, solicitors, court welfare officers, social workers, or doctors, without the express consent of each participant or an order of the court (UK College of Family Mediators, 2000a).

---

1   The Code of Practice of the UK College of Family Mediators sets out the parameters of confidentiality and legal privilege for family mediators in the UK (2000a, sections 4.5 and 4.6).

Exceptions to confidentiality

Confidentiality is, of course, not absolute as it is always subject to the requirement that the law of the land shall be complied with (*Parry-Jones* v. *Law Society* 1968). The limits are those pertaining in all confidential or professional communications, whether between doctor and patient, priest and penitent, or journalist and informant. Therefore, the promise of confidentiality does not prevent the mediator from disclosing information in the exceptional circumstances where there is substantial risk to the life, health or safety of the parties, their children or anyone else. The risk of child abuse highlights the special need to define explicitly the limits of confidentiality in family mediation, given its serious implications. As the Code of Practice of the UK College of Family Mediators (2000, 4.5.3) specifies: 'Where a mediator suspects that a child is in danger of significant harm, or it appears necessary so that a specific allegation that a child has suffered significant harm may be properly investigated, mediators must ensure that the local Social Services (England and Wales) or Social Work Department (Scotland) is notified.'

Family mediators in the UK are expected to follow strict guidelines on what courses of action to adopt when a child protection issue arises in mediation – 'where it appears to a mediator that a child is suffering or is likely to suffer significant harm' (The UK College of Family Mediators Code of Practice, 2000, 4.7.4 and 4.7.5). In the first instance, the parties themselves should be encouraged to seek help from an appropriate agency. The mediator should take action in accordance with local child protection guidelines and should only report the matter to both solicitors or to the Social Services department or the welfare service of the court, if already involved, only where neither party is willing to do this, and normally after discussion with both parents. The mediator must advise the parties that whether or not they seek that help, the mediator will be obliged to report the matter to the relevant authorities (UK College of Family Mediators Code of Practice, 2000, 4.7.4). Where it appears to a mediator that the participants are acting or proposing to act in a manner likely to be 'seriously detrimental to the welfare of any child of the family', the mediator may withdraw from mediation (UK College of Family Mediators Code of Practice, 2000, 4.7.5).

Although mediators, when outlining the limits to confidentiality, refer specifically to the risk of harm to children, the limits apply too, to other equally applicable life or health-threatening risks associated with situations of great stress, such as self-harm, suicide or physical violence between adults.

A second exception to the promise of confidentiality in family mediation relates to the requirement, under the Proceeds of Crime Act 2002 and/or the relevant money laundering regulations, to make disclosure to the appropriate government authorities in respect of transactions in criminal property. While there is some lack of clarity over the remit of the Proceeds of Crime Act 2002, the general advice to mediators is to err on the side of caution and to clarify this exception explicitly to the parties, discontinuing mediation if necessary. The responsibility of the mediator under this legislation is that of any good citizen should they uncover criminal activity while undertaking their duties (for guidance on this matter, see UK College of Family Mediators Guidance, 2006c).[2]

A third, different order exception to the promise of confidentiality occurs when one or both of the parties are legally aided. Where there is a legal aid component in the case, the parties need to know that, in the course of an audit by the Legal Services Commission, their files might be examined. The purpose of the audit is, of course, to ensure that the proper quality assurance standards are being met by the mediation provider, and the parties' personal file details are not the concern of the auditors.

In addition to the exceptions already referred to, another exception relates to factual disclosures made in the course of mediation on financial or property issues. Factual data of this kind may be disclosed in any subsequent legal proceedings (see UK College Code of Practice, 2000, section 4.6.2).

The problem for mediators is not whether confidentiality is absolute nor whether its limits – implied, as they generally are, in the confidential relationships described above – should be spelt out. The question that arises is *how* this should be done without at the same time stigmatizing decision-making processes with inappropriate criminal or pathological overtones, or damaging the wholehearted commitment of the mediator to the principle of confidentiality by hedging it about with too many restrictions and reservations.

The dilemmas of confidentiality

Confidential information vouchsafed separately to the mediator by each party is recognized to be problematic in the context of the caucus (Moore, 1986; Folberg and Milne, 1988). It can be difficult to maintain impartiality in circumstances when information is being imparted to the mediator in the absence of the other. Some mediators pre-empt this by stating in advance that all information disclosed separately must be able to be

---

2   The Court of Appeal decision in *Bowman* v. *Fels* 2005 has now clarified that the Proceeds of Crime Act 2002 (sections 327 to 329) does not override legal professional privilege. It is argued too that this decision must apply equally to mediations (Kallipetis and Bootle, 2005). The related policy issue, of whether or not mediators who are also qualified as lawyers provide 'legal services' when they mediate, has also been resolved. There is now consensus amongst all the relevant bodies, including the Law Society, the Bar Council and the leading mediation providers, that mediators, whatever their profession of origin, do not provide 'legal services'.

shared in the joint session. There shall be no 'secrets'. This is intended to prevent alliances, or the perception of alliances, being formed between the mediator and one party. Other mediators engage the caucus on the basis that its benefits outweigh the disadvantages and that separate confidential communication can enhance the potential for subsequent constructive exchanges – in commercial mediation, confidentiality is a primary requirement of the caucus.

Where mediators do allow separate confidential communications in the context of an early and established stage within the structure of the joint session (see Chapter 8), the parties need to be informed about its nature and purpose in advance. Commonly, confidential disclosures have little bearing on the resolution of the matters in hand, in which case there need be no problem (for example, where there is an expression of negative views about another family member, or past facts about the ex-partner).

There is a problem, however, when information imparted in confidence to the mediator by one party is central to subsequent joint discussion of the dispute. If that party cannot be persuaded to make the necessary disclosure to the other party, then it may be necessary to end the mediation session. This may be preferable to negotiations taking place fettered by the concealment of vital information, unbeknown to the mediator and one of the parties, which might occur if separate confidential communications were not allowed in the first place.[3]

All communications made in the course of mediation – whether between the parties themselves, or between the parties and the mediator(s), or between mediators or the parties' solicitors – are confidential, subject to certain exceptions, and will not be disclosed. Mediators shall not discuss or correspond with any party's legal adviser without the express consent of each party and nothing must be said or written to the legal adviser of one, which is not also said or written to the legal adviser of the other(s) (UK College of Family Mediators Code of Practice, 2000, section 4.5.2).

---

3   The Code of Practice of the UK College of Family Mediators (2000a, section 6.6) states: 'Mediators must not guarantee that any communication from one participant will be kept secret from the other(s), except that they may always agree not to disclose one participant's address or telephone number to the other(s). They may see participants separately, if both agree, but if any relevant information emerges which one participant is not willing to have disclosed to the other(s), mediators must consider whether or not it is appropriate to continue with mediation'.

Confidentiality of communications between the parties and third persons outside the process

While confidentiality can be promised by the mediator, confidentiality belongs to the parties. It is a matter of their own discretion and their decision what information they impart to their solicitors or anyone else. All these matters should be clarified explicitly at the outset, as should the fact that the court will be very reluctant to allow confidential exchanges between the parties to be used as evidence in any subsequent proceedings (see below).

Confidentiality in relation to legal proceedings (privilege)

Mediation as an alternative to litigation occurs nonetheless within a legal framework. Legal proceedings may follow mediation or take place concurrently over other disputes (for example, finance). Agreements may break down, and litigation may be resorted to subsequently. Variation proceedings may follow changes of circumstance. Details of proposed arrangements for children have to be provided before a decree absolute may be granted by the court (Matrimonial Causes Act 1973, section 41).

Public policy has always favoured the settlement of disputes – it is in the public interest that disputes be settled and litigation reduced to the minimum. The privilege of 'without prejudice' negotiation (that is, without prejudice to the legal rights of the maker of the statement) has long been a principle of English law. It attaches to statements and offers of compromise made by the parties and their legal advisers in negotiations for settling disputes. These disclosures may not be used in subsequent legal proceedings without the consent of both parties. The policy of the law has also been in favour of enlarging the cloak under which negotiations may be conducted without prejudice (Cross and Tapper, 2007).

Over the years, the 'without prejudice' privilege was extended to cover new categories of cases. The privilege was accorded to confidential communications between a mediator and two parties where the purpose of negotiations was designed to effect a reconciliation between them (for example, *Mole* v. *Mole* 1950; *Henley* v. *Henley* 1955; *Theodoropoulos* v. *Theodoropoulos* 1964; *Pais* v. *Pais* 1970). The protection derived from the activity engaged in, and not from the office of the mediator involved (a clergyman in one instance, a probation officer in another). In the earlier case of *McTaggart* v. *McTaggart* [1948] 2 All ER 755, Lord Justice Denning stated:

The rule as to without prejudice communications applies with especial force to negotiations for reconciliation. It applies whenever the dispute has got to such dimensions that litigation is imminent. In all cases where estrangement has reached the point where the parties consult a probation officer [the mediator in this case] litigation is imminent.

The public policy considerations behind this ruling were based on the interest of the state in preserving the stability of marriage.

In 1971, a Practice Direction on Matrimonial Conciliation issued by the President of the Family Division of the High Court, provided that both reconciliation and conciliation negotiations should be legally privileged. *Practice Direction* [1982] 3 All ER 988 provided that discussions at 'conciliation appointments' before a registrar attended by a court welfare officer and at a private meeting with the court welfare officer be privileged. Conciliation that was not part of court proceedings was not covered by this direction. The critical issue of how the same officer could engage in the privileged communications of conciliation and at the same time the non-privileged welfare investigation and report-writing was not addressed.

The Booth Committee, on the other hand, made clear the incompatibility of the same officer carrying out both conciliation and report writing in the same case (Booth Committee, 1985, para. 41.2). It also recommended that conciliation in court proceedings be absolutely privileged (Booth Committee, 1985, para. 4.60).

The current practice is that if a CAFCASS officer acts as a mediator, that officer cannot prepare any subsequent report should the parties fail to reach agreement (Walsh, 2006, p. 2.74). It is now stipulated that when a CAFCASS officer acts as a mediator, the information given by the parties is privileged, whereas when s/he acts as an in-court conciliator, it is not privileged, and can be reported to the court (Walsh, 2006, pp. 2.63; 4.54). However, given the acknowledged terminological and practice confusion currently surrounding the varieties of 'dispute resolution' functions carried out by CAFCASS officers (see Chapter 2), the critical issue now, if the public is to be protected, is how the practice of 'mediation' by a CAFCASS officer, can be meaningfully distinguished from the practice of 'in-court conciliation'.

There is, in fact, no legislation in England and Wales – and, until 1993, no case law – to clarify the issue of privilege in mediation where reconciliation was not an issue.[4] That is why the decision of the Court of Appeal in *Re D. (Minors)* was such a landmark. This case established for the first time that, in mediation where reconciliation is not the purpose of the negotiations, discussions in relation to disputes involving children are privileged. The

---

4   In Scotland, admissibility as to what occurred during family mediation is protected by the Civil Evidence (Family Mediation) (Scotland) Act 1995 in any subsequent civil proceedings.

case established that statements made by either of the parties in the course of mediation cannot be disclosed in proceedings under the Children Act 1989, except in the rare case that such a statement clearly indicated that the maker had in the past caused or was likely to cause serious harm to the well-being of a child. Even within that narrow exception, the trial judge would admit the statement only if, in his/her judgment, the public interest in protecting the child's interest outweighed the public interest in preserving confidentiality.

This Court of Appeal decision was significant in three further respects:

- The privilege of exchanges relating to the resolution of disputes over children exists as an independent head of privilege based on the public interest, both in sparing children unnecessary suffering by encouraging the settlement of issues concerning them, and in reducing the burden of the cost and delay of litigation.
- Their Lordships stated explicitly that mediation did not form part of the legal process, though, as a matter of practice, it was becoming an important and valuable tool in the procedures of many family courts.
- The Master of the Rolls stated that the privilege belongs to the parties themselves, and that they may, if they so choose, waive it. In such circumstances the implications are clear – the mediator may be compelled to testify.

McCrory (1988) has argued for the removal of this limitation by the extension of privilege to matrimonial mediation on the basis of public interest immunity. This is founded on the principle that mediation serves an important public interest in promoting co-operative decision-making and the reduction of conflict, and that the privilege should attach therefore to the *mediation process* itself, immunity from disclosure being essential to the effectiveness of the process.[5]

Notwithstanding this limitation, the judgment of the Court of Appeal in *Re D. (Minors)* (1993) is a valuable clarification of the legal position in relation to the confidential exchanges that occur in family mediation. The decision is confined to the circumstances of the case – that is, to matrimonial disputes over children in proceedings under the Children Act 1989. It may be assumed that the privilege of 'without prejudice' negotiations still attaches to mediated negotiations relating to finance and property issues.

This 'without prejudice' privilege is subject to three limitations when applied to mediation (Cross and Tapper, 2007):

---

5   In the new European Mediation Directive concerning civil and commercial matters in cross-border disputes, approved in April 2008 by the European Parliament, Article 7 introduces provisions confirming confidentiality and privilege in mediation matters – a privilege enacted in relation to mediation for the first time.

- The privilege belongs to the parties jointly, and not to the mediator or the process. It can therefore be waived by both parties, expressly or otherwise, in legal proceedings, and then the mediator could be compelled to testify.
- The cloak of the privilege does not cover statements that are not sufficiently related to the dispute which is the subject of negotiation.
- A binding agreement that results from privileged negotiations is not itself privileged. It is therefore important that the status of any mediated agreement be clear to all concerned. In most cases, the parties will not intend their agreements to be legally binding in any event.

In practice, the court is unlikely to allow either party to make use of evidence derived from failed negotiations. Agreements are encouraged by the court, which will not wish either party to be disadvantaged by prior attempts to reach agreement. Although, for example, no privilege exists as a matter of law to protect confidential communications (except between lawyers and their clients and in proceedings under the Patents Act 1943), in practice, these are frequently protected. The judge has a discretion to disallow questions concerning them and witnesses are not in fact pressed to disclose confidential information (Cross and Wilkins, 1996).

The UK College of Family Mediators (2000) has clarified the requirements of privilege in relation to legal proceedings for family mediators. Subject to the qualifications below, all discussions and negotiations in mediation must be conducted on a legally privileged basis. Participants must agree that discussions and negotiations in mediation are not to be referred to in any legal proceedings and that the mediator cannot be required to give evidence or produce any notes or recordings made in the course of mediation, unless all participants agree to waive the privilege or the law imposes an overriding obligation upon the mediator (Code of Practice 2000, 4.6.1). This is subject to the following qualifications: that participants must agree that any factual disclosure made with a view to resolving any issue relating to their property or finances may be disclosed in legal proceedings; and that mediators must be aware of the exceptions to the general rules of inadmissibility, including where there are civil or criminal proceedings related to the care or protection of a child (Code of Practice 2000, 4.6.2 and 4.6.3, see also the current chapter's footnote 4 for the legal position in Scotland).

10 Children and the mediation process

Childhood is entitled to special care and assistance. (UN Convention on the Rights of the Child, 1989, Preamble)

The subject of children, in whatever professional context, always provokes important, delicate and complex questions – about their rights and their welfare; about the kinds of decisions that have to be made, often profound and far-reaching in their life-changing effects, particularly in circumstances of family breakdown; about the participation of children in decision-making, and what is meant by 'participation'; about ethnic, cultural, social, economic, and gender factors and differences; about what children themselves think and want; and about balancing respective and possibly competing interests within families.

The focus on children and family mediation brings to the fore general themes that emerge in mediation in all fields of practice, for example:

- the role of third persons in mediation – those not involved directly in the negotiations but who are directly affected by the process and its outcome;
- the ways in which mediation differs from other interventions and the importance of maintaining clarity of boundaries with other interventions – for example, the distinctive, mediation-specific role of children in mediation needs to be clearly differentiated from their involvement with other forms of intervention, such as child counselling, advice-giving, guidance and advocacy;
- the tension between the pursuit of individual rights and the ethics of collaboration and consensual forms of decision-making that distinguish mediation.

191

Children in mediation

The place of children in the mediation process has generated much debate ever since family mediation was first introduced in the UK in the late 1970s. There has long been a consensus that mediation can enhance children's interests. The process and outcome benefits of mediation – collaborative approaches to decision-making, improved communication between parents, reduced misunderstanding and conflict, and parents retaining control over the fashioning and content of their own agreements – have recognized advantages for children (Trinder et al., 2002; Kelly and Emery, 2003; Hunt with Roberts, 2004; Kelly, 2004). Research also highlights the negative consequences for children of the competitive, adversarial approaches of litigation and adjudication, which require the disputants (parents in this case) to take up opposing stances in order to achieve their objectives (Lund, 1984; Wallerstein and Kelly, 1980; Maccoby and Mnookin, 1992; Cockett and Tripp, 1994; Trinder et al., 2002; Kelly and Emery, 2003).

Family mediation has long been identified with a greater concentration on the needs of children (Davis and Roberts, 1988; Kelly, 2004). One of the special features of family disputes referred to earlier (see Chapter 2) is the continuing and interdependent relationship of the adult disputants who, as parents, are bound together forever through their children (Fuller, 1971). Children provide the common interest and the mutual inducement for collaborative effort. Children may be seen to be, simultaneously, the cause of dispute, the weapons of dispute, the main casualties of dispute, *and*, therefore, the best reason for ending the dispute (Davis and Roberts, 1988). Disputes over children frequently reflect this complex and paradoxical predicament.

There is also a common view that mediation can offer the 'best setting' for the voice of the child to be heard (Simpson, 1989). This is linked to the presumption, embodied in the UN Convention on the Rights of the Child 1989, the Children Act 1989 and the now defunct Family Law Act 1996, that greater awareness of and greater attention to the views and feelings of children both acknowledges their worth and significance and alleviates distress at the time of separation and divorce.

On the other hand, the vexed question of children's *direct participation* in the mediation process – whether, when and how this should take place – has excited controversy rather than consensus. Discussion on this issue in the 1980s was characterized by two features: a polarization of positions lined up for and against the direct 'involvement' of children in mediation, and the importation into family mediation of the child-saving and paternalist aspects of social work and family therapy practice. There has always been a danger that the preoccupation of professionals regarding the issue of 'children's interests' could give rise to a conflict – not between the interests of parents and their children, but between parents and the various professionals who claim to know and represent the best interests of children (Berger and Berger, 1983). The fundamental issue at stake here has been whether divorcing parents, like parents in intact families, should be trusted to make decisions about the future of their own children.

By the 1990s, the convergence of the long practice experience of family mediators, the clarification of the nature of the mediation process that had by then occurred and a fresh climate of thinking about the 'voice' of the child in decision-making (for example the UN Convention on the Rights of the Child 1989 and the Children Act 1989), resulted in a new appreciation of the distinctive and precise role of children in mediation (NFM, 1994). More recently, researchers have examined how children are listened to in legal, administrative and mediatory processes and they have reported on the most effective ways of listening to children so that they can be fully involved in the processes that affect them (O'Quigley, 1999; Wade and Smart, 2002).

The discussions in the 1980s

Arguments in favour of 'involving' children

Those who argued in favour of the direct involvement of children in the mediation process did so on two counts. First, the physical presence of the children was a reminder to the parties of their parental responsibilities (James and Wilson, 1986). Second, research findings suggested that parents' views of what their children thought might differ considerably from what the children themselves thought (Wallerstein and Kelly, 1980; Walczak with Burns, 1984; Mitchell, 1985). It was claimed that stress-induced incapacity and poor communication, especially in the immediate aftermath of separation, could account for this discrepancy of perception. The presence of children was necessary therefore to give the parents first-hand information (Saposnek, 1983).

It was also argued that although children should not have a final say in the decisions that were made, they should be involved in the making of arrangements that affected them. This helped them to happier adjustments following the disruption of their families (Walczak with Burns, 1984). The 'real' feelings of children, it was also claimed, could only be ascertained when children were seen 'within the context of their parenting rather than taken from it' (Howard and Shepherd, 1982, p. 92).

Furthermore those who advocated a 'family systems' approach to mediation required the presence of *all* family members as 'contributors to the interactional process' at least at some stage, in order that the mediator 'maximizes her leverage as a result of her more comprehensive view of the functional rules of the family system' (Saposnek, 1983, p. 120).

Arguments against the direct 'involvement' of children in the mediation process

Those who argued against children participating directly in the mediation process did so for the reasons set out below – underpinned by the adverse impact on those most affected, namely, the children, the parents and the mediators.

The impact on children:

- it was stressful for children;
- it placed an unfair burden on children to make a decision when parents were in dispute;
- it was difficult, if not unfair, to expect children, at a time of crisis, to make informed judgements about what was in their own best interests in the future.

The impact on parents:

- this was in line with parents' own preferences on the matter;
- their decision-making authority could be undermined;
- children's views could be imposed on parents.

The impact on mediators:

- incompatible demands could be placed on the mediator, complicating or distorting their role;
- the mediator was not a spokesperson for the child yet when called upon to voice the views of the child could be seen to take on the role of child advocate, a role incompatible with the mediatory role. The child's views could also be, or be perceived to be, taking precedence over and above both parents' views;
- where great weight was attached by one or both parents to what the child said, as was likely where there was a clash of views between the parties as to what the child was saying, then the mediator, in acting as spokesperson for the child, could be forced into an arbitrating role;
- impartiality could be compromised – for example, where a child's views, when voiced by a mediator, corresponded with the views of one parent. The mediator could become identified with the position of the child and therefore with one of the parent;
- confidentiality could be compromised. The mediator could be placed in an impossible position vis-à-vis the confidentiality of the information vouchsafed by a child. The mediator might hold information and yet be unable to use it. There could therefore be

serious difficulties for the mediator in both conveying and not conveying information revealed by a child.

Judges, it was argued, were reluctant to see children in disputes that were affecting them for two main reasons, both of which applied in mediation. First, an unfair burden was placed upon the child to express a preference on an issue, knowing that his/her parents were in dispute over it. Second, where a decision would be reached (by the judge or, in mediation, by the parents) that was likely to be contrary to the wishes of the child, this also placed the child in an unfair position (Poulter, 1982).

Families, it was noted, made decisions in their own way. These decision-making processes of the autonomous intact family should be encouraged to continue after separation and divorce. In that process, parents do commonly impose decisions on their children. The decision to divorce is a stark example of this and one which 'society sanctions through its non-intervention' (Maidment, 1984, p. 273). Why, it is asked, if children's views are so important, are they accorded greater significance in relation to decisions over family breakdown than in relation to other decisions taken by intact families that also profoundly affect their future – for example, moving house or a parent's return to work (King, 1987)?[1] In circumstances such as these, the state has no power to force parents to act in ways that respect children's rights or even take their views into account – for example, the state cannot require parents to have a continuing relationship with their children even though this is what the children may want and is likely to be in their best interests.

In conclusion, it was argued that the disadvantages of involving children directly or indirectly in the mediation process far outweighed any advantages. The boundaries between mediation and therapy might become dangerously blurred. The parents' authority might be undermined. The children might become embroiled in an anxious and unnatural situation, feel obliged to make unfair choices, and carry some of their parents' responsibility to reduce conflict.

However, there were specific, relatively rare occasions when, it was argued, it might be appropriate to see a child – for example, when that child (particularly the older child) was creating obstacles to any agreement the parents might wish to make, or had access to information unavailable elsewhere. With the consent of both parents, and, of course, that of the child, s/he might be appropriately interviewed in order that these obstacles might better be understood and overcome – for example when a child suddenly and for no apparent reason refused to see one parent. There were also occasions

---

1   Questions such as these continue to be raised – for example, why should disagreement between parents act as a trigger for asserting children's rights? (See King, 2007.)

when one parent, voicing the child's point of view, was disbelieved by the other parent. This problem might arise when the parent with residence had to express his/her own position and act as the spokesperson for the children at the same time. In these circumstances, the mediator, after seeing the child separately, could validate independently, the views of the child, also enabling the non-resident parent to accept the message because it came from an impartial third person.

Arguments in favour of indirect 'involvement' of children in mediation

It was also argued that children do have independent views which should be heard, but it is the parents who should talk to and listen to their children as far as possible. It was not appropriate for the mediator to decide at the outset that children have the right to be present at the discussions between their parents. This could undermine the adults' authority before they even start. Rather than take over these decisions and responsibilities, the mediator should encourage parents to fulfil these tasks themselves – assuming of course that they had not already done so.

While research has pointed to a need for greater recognition, among parents who separate, of their children's likely needs and feelings (Utting, 1995), findings also showed that many parents were very concerned about the harmful effects of separation on their children, and positively welcomed the explicit focus on their needs that the mediator might provide (Davis and Roberts, 1988; Saposnek, 1983). There was no evidence to suggest that, in most cases, parents, however angry or distressed, were less committed to their children's welfare than the mediator, and that without the intervention of the mediator they would tend to disregard their children's interests or treat them as 'inanimate objects to be collected and deposited as parcels' or 'sacks of corn to be haggled over or split in half' (for example, Parkinson, 1986, pp. 116, 161).

Children did not have to be present at the mediation session to have their views taken into consideration. As already noted, the mediator had an ethical responsibility to ensure that the needs of children – and of all those not at the negotiating table yet who were affected by the decisions made there (including grandparents and step-parents) – were taken into account as part of the parents' examination of various options and their consequences. The knowledge that their parents were actually talking together was, of itself, often reassuring to children. They might be helped too by the removal of the uncertainty that decision-making often achieved. Parents themselves often did not know what was or would be happening. This objective uncertainty itself inevitably contributed to the problematic communication between adults and their children in the post-separation period, as well as to the confusion and insecurity of their children.

The wishes of children (certainly those under 16) were not conclusive. They could not be reliable judges of their own best long-term interests, and their expressed opinions and preferences at the time of the divorce crisis, however strongly felt, could not be decisive when arrangements over contact and residence were made (Wallerstein and Kelly, 1980). Some parents appeared only too ready to absolve themselves from the difficulty of decision-making and let the child decide. This frequently arose when a child was refusing to see the non-resident parent. The child should not be expected to shoulder such responsibility. There was a risk in such cases that the child might find her/himself ultimately alienated from both parents – cut off from the non-resident parent as well as resentful in later years that the resident parent had allowed this situation to come to pass.

Children could be pressurized or deliberately coached. In any event, they were usually most influenced by the parent with whom they were in closest contact. Where one parent (usually the parent with residence) insisted on the child being seen by the mediator, the possibility existed that the parent wanted their child's views elicited precisely because, at that moment, they coincided with their own views. But children's views do change. Mitchell (1985), for example, described how when first interviewed, children expressed strong preferences for keeping their parents together even if they did not get on, rather than have them separate. Interviewed five to six years after divorce, only 6 out of 50 still thought their parents were wrong to have divorced. Family life was happier as a result of separation and divorce but it had taken them a long time to appreciate this. Wallerstein and Kelly (1980) also found that many of those children with the most passionate convictions at the time of break-up came later to regret those statements.

Developments in the 1990s

In the 1990s, with the convergence of policy and practice developments – the greater experience of family mediators; the clarification of the nature of the mediation process in relation to family disputes; and a fresh climate of thinking about the significance of the 'voice' of the child in decision-making – there was a new appreciation of the distinctive and precise role of children in the mediation process (Children Act 1989; UN Convention of the Rights of the Child 1989).

By the late 1980s, a productive interaction between researchers and practitioners in the field began to shed light for the first time on the delicate and complex role of children in mediation. For the first time too, children's own views were canvassed (Garwood, 1989). For researchers, the very dilemmas of mediation practice in relation to children – for example, the multi-party consent requirements – both informed and complicated, even stymied, the research endeavour itself (Ogus et al., 1987; Simpson, 1989). For practitioners, greater awareness of research, its value as well as its limitations, resulted in a more careful and focused approach (Davis and Roberts, 1988; Collinson and Gardner, 1990).

Practitioners, for example, no longer, regarded the parents' right to determine their own decisions about their children as an abstract principle at odds with child welfare considerations. As far as their own children were concerned, parents may well be the true experts as to the best arrangements for the children, knowing their children better than anyone else and caring about their welfare. While, in one research study, the mediators' focus on children (encouraging the parents to adopt the *child's* perspective on the matter) was welcomed by parents, the mediators would limit themselves to the question; 'what is best for the child?' The answer remained a matter for negotiation between the parents who were presumed to be the most competent judges of the issue. This did not mean the mediators had no useful specialist knowledge to offer but there was greater recognition that this knowledge was, at best, tentative, that the general principle might not apply in the individual case, and that this expertise should not be paraded in such a way as to brow-beat parents. Disagreements over arrangements for children (residence and contact, in the main) did not arise simply from parents' own hurt, grief or bitterness – what might be termed their 'selfish' preoccupations with the past marital history. They might genuinely differ in their assessment of the children's interests. Furthermore, this study found that the mediators no longer regarded a failure to reach agreement, or a preference for court adjudication, as an indication that parents did not have the best interests of their children at heart (Davis and Roberts, 1988).

The National Family Mediation (NFM) report

In 1994, following a study of its services' practices in relation to children, NFM, supported by a grant from the Calouste Gulbenkian Foundation, published a definitive report, *Giving Children a Voice in Mediation*, with the purpose of devising a policy and practice guidelines on the subject. The study yielded several specific findings:

- There was a continuum of views among mediators ranging from those who were against direct inclusion of children, seeing mediation as an adult decision-making process, to those who were committed to their inclusion either on the basis that it was the child's right to be included or that it was in their best interests. The largest number of mediators were situated in the middle of this continuum and, whether reluctant or enthusiastic, adopted an approach of caution. The words 'only if appropriate' were frequently used.

- While most mediators and mediation services believed their primary concern was to protect the interests of children in divorce, it was rare for children to be directly involved. The average percentage of cases in which children were directly involved was 8 per cent and there were only two services (out of 30 that responded) that saw children frequently. 'Apart from these exceptions, it is significant that those at the enthusiastic end of the continuum did not, in fact, appear to see children more frequently than those at the reluctant end' (NFM, 1994a, p. 12).
- There was no evidence to suggest that those most in favour of direct inclusion of children were more experienced or better trained than those who least favoured it. Those who were specifically trained as mediators to see children, did not in fact see children more frequently.
- Most actual practice involved children being seen by mediators outside the mediation process and purpose.
- The language used to describe this practice was varied and unspecific, for example, 'working with' [children]; 'involving' [children]; 'seeing' [children]; 'including' [children]; [children] 'participating in', and so on.
- All mediator respondents, despite strong differences of approach, were agreed that the decision-makers were the adults, not the mediator nor the children, and that an approach of caution in relation to children was appropriate (NFM 1994a).

The policy question to be resolved was therefore: 'How can children's perspectives best inform a process in which the parents are the ultimate decision-makers?' The answer lay in the concept of *consultation*, which clarified language use as well as resolved the substantive question – children can be consulted as part of their parents' decision-making within mediation. Consultation could take place in two ways:

- Indirect consultation by means of the parents themselves bringing their children's views into the process – the preferred form of consultation, because it encouraged parents themselves to consider their children's views and perspectives fully.
- Direct consultation with children by the mediator within the process – of great assistance particularly where the perspective of the child might be missing form discussions. Whether children should be consulted directly, how, and at what stage, were matters to be agreed jointly by the mediator and the parties also requiring the child's consent.

To implement its policy, NFM developed training modules covering both the indirect and the direct consultation of children in mediation.

There is a view (for example, Richards, 1994b) that mediators should go further than giving children a voice in parental decision-making. Mediators should assist both in ensuring that the emotional needs of children are being met by others, such as counsellors, and in educating parents in better communication with their children.

There is no doubt that children will, on occasion, need specialist help in coping with the separation of their parents. Counselling, advice-giving, information, assessment and therapy should be available in these cases (Ross, 1986). But these forms of intervention, vital as they may be, should not be confused with mediation or be attempted at the same time by the same person. While every effort should, of course, be made to mitigate the unhappiness of loss and change, especially for children, misfortune in family life is, sadly, often unavoidable.

The legislative framework

There is now near universal acceptance of the importance of the view that children are people entitled to basic human rights. In 1989, the United Nations General Assembly adopted the UN Convention on the Rights of the Child 1989 which was ratified by the UK Government in 1991 and, since then, at least 177 countries. In so doing, these countries made an explicit commitment to respecting and promoting children's rights. These embrace not only the survival, development and protection of children, but also their basic civil rights – the right of children to freedom of expression, religion, conscience, association, information, physical integrity and to participation in decisions on matters that affect them. Because the Convention is not incorporated into English law, English children cannot rely on its provisions in the English courts. However, as international standards are becoming increasingly important, the Convention has been endorsed by the European and domestic courts (Walsh, 2006).

Most pertinent to family decision-making, and therefore to family mediation, are articles 2, 3, 5, 9 and 12, which are summarized briefly below:

- Article 2 affirms the principle that all rights guaranteed by the Convention must be available to all children without discrimination of any kind.
- Article 3 sets out the principle that in all actions concerning children the best interests of the child shall be a primary consideration.

- Article 5 sets out the state's duty to respect the responsibilities, rights and duties of parents and the wider family to provide appropriate direction and guidance appropriate to the child's evolving capacities.
- Article 9 sets out the child's right to live with his/her parents unless this is deemed incompatible with his/her interests and the right to maintain contact on a regular basis with both parents if separated from one or both, except if it is contrary to the child's best interests.
- Article 12 states the child's right to express an opinion freely where capable and to have that opinion taken into account in any matter or procedure affecting the child. The views of the child are to be given due weight, in accordance with the age and maturity of the child.

The UN Convention provides international affirmation, therefore, of the principle that children, rather than being treated as the property of their parents, are individuals with their own needs and rights.

The Human Rights Act 1998 introduced the right to raise in court any breaches of the European Convention on Human Rights. Article 6 (the right to a fair and public hearing of both civil and criminal cases) and article 8 (the right to respect for family and private life) are the most used articles. The Act has also been successfully used to challenge certain decisions made by the local authority in connection with Articles 6 and 8.

The Children Act 1989 recognizes the importance of respect for the child's perspective in family proceedings and in local authority decision-making, as does the European Convention on the Exercise of Children's Rights produced by the European Council in 1994. The Children (Scotland) Act 1995 goes further and incorporates into primary legislation a specific provision requiring *all* those with parental responsibility:

> to have regard so far as practicable to the views (if he wishes to express them) of the child concerned, taking account of the child's age and maturity … and without prejudice to the generality of this subsection a child twelve years of age or more shall be presumed to be of sufficient age and maturity to form a view. (Section 6)

This Act therefore extends the obligation to take account of the views of the child into the private sphere of the family.

In addition to the rights of participation in decision-making, embodied in the Children Act 1989, the House of Lords, in the 'Gillick' judgment, clarified the extent of parental authority in relation to decision-making on behalf of a child. Their Lordships' ruling (*Gillick* v. *West Norfolk and Wisbech AHA* [1986] AC 112) included the following:

> … parental rights to control a child do not exist for the benefit of the parent. They exist for the benefit of the child and they are justified only in so far as they enable the parent to perform his duties towards the child, and towards other children in the family.

And:

> ... parental rights yield to the child's right to make his own decisions when he reaches a sufficient understanding and intelligence to be capable of making up his mind on the matter requiring a decision.

In *Re W.* (1993), the Gillick decision was redefined as extending only to the child's right to *give* consent, not to *refuse* treatment. Until a child reached the age of 18 years, a parallel right of consent continued to be vested in the parent, and would prevail if the child refused consent, irrespective of the competence of the child.

Striking the right balance between the rights and obligations of articles 3, 5, 9 and 12 – rights to care, protection, direction, guidance and consultation – is one of the many challenges involved in decision-making in separating and divorcing families. If children have the right both to express a view on matters of concern to them and to have those views taken seriously, then parents have a corresponding obligation to consult their children. This right of the child to participate in decision-making does not remove the ultimate authority of the adults to make the decisions in relation to the child. It does, however, significantly affect the process by means of which those decisions are made (Lansdown, 1995).

If striking the right balance within families is not without difficulty, then what of the difficulties of striking the right balance between families and professional interveners? Official judicial and legal endorsement of private ordering and mediation has already precipitated warnings by some children's rights advocates about the dangers of parental agreement for children. Such advocates have urged the need for the greater welfare surveillance of family decision-making in divorce (Timms, 1995). This contradicts the ethos of mediation, premised on the principle of party competence. It cannot be presumed that professionals care about children more or better than parents themselves. Nor is there any reason to presume that the implementation of Article 12 in respect of divorce or separation requires there to be a professional involved rather than a parent or parents in non-contested or out-of-court decision-making. There is something of a paradox in advocates of children's rights presuming the competence of children (that children will behave sensibly and reliably in participating in the making of serious decisions affecting them) and yet at the same time denying such a presumption of competence in relation to the parents of those children.

Furthermore, even where there may be an acknowledged conflict of interest between a child and parent(s), it is arguable that the interests of children are necessarily safeguarded by their separate legal representation by social workers in adversarial legal proceedings.[2] Those who argued for a new expanded role for *guardians-ad-litem* in private law proceedings sought to deny the fundamental difference between private and public law proceedings involving children (Timms, 1995). Unlike child protection public law cases, parental competence is not, by definition, legally challenged in private law proceedings. It has long been recognized that the costs of such professional intervention are great in the risks entailed of undermining family autonomy, stability, privacy and competence with concomitant increased conflict and serious effects on children (Freeman, 1983). The parental role in child-rearing needed reinforcing and strengthening, not undermining and weakening (Freeman, 1983).

The Adoption and Children Act 2002, implemented in 2005, has now made provision for the representation of children in private law cases. Children may be made parties and be represented by both a solicitor and a children's *guardian-ad-litem*. The President's Direction (2004) 1FLR 1188 contains guidance on the circumstances in which the court may consider making children parties under Rule 9.5 of the Family Proceedings Rules 1991.[3]

Developments from 2000

Policy and professional issues

The increasing political focus on the rights to citizenship of children (UN Convention on the Rights of the Child and the European Convention of the Rights of the Child) has strengthened the presumption – in a number of areas such as law, public policy and professional practice generally – in favour of involving children in decisions on a range of matters that affect them directly.

---

2   Guggenheim (2005) controversially challenges accepted views that govern the legal process and legitimate decision-making in children's cases in terms of securing their rights and promoting their best interests. In particular, he argues that the prevailing belief, that giving children legal rights actually improves their lives, cannot be substantiated by empirical evidence. It may, he argues, have made things worse, for example, by imposing a responsibility on children for their actions, which, at their age, they should not be required to bear. He argues that the invocation of legal rights in children's cases – claimed to protect them, to promote their welfare and their autonomy – operates, ultimately, to serve the interests of adults and does little to improve children's lives.

3   The National Youth Advisory Service (NYAS) is a charity that represents children in family proceedings under rule 9.5 of the Family Proceedings Rules 1991. In 2006, NYAS agreed a protocol with CAFCASS clarifying when each would act in particular cases where children are made parties in private law proceedings. NYAS usually deals with cases involving intractable contact disputes.

The repercussions of these developments have influenced debates in the field of family mediation practice in respect of these policy questions:

- Whether separating/divorcing parents can be trusted to make decisions in the best interests of their children? The issue is not whether or not children should be consulted in the decisions that affect them, but what is the role of professionals in the consultation process. There is a view that agreement *per se* between parents may not be beneficial for children who, therefore, require to be separately represented in private law cases. On the other hand, it is argued that there is no reason to presume that in respect of the implementation of Article 12 (of the UN Convention on the Rights of the Child) in relation to divorce and separation issues in non-contested or out-of-court decision-making, a professional is required to be involved, rather than the parents themselves. The difficult question, in each unique, delicate and complex family situation, is how best to strike a balance between the rights and obligations both within families, and between families and professionals.

- What other services should be available for children going through separation and divorce? Mediation services should not be expected to be responsible for meeting a lack of provision of other, more appropriate services for children (such a counselling, therapy or guidance) nor be criticized for failing to fulfil objectives that are not its business to fulfil.

- What do children themselves think about what they need and want? A number of recent research studies have interviewed children, including those that have shed valuable light on children's own views – about their involvement in family proceedings and mediation; about parental separation and family change; and about everyday family decision-making (see for example, O'Quigley, 1999; Wade and Smart, 2002; Butler et al., 2005).

Policy on children and young people of the UK College of Family Mediators

This policy and it practice guidelines (*Children, Young People and Family Mediation: Policy and Practice Guidelines*, 2002) was the product of an extensive consultation process amongst family mediators representing all the sectors of provision and professional backgrounds. It culminated in two achievements: first, consensus on a highly controversial subject – the consultation of children in family mediation – that was characterized by a powerful polarization of views influenced by the profession of origin of the practitioner; and second, the realization of the requirements of best practice, reflecting too, the core principles of a discrete and distinctive intervention.

The policy upholds six principles, set out below:

- The policy positively encourages parents (and other participants) in mediation to talk to and listen to their children.
- There is a central focus on understanding and taking account of children's perspectives so that the decisions parents make are informed by their children's views.
- The parents are the decision-makers.
- Central importance is attached to the parents themselves, rather than any professional, informing and consulting their children (in line with the code for mediators set out in the Family Law Act 1996)[4].
- The policy encourages family mediators to be imaginative and flexible in considering the variety of ways children can be consulted or involved.
- This consultation includes the option of direct consultation between the mediator and the child.

Three main features distinguish the UK College policy and practice guidelines:

- These embody an acknowledgement of the worth and significance of children. In recommending that they be talked to, and listened to, they are accorded their dignity. The adults too, their authority for decision-making recognized, are accorded their share of dignity and respect.
- The policy recognizes, implicitly, that this acknowledgment is part and parcel of the aim of seeking to alleviate and minimize the distress for children arising from the break-up of their parents' relationship.
- The policy identifies the distinctive, flexible and precise ways in which it could be appropriate for family mediators to incorporate children, directly and indirectly, in the process.

---

4   The Family Law Act 1996 (Part 2, section 27 (8)) *required* mediators, where there were one or more children of the family, to have arrangements designed to ensure that *the parties* would be encouraged to consider; (a) the welfare, wishes and feelings of each child; and (b) whether and to what extent each child would be given the opportunity to express his or her wishes and feelings in the mediation (emphasis added).

The 'child inclusive' approach to family mediation practice

This refers to a specific practice approach and model, piloted in two sites in Australia (Darwin and Melbourne), that aimed to embrace children's concerns and interests in all aspects of overall practice, whether counselling or mediation (Commonwealth Department of Family and Community Services Report 2002; McIntosh, 2000). Recommended as a 'good practice' rather than a 'best practice' approach, it could consequently be realized in different models of practice. Concerns were raised that 'child inclusive' practice might be understood to mean that *all* children would be seen in *all* cases, an assumption explicitly refuted by the consultants to the pilot scheme (Commonwealth Department of Family and Community Services Report 2002). Rather, what was envisaged was that throughout the process of mediating with parents, both the parenting role and the needs of the children would be supported. It was recognized that children's needs could be considered in a variety of ways – direct child consultation being one critical option, as well as other, indirect ways, such as working with parents, in group programmes, or with families (in family therapy).

Findings highlighted the vital resource, expertise, training and infrastructure implications entailed in the two pilots. An extra six to eight hours of worker time per case were needed to be funded, and staff trained for direct consultation already had graduate training in psychology and social work and prior therapeutic work experience with children. Supervision was conducted by a clinical child psychologist.

It is noteworthy that the 'child inclusive' approach and that of the UK College of Family Mediators are entirely consonant – in terms of objectives, definitions, terminology, principles, guidelines, the delineation of the basic stages of the process of direct consultation of children, and in terms of concerns both for safeguards and for clarity of limits and boundaries (UK College of Family Mediators' policy and guidelines on children and young persons 2002; see also Astor and Chinkin, 2002).

Mediation and children: Developing applications of practice

International child abduction and mediation

International child abduction may not appear obviously to be suitable for mediation – the high levels of conflict, cultural differences that exacerbate misunderstanding, different languages, and the involvement of different legal systems, are all complicating factors. Notwithstanding such unpromising circumstances, *reunite*, informed by years of experience, recognized early on the potential for mediation, recently pioneering a model of mediation uniquely adapted to the specific legal and practical conditions of international child abduction.

In 1990, the Parliamentary Working Party on Child Abduction was set up in response to the rising numbers of children being abducted by their parents and taken abroad without the consent of the children and of the other parent. Administered by *reunite*, the National Council for Abducted Children, the All Party Group of MPs on Child Abduction and the specialist subgroups (prevention and mediation; law; Scotland; and diplomacy) published a Report entitled *Home and Away: Child Abduction in the Nineties* (PWPCA, 1993). Prior to the report, little information about child abduction had been available.

One of the recommendations of the prevention and mediation subgroup was that mediation could have a role to play at different stages in the developing dispute that escalates into an abduction. In particular, it recommended a pilot study to test the demand for and feasibility of mediation projects along the lines of the successful US Child Find Project. This free telephone mediation scheme was set up with two clearly-defined goals: the return of the child to the pre-abduction position; and the parties' agreement on a forum in which to resolve their differences. One unexpected finding was the preventive value of the project. A large number of parents *contemplating* abduction contacted the mediators even though the scheme was not aimed at them.

More recently, the potential for mediation has been recognized in the context of the kind of abductions now taking place – many typical cases (60 to 70 per cent of Hague Convention cases) involve abduction by the child's primary carer, usually their mother. In these cases, although a speedy return would be inevitable, often there are other relevant issues that have to be considered. In many cases, for example, the left-behind parent might want secure contact arrangements rather than primary care or the permanent return of the child, yet an application under the Hague Convention for the pre-emptory return of the child might appear to be the only option available and the only way to secure contact with the child. There exist, therefore, strong incentives for mutually agreed outcomes that could limit damage, delay and expense; avoid disruptive physical relocations; and reduce continuing conflict and trauma, especially for children. For the abducting parent, too, their unilateral, non-consensual act of abduction could be re-characterized as an agreed relocation (*reunite* Report, 2006).

With funding from the Nuffield Foundation, *reunite* developed a mediation pilot scheme for use in such cases, publishing its final report in

2006.[5] The project set out to determine whether mediation could provide a realistic, practical alternative to the court process in cases of international child abduction. The main objectives of the project were, therefore, threefold:

- to establish how mediation could work in legal conformity with the principles of the Hague Convention;
- to develop a mediation structure that would fit in practically with the procedural structure of an English Hague Convention case;
- to test whether such a model would be effective.

One important feature built into the pilot mediation scheme was that it had to be complementary to a court application for a return under the Hague Convention 1980. Mediation was embarked on only once an application for a return had been issued and there had been an initial hearing by the court. This integration into the court's return proceeding was considered to be essential for the effectiveness of the scheme. The design of the scheme also ensured that participation in mediation could not be construed as acquiescence (Re: H (Abduction: Acquiescence) Re: HL [1997] 872 1 FLR).

The main findings of the scheme, extremely positive overall both about the mediation process and the effectiveness of the mediation model, include the following:

- that it is crucial that mediators undertaking this work have expertise in the field of international child abduction and the 1980 Hague Convention, although it is not necessary to have a specialist family law background;
- that the quality and professional skill of the mediator are key requirements for effective practice;
- that these cases should always be co-mediated and that, from the parents' perspectives, it is the expertise of the mediators that matters rather than their gender;
- that pre-mediation screening for suitability for mediation is crucial.

Adoption and mediation

An innovative mediation service, initiated to address the complex and controversial area of contact in the adoption of older children with histories of neglect or abuse, was set up by the Post Adoption Centre (1995, p. 3):

---

5   *Mediation in International Parental Child Abduction: The reunite Mediation Pilot Scheme* 2006. A total of 28 mediation cases progressed to completion with a Memorandum of Understanding reached in 75 per cent of all cases mediated.

Mediation seeks to return decision-making processes back to the people at the centre of adoption, whilst taking very careful account of child protection issues. Mediation is a process that can potentially promote a broader view of the concept of parenting in adoption by emphasising the mutuality of the relationship between the relinquishing parent and adoptive parent. Both are parents supported in co-operating directly, and there is a move away from having their relationship fragmented and defined by the intervention of outside agencies.

Mediation can involve birth parents and social services departments over care plans (once plans to rehabilitate the child with birth parents have been abandoned). Birth parents, engaged in the preparation of the care plan, are less likely to contest the adoption order later on.

Deploying mediation with the goal of replacing conflict with agreement in the context of the negotiation of contact arrangements between prospective adopters and birth parents, can involve a number of parties, including birth mothers, fathers and grandparents in the process of losing, or who have lost, a child to adoption, carers, adoptive parents or professionals. All aspects of contact between adopted children and their relatives can be negotiated – letterbox arrangements, re-opening of contact with older children, support during contact visits, and consultation with children about their wishes, both before and after adoption.

A number of difficult and important concerns have to be addressed in these situations. For example, what issues are or are not negotiable must be clarified at the outset. Intrinsic power inequalities (the birth parent starts off from a disadvantageous position vis-à-vis the adoptive parent whose position is endorsed by the law) must be recognized and offset. Child safety parameters must be established, and reviewed in the light of changing circumstances.

While the Post Adoption Centre originally developed mediation as a way of facilitating post-adoption contact, what has emerged is the need for such a service at a much earlier point in the adoption process particularly at the court stage. With increasing numbers of referrals, practice findings have provided a valuable fund of learning in this pioneering field and an independent mediation service has proved to be effective in the difficult and conflict-ridden area of adoption practice.

Child protection and mediation

Several pressures influenced the development in the UK of a pioneering project piloting mediation in the context of public law child protection cases. North American studies (for example, Mayer, 1989) had testified to the advantages of mediation as an alternative to litigation and adjudication in public law cases. Mediatory approaches had begun to operate in Review and Complaints proceedings under the Children Act 1989 (s.26). King and Trowell (1992) had used case histories to point out the deleterious effects for the children (in many cases) of using the legal system as the only or the main forum for protecting children and promoting their welfare.

In a unique collaboration in the 1990s, National Family Mediation and the Tavistock Clinic, bringing together their separate areas of expertise, set up a joint and independent project, funded by the Department of Health, aimed at identifying the knowledge and skills applicable for Alternative Dispute Resolution (ADR) in child protection and child welfare cases within public law, applying these to a pilot case study and preparing a specialist training module.

One of the first tasks facing the interdisciplinary team in exploring the application of ADR to public law child cases, was to reach a common understanding on how the respective contributions that each brought to the task, could best be utilized in a new, then untried (in the UK) intervention. This involved identifying a preferred practice approach; exploring, clarifying and reconciling a new and different application of complementary knowledge and skills; as well as defining the task itself precisely. A new term for the intervention was agreed – 'specialist child care mediation' – which resolved the hitherto undecided question of what to call the combination of skills of two different professions in their application of ADR to this new field of practice. This clarification was also of benefit to referrers and families for whom 'ADR' was an unfamiliar term (National Family Mediation and the Tavistock Clinic, 1998).

The experience of the project was positive despite the low level of referrals from social workers and the late stage at which many cases were referred (National Family Mediation and the Tavistock Clinic, 1998). It was possible, in several cases, to reduce hostility, increase understanding and improve communication. Recommendations in the Final Report highlighted the suitability of specialist child care mediation for complex cases involving a range of severe and entrenched conflicts, legal issues, and fears about the safety of individuals, in a wide range of child care cases. Early referral was likely to offer the greatest chance of successful resolution and co-mediation was considered necessary for effective practice, the task requiring a combination of complementary knowledge, experience and skills (National Family Mediation and the Tavistock Clinic, 1998).

While it was not possible to obtain further funding to build on the work of the pilot, or implement its specialist training module, many family mediation services do receive referrals from social workers and some mediation in the child protection field is taking place throughout the UK.

Young people and homelessness mediation

Alone in London was one of the first organizations to set up a mediation service to assist young people (under 26 years), alienated from their families, to re-establish communication and resolve disputes with their families. With family breakdown a major cause of youth homelessness, the Family Mediating Service aimed both to prevent a young person running away or being ejected from their home, as well as to re-establish positive contact (where this was safe and appropriate) with family members where there was already homelessness or a young person was in care. *Alone in London* has expanded its prevention work, developing partnerships with schools to create greater awareness amongst young people about family issues and homelessness and has set up advice and training programmes in mediation in this context.

Many local authorities have now introduced mediation schemes, often contracted out to local not-for-profit community or family mediation services, to address the linked problems of broken family relationships and homelessness for young people.[6] Current legislation places a duty on local authorities to provide temporary accommodation for young people in priority need (while their case is assessed) – 16 to 17 year olds being automatically in priority need for housing purposes unless they are 'intentionally' homeless. Introducing mediation at an early stage of the homelessness application has been found to be effective in reducing the number of homelessness applications as well as the number of young people in temporary accommodation, both targets of local authorities. However, the Court of Appeal has criticized a local authority for using the attempt at mediation to justify delaying their decision in order to avoid their housing responsibilities (*Robinson* v. *Hammersmith and Fulham London Borough Council* [2006] 1 WLR 3295).

> It goes without saying that mediation is an enormously valuable tool in the resolution of problems of homelessness. However, the process of mediation is not to be confused with the duty of a local housing authority under section 184 of the Act to make inquiries as to what (if any) duty it owes to an applicant under Part 7 of the Act. In my judgement, the process of mediation is wholly independent of the section 184 enquiry process. (Lord Justice Parker, 42)

---

6   The Homelessness Code of Guidance (section 12.7) issued by the Department for Communities and Local Government on 24 July, 2006, states that 'generally it will be in the best interests of 16 and 17 year olds to live in the family home, unless it would be unsafe or unsuitable'. The Code encourages mediation to promote this aim.

As this case illustrates, mediation can be deployed to serve the interests of local authorities rather than the best interests of a young person. Other concerns about mediation in respect of homelessness have been highlighted – mediation may not be suitable in all circumstances (for example, where violence or abuse is reported); funding of mediation providers by local authorities can compromise their independence and neutrality; confidentiality may be jeopardized where information in reports by mediators on outcomes can be used by local authorities to assess whether or not homelessness in such cases is 'intentional' (Advice Services Alliance, 2006).

11 Fairness

Perhaps that is what love is – the momentary or prolonged refusal to think of another person in terms of power. (Rose, 1985, p. 16)

The very advantages of mediation over the adversarial legal system also create potential risks (Folberg and Taylor, 1984). Mediation is held in private. No legal representatives are usually present (certainly not in out-of-court agencies). Procedures are informal and flexible. The safeguards of due process do not apply. There is always a danger that the more powerful interests will prevail over the weaker ones. Therefore, fairness is a matter of central importance in mediation. The parties must feel that they have been treated fairly and that any agreement they reach is fair, or as fair as is practicable in all the circumstances, not only to them, but to their children and whoever else is affected by their arrangements. Given that, in mediation, the issue of party authority for decision-making is so central and delicate, it is also only in the independence of mediation from other forms of intervention that the essential ethical and professional principles that fully safeguard the interests of a fair process can be realized (see Chapter 2). In addition, a range of safeguards are necessary – procedural, structural and professional.

Justice and the law: Fairness and mediation

An important dimension of the political critique of mediation revolves around the debate about justice and fairness in mediation. This debate is complicated further in its application to international mediation where understandings about power, its distribution and dynamic, take complex and contradictory forms when applied to mediation.

A core aspiration of mediation, already discussed, manifests itself in the responsibility of the mediator to treat each person with respect, in particular with respect for that person's own meanings and for his or her capacity to decide and make choices, through critical reflection and the awareness of alternatives. Mediators themselves consider that this principle of respect interlocks not only with other principles of mediation (such as impartiality and the autonomy of the parties), but also with other central aspects of practice, in particular, the quality of outcome, its fairness or justness (Roberts, 2007).[1]

While justice and fairness may sometimes be conflated in ethical discussions about mediation, their differences are explored below.

Justice

Justice is symbolized in western cultures by a blind goddess holding the sword of state power in one hand and, in the other, balancing the scales of justice exactly. This symbol of justice embodies three principles:

- justice is bestowed by a third party – an official state-sanctioned judicial authority;
- that third party must be strictly impartial;
- impartiality is achieved by means of the application of consistent rules to each case.

Access to justice has traditionally meant equal, adequate and ready access to legal services and the courts. Access to justice, since alternative dispute resolution (ADR) processes are now available, also includes access to choice in relation to the dispute resolution process most appropriate to the type of case (Labour Party Report, 1995; European Mediation Directive, 2008).

Strictly speaking, justice – understood as impartial, rule-determined, consistent, third-party decision-making – is not applicable to mediation, where authority for decision-making lies with the parties themselves. Justice involves a finding. For example, in relation to marital breakdown, it has traditionally been taken to mean the accurate allocation of blameworthiness.

---

1   Shah-Kazemi (2000, p. 305) affirms this core aspiration of mediation with an emphasis on the essential significance of the cultural and normative context that shapes the mediation process:

The mediation process is predicated on achieving an initial consensus, which will ultimately succeed because of the mutual respect between not just the parties themselves, but also between each party and the mediator. This respect entails, at its most fundamental level, the acknowledgment of the universal human capacity to act with dignity in the pursuit of fairness, at the same time as being understandably orientated towards what is in their [and their dependents'] best interests. This respect can only be authentic when the cultural and ethical norms upon which it is based can be shared by both the mediator and the parties.

Fairness

In mediation, on the other hand, fairness is determined by the parties themselves, and involves personal norms (including ethical and psychological aspects) as well as legal norms. Fairness in mediation embraces the necessity for a fair process, fair procedures and structural fairness, as well as a fair outcome – although not all may be significant in each case (Menkel-Meadow et al., 2005; see Chapter 7 on the requirements for structural fairness).

One of the advantages of mediation is its procedural flexibility, which provides the opportunity for powerful concerns about fault and fairness to be addressed. This frequently necessitates consideration of the particular historical context of the dispute. Fairness, when it is equated with formal equality, excludes this context by discounting concerns about the past or disallowing their expression. For fairness to operate in mediation, this context may well be relevant.

The future as well as the past is relevant for considering fairness. Fairness in relation to outcomes refers to the principles that underlie the negotiated agreement – principles of equity, of equality and of need – as well as to the extent to which parties actually consider the outcome (which usually involves some allocation of benefits and burdens) to be fair thereafter (Menkel-Meadow et al., 2005). When do the parties determine fairness – at the time the outcome is reached, or subsequently? The settlement of the family arrangements is, as noted earlier (see Chapter 4), not a 'closed episode' but part of 'the flow of time' (Falk Moore, 1995, p. 31). It must be remembered both that the intervention of the mediator within this dimension of time is limited and modest, and that the value and effectiveness of mediation lies as much in an improved understanding and improved capacity to negotiate together in the future, as it does in the reaching of specific agreements.

A family systems approach and fairness

For mediation to have value, it must be fair to *all* those concerned – parties, participants and non-participants. Respect for the interests and objectives of each party and for those affected by any agreement, notably children, is not easily reconciled with the family systems approach that analyses the family in terms of functional needs and services. It is an approach that, in claiming to be value free, can imply, at the same time, that all family members are responsible for the ills of the family (Grillo, 1991). Advocates of the family systems approach to mediation have this to say about fairness.

> 'Fairness' is another of those unfortunate concepts that appears so obviously to be a 'good thing' that seldom is its appropriateness in a particular context questioned. At the risk therefore of appearing to support unfairness we nevertheless wish to question this notion … [Fairness] represents a (perhaps legalistic?) distortion of the way in which relationships actually work … [R]elationships are not fair or unfair, they are what they are. (Howard and Shepherd, 1987, p. 17)

Such an approach confuses what *is* with what *ought to be*, which is precisely what 'fairness' reminds us about. It ignores the ethical implications of situations in which the interests and rights of individual family members may be in direct conflict or where there are significant disparities of power between the parties. Systemic levelling, through the application of techniques such as positive connotation, often 'flies in the face of common conceptions of justice' (Walrond-Skinner, 1987, p. 3). As some systems thinkers have themselves described it, 'the positive connotation [as an intervention technique] is not related to truthfulness, but to the strategy of being therapeutic' (Campbell et al., 1989, p. 46).

Reframing techniques can elevate reinterpretation over action for change. Such techniques are designed to challenge the parties' different values and can not only devalue what the parties regard as significant, but also collude with and perpetuate unfairness by denying relevance to objective circumstances such as the political, economic, social or gender factors of a dispute. One of the mediator's primary ethical responsibilities is to ensure that where these factors (or others) significantly affect the respective balance of power between the parties, this imbalance is recognized explicitly and duress prevented – if necessary, by ceasing mediation.

Bargaining power

There is no precise definition of bargaining power. This is because there is no simple construction of the issue of power inequality, just as there is no single truth about relationships (Lukes, 1974). There is, rather, as Seidenberg (1973, p. 97) views it, a 'repertory of truths'.[2] The richness and irreducibility of personal relationships is exemplified too in Rose's view of marriage as a shared imaginative construct, a 'subjectivist fiction', as well as the primary political experience of those adults involved:

---

2   See also Updike (1965, p. 120):

Perhaps they were both right. All misconceptions are themselves data which have the minimal truth of existing in at least one mind: Truth, my work has taught me, is not something static, a mountain top that statements approximate like successive assaults of frostbitten climbers. Rather, truth is constantly being formed from the solidification of illusions.

Whatever the balance, every marriage is based upon some understanding, articulated or not, about the relative importance, the priority of desires, between its two partners. Marriages go bad not when love fades – love can modulate into affection without driving two people apart – but when this understanding about the balance of power breaks down, when the weaker member feels exploited or the stronger feels unrewarded for his or her strength. (Rose, 1985, p. 15)

Unhappiness in marriage may occur therefore when 'two versions of reality rather than two people [are] in conflict' (Rose, 1985, p. 15). This realm of personal power relations is for the most part inaccessible to outsiders, and may also be, if not unperceived by the parties themselves, unacknowledged by them.

The picture is further complicated, as Gilligan (1982) suggests, by the different perspectives that women and men can bring to relationships and to moral problems. Speaking different languages yet employing a common moral vocabulary, they are likely to mistranslate and misunderstand one another, thereby limiting the possibilities for co-operation (see also Menkel-Meadow, 1985b; Tannen, 1990, 1998). It is argued that women, for example, will tend to associate power with the capacity and strength to nurture, while for men, power is associated with assertion and aggression. Other feminists (for example, Williams, 1989) criticize what they view as gender-constructed dichotomies, denying such differences exist, or arguing that differences result from socialization, rather than innate and therefore inevitable differences between the sexes. Any examination of bargaining power needs, nevertheless, to take into account the tension between the complementary ethics that might motivate individual women and men – an ethic of care and responsibility, and an ethic of rights and self-advancement respectively.

A consideration of what factors make up any assessment of bargaining power must include the following:

- financial and material circumstances;
- the legal 'endowments' – for example, legal rulings in relation to children and property (Mnookin, 1984);
- emotional and social vulnerability;
- de facto care and control of the children;
- the presence of new partners;
- readiness and ability to negotiate;
- personal attributes;
- access to legal and other advice and support, including access to Legal Aid;
- the family history (violence as a feature of family life, for example).

Furthermore, the perceptions of each party of their predicament must be taken into account. It is not uncommon for each party to feel they are the more vulnerable and to see their former partner as all powerful, whatever the objective circumstances. Bargaining power therefore involves a complex and subtle interplay of forces, objective and subjective, perceived or otherwise. Nor are situations static. The decision to separate can bring about a radical shift in the balance of power, psychologically, and in relation to the children. Yet rarely are the disadvantages or advantages stacked all one way, nor should it be assumed either that, where one party has superior 'endowments' of one sort or another, that power will necessarily be used, let alone exploited.

Feminist fears about mediation

Early fears about mediation damaging women's interests were resurrected when the Family Law Bill 1996 made its way through Parliament (Roberts, 1996). Feminist lawyers (for example, Bottomley, 1984, 1985) first voiced these theoretical concerns in the UK in the 1980s. Mediation, it was argued, was disadvantageous to women because:

- Individual women faced their former partners as unequals.
- Women faced a mediator whose dominant social values, it was claimed, were oppressive to women. The focus on children was seen as a denial of rights for women as distinct from their children and their mothering role. Furthermore, the presumptions of many mediators in favour of access and joint custody (the terms then in use) served, it was claimed, to perpetuate the dominant role of the father in the reconstructed family.
- Women as a group suffered fundamental power inequalities in the family and these were ignored. Mediation 'privatized' family disputes which were therefore concealed instead of emerging in the 'public sphere of formal justice' (Bottomley, 1985, p. 180). Consensus masked and therefore perpetuated the conflict that characterized the power inequalities of relationships within the family.

Similar fears were raised again in the 1990s:

They (women) are more likely in this situation to be inarticulate and ill-informed about their rights, more likely to be timid, suffering from depression and possibly in fear of their husbands. Women mediators, it is said (and most of them are women) are more likely to side with the husband's account of affairs than the wife's. The husband is more likely to be able to afford legal advice in the background, to have some experience of negotiation and to know his rights. Most seriously of all, it is not the job of the mediator, who may have no legal training at all, to inform the couple of their rights under the law. (Deech, 1995, p. 12)

These views formed part of a feminist critique of mediation underpinned by two assumptions: first, that women do not know what they want and cannot speak for themselves and, second, that where women do make certain demands – for example, for co-operation with their former partners, for maintenance, or for increased contact for their children with their fathers – these are mistaken, reactionary or contradictory. While these assumptions have been unsubstantiated by empirical evidence, they did raise important concerns about the problems of bias, fairness and power in mediation that mediators have had to recognize, and have indeed addressed in their writing, training and practice over many years (for research findings on the subject, see below). It is ironic too, that these assertions have been made in the absence of empirical studies assessing the fairness and impact of adversarial processes on women, including those with a history of domestic abuse (Kelly, 2004).

One of the difficulties with this critique of mediation has been its oversimplification of issues that are, in fact, complex, multifaceted and interdependent. One also needs to bear in mind the complex and highly problematic nature of the circumstances that characterize the divorce process and the complexity and interrelated nature of the disputes that frequently attend divorce and separation. Usually there is no one cause of difficulty, but numerous obstacles and sources of tension. In addition, it is necessary to recognize and acknowledge the uncertainty, the ambivalence, the inconsistency and the ignorance that often characterize situations, as well as perceptions, at times of conflict and change. Disputes also concern many interconnected issues, which are themselves affected by multiple variables and attributes.

Mediation as an alternative to other dispute resolution processes

While it has been important to raise questions about fairness in mediation, the same questions also arise in connection with all methods of dispute resolution – whether private negotiations, solicitor negotiations, door-of-the-court settlements by barristers, or adjudication: 'No dispute resolution mechanism is devoid of problems concerning fair outcomes, and none of the alternatives is best for every dispute' (Folberg and Taylor, 1984, p. 247). Private negotiations between parties lack the checks of due process or third-party presence. Such negotiations may be coerced by the expense and uncertainty of litigation (Wishik, 1984). Many family disputes following matrimonial breakdown are negotiated by lawyers with only a minority reaching the stage of adjudication. But neither bilateral lawyer negotiations nor adjudication avoids the problems of power differentials. If anything, new inequalities may be created – for example, of unequal resources, professional competence of a lawyer or idiosyncratic judgments. Guilt and the extent of the non-mutuality of the decision to divorce are important determinants of both the dispute and its processing (Ingleby, 1992; Mather et al., 1995; Chin-A-Fat and Steketee, 2001). Guilt – and this is an issue unrelated to gender – is a prime cause of unwillingness to claim legal entitlements (Mather et al., 1995).

North American research shows that 'in divorce, lawyers and clients negotiate power but they do so on uneven terms' (Felstiner and Sarat, 1992, p. 1497). Divorcing clients are typically the weaker parties, their situations characterized by personal crisis, vulnerability and inadequate resources, with critical issues in their lives at stake. Other North American studies into divorce negotiations between lawyers reveal imbalances of power as far as the clients' interests are concerned (Menkel-Meadow, 1993a: see also Chapter 3).

It is acknowledged that court intervention is likely to be most appropriate 'in a setting where conflict occurs among unequal strangers, when a court can, at least in theory, rectify an imbalance by extending the formalities of equal protection to weaker parties' (Auerbach, 1983, p. 120). Research also exposes the fact that this ideal of equal justice is incompatible with the social and economic realities of unequal wealth, power and opportunity: '... The austere neutrality of law is constantly eroded by the special protection that its form and substance provide to privileged members of society' (Auerbach, 1983, pp. 143–4).

Furthermore, the law is acknowledged to be patriarchal in its assumptions and the legal profession male-dominated (Smart, 1984). Lord Woolf's general indictment (Woolf, 1995) of a civil justice system where exploitation of the weaker party by the stronger party is endemic, is just as applicable in family proceedings where imbalances in gender power are unlikely to be considered, let alone pointed out by predominantly male lawyers to women clients. In fact, the experience of legal proceedings of many people (men and women) is of being caught up in a process over which they have no control. People experience their disputes as being taken over and transformed by legal professionals, leaving them feeling impotent and irrelevant (Christie, 1977; Auerbach, 1983; Davis and Roberts, 1988). Ingleby (1994) speculates that the conflict between what the client wants and what the client is entitled to, might account for these feelings of alienation and loss of control.

Disparity of bargaining power is not, of itself, a ground for the court setting aside a private agreement, if there has been no unfair exploitation of superior bargaining strength and both parties have had the benefit of professional advice (*Edgar* v. *Edgar* 1980). The parties are not required to be represented in matrimonial proceedings, nor is the respondent required to attend the Children's Appointment. Any bias shown to women in relation to decisions over children gives priority to them, it is argued, not as women, but as mothers (Smart, 1984).[3]

Research evidence

The field of alternative dispute resolution, and of mediation in particular, has been the subject of research to an unusually large extent since the early 1980s. In the field of family mediation, early research, conducted in the United States, Canada, England and Australia 'constitutes the largest body of empirical research among any of the mediation sectors' (Kelly, 2004, p. 3). At the same time, it is acknowledged that a number of methodological and other research difficulties (for example, variations in research populations, measures, and dispute settings) have made generalized findings, or reliance on a single study, problematic (Kelly, 2004). Despite these problems, over two decades of research, convergence has emerged on many questions indicating that some of the major findings on family mediation are 'robust and replicable across settings' (Kelly, 2004, p. 4).

On the controversial subject of gender disadvantage, there is no empirical evidence in the UK or elsewhere, to substantiate allegations that women are disadvantaged by mediation. On the contrary, there is a growing body of research showing high levels of satisfaction among women in relation both to the process and outcomes of mediation. The main research studies that attempt a gender analysis of their findings are set out below.

Initial findings of consumer research in the UK suggested that:

- Fairness mattered very much to both parties.
- Women did not regard themselves as disadvantaged by mediation. In fact, some felt 'empowered' by their experience of the process. Women in particular regarded the agreements they reached as fair.
- Social and economic aspects of the dispute were not ignored in mediation. On the contrary, women themselves exposed these topics for discussion. They demanded express acknowledgement of their predicament from their former partners.

---

3   In the UK there is no legal presumption that young children should reside with their mother, although, in practice, if the father is in full-time work, it is more likely that young children will stay with their mother, whether or not she works. As a general rule, the courts do not alter the status quo relating to the residence of the children unless there is a very good reason to do so (Walsh, 2006).

- The explicit focus on children's needs by the mediator (reflecting as well the values of the court in disputes involving children) was positively welcomed by the majority of the couples (both men and women), according as it did with their own priorities (Davis and Roberts, 1988).

In the UK, the bulk of the evidence offers no support for feminist fears (David and Roberts, 1988; Walker et al., 1994; McCarthy and Walker, 1996b).[4] This has been confirmed more recently in an extensive review of the empirical literature surrounding the practice of mediation; Conneely (2002, p. 255) concludes that, while the feminist critique of mediation 'represents the most sustained attack on the practice since its recent rise to prominence in Western dispute resolution', this is not supported by empirical evidence. Research shows, instead, that women do not perceive themselves to be disadvantaged in mediation and are commonly satisfied with their experience. Furthermore, there is no evidence of financial disadvantage for women who choose mediation over lawyer negotiation or adversarial settlement (Conneely, 2002).

In their Californian study, Kelly and Duryee (1992) found few differences of significance between men and women in their perceptions of the mediator, the process and the outcome. Where there were differences, they found that women rated the mediation experience more favourably than men because they benefited both from the opportunity the process provided to express their views and be heard, and from the increased confidence to stand up for themselves in relation to their ex-spouses. They also benefited from the opportunity mediation provided to put their anger aside and focus on the children.

The major Australian Research Report (Bordow and Gibson, 1994) also dispels several myths about mediation, finding in summary that 'separated couples come to mediation with the hope of reaching a fair and mutually satisfactory agreement and most did just that' (Bordow and Gibson, 1994, p. 11). More specifically, the research data does not support the notion that women feel disadvantaged in the mediation process. On the contrary,

---

4   A small, recent study in the UK, focusing on five women's experience of all-issues mediation subsequent to two significant changes in the law – the introduction of pension sharing and the decision in *White* v. *White* [2000] 2FLR 981 (see Chapter 3) – has concluded that there are circumstances when women can be disadvantaged in mediation (Tilley, 2007). Differences of negotiating style, feelings of guilt, concern for a former partner and a desire to put the children's interests first, mean that women do not necessarily consider their own interests in the negotiation, compared to men who can be more concerned about legal and financial issues (Tilley, 2007). The study concludes that awareness of these gender differences should alert mediators to the need to intervene where women are acting to their own detriment, particularly in the context of mediating all issues (Tilley, 2007).

women felt they had equal influence over the terms of their agreements and reported increased confidence in their ability to stand up for themselves and handle future disagreements with their ex-spouses.

This research finds that, in most respects, women's perceptions of the mediation process and outcomes (on all issues – financial, property and children) are as favourable as, and sometimes better than, those expressed by their partners. Where significant gender differences occurred, 'women felt more empowered by the mediation process and reported feeling more confident about their ability to stand up for themselves' (Bordow and Gibson, 1994, p. 144). The most positive finding was the high level of client satisfaction with all aspects of the mediation service and this was largely independent of whether or not agreement was reached. This confirms the earlier North American findings of Pearson and Thoennes (1989) and Emery et al. (1991), and is confirmed in the UK by the research of Walker et al. (1994). In particular, both men and women who mediated were satisfied that their rights were protected (Emery et al., 1991).[5] One 'astonishing' finding (Kelly, 2004, p. 29) has been that fathers who mediated remained more involved with their children one year *and* twelve years later, following divorce, compared with fathers who litigated (Emery, 1994; Emery et al., 2001).

The North American research of Maccoby and Mnookin (1992) and Pearson (1993) was unable to detect negative financial consequences for women in mediation. More specifically, there was no ground for the fear that, in mediation, fathers commonly persuade mothers to accept less financial support by using custody as a bargaining chip or that women bargain away important and needed property in order to gain custody and avoid excessive visitation.[6] The only difference Pearson found in relation to dispute resolution forum had to do with legal fees and respondent satisfaction with the agreement, both of which were more favourable for the mediation group. Agreements were perceived to be fair, even among those who objectively might be viewed as the 'losing party' (Pearson, 1993, p. 284).

Bohmer and Ray's (1994) comparative Georgia and New York study, designed to evaluate the relative benefits of mediation for women and children as compared to other methods of dispute resolution, also found that women who chose mediation did not lose out in terms of outcome. The

---

5   Emery (1994) has highlighted how, despite the clarity and consistency of these findings, they have nevertheless been misrepresented as indicating that mediation is 'bad' for women. The results, across a range of items, showed high average levels of satisfaction for mothers who mediated, mothers who litigated, and fathers who mediated. However, across these same items, fathers who litigated reported a notably lower level of satisfaction.

6   On the other hand, informants in the Australian Keys Young (1996) study expressed the view that, particularly when there was a history of abuse, mediation on property and mediation on child access/custody matters, need to be completely separate processes.

use of child support guidelines and the professional training of mediators were significant variables. Grillo's (1991) important North American work has highlighted several dangers for women in mediation (mandatory and voluntary) when essential safeguards are abandoned and context is insufficiently addressed. For example, *mandatory* mediation requires women and men to speak in a setting they have not chosen, and in some mediation practice, reference to 'the past' is disallowed. This can deny women the opportunity for the expression of fault and anger, therefore excluding powerful aspects of the historical context that makes up the dispute (see above). Grillo also warns of the dangers for either spouse, of a family systems approach to mediation where each takes on the burden of the other's irresponsibility and every family member becomes equally responsible for everything. Grillo (1991, p. 1550) states, 'Although this article cautions against mediation's dangers I should emphasise at this juncture that mediation is the work I most like to do.'

All these findings suggest that mediation does not have the detrimental effects for women that were feared (or hoped). As a process, mediation is not inherently good or bad for women's interests (Menkel-Meadow, 1985a). It is increasingly clear that what is crucial is that the necessary screening, structural and procedural safeguards are in place, and that the mediator practises with the necessary skill and competence.

The limits of mediation

It must be acknowledged that mediation should not be criticized for failing to remedy those ills which it cannot and never set out to solve in the first place (Felstiner and Williams, 1985). But social and economic inequalities (as well as deep-seated emotional problems) do, of course, exist and their impact on disputes must be recognized – for example, the division of labour in the family; limited job opportunities, especially for women; and unequal rates of pay. In the majority of cases, women with children – especially older women with dependent children, for whom remarriage is not easy – do suffer economic deprivation on divorce even if they have jobs (Eekelaar and McLean, 1986). But while inequalities exist and cannot easily be legislated or negotiated away, it is misleading to define these simply in terms of a battle between men and women (Smart, 1982). Solutions to economic disadvantage and other inequities lie outside mediation in reforms to tax, welfare, housing, child care and employment provision.

Fault and mediation

One of the advantages of mediation is the opportunity it affords for the expression of personal (that is, non-legal) norms of fairness. These may be of great importance to the parties in arriving at an agreement that they deem fair and therefore acceptable, although these norms may have no legal validity – for example, the relevance of emotional vulnerability, or the accommodation of individual ethical standards of fault and responsibility (Folberg and Taylor, 1984). Unfairness may have to be accepted as a fact of life by one party if the children's needs, especially their need of a home, are to be satisfied.

The intention of the Family Law Act 1996, unrealized, was to remove the need to establish irretrievable breakdown by means of any fault-based facts such as adultery or unreasonable behaviour. It has long been recognized that fault-based allegations create conflict, and that, in any event, the court is too blunt an instrument for allocating blameworthiness in this complex and sensitive area of family life. The White Paper (1995) on divorce reform, in arguing for the removal of fault as a legal construct, recognized, nonetheless, that fault remained a powerful issue in marriage breakdown, but that this was an issue that the couple *themselves* had to deal with. Mediation was seen as the proper forum for couples to address fault directly together:

> Such a process requires each party to accept that the marriage is over before proceeding to address the future of a life apart. In this way, *the couple* have to deal with issues of fault, acknowledge that the marriage has broken down irretrievably, and take responsibility for the consequences. (White Paper, 1995, para. 2.18; emphasis added)

Mediators are accustomed to seeing couples at a bitter time in the divorce and separation process. On occasion, one of the first decisions to be made is over whether or not the marriage or relationship is over. Feelings of injustice are often related to a belief that some moral obligation has been violated. The resolution of the issue then requires acknowledgement of these powerful feelings of fault or blame, of being wronged as a 'good' mother and wife, or as a 'good' father and husband; or in the aftermath of separation or divorce, acknowledgment of its almost inevitable inequitable impact on one or both parents' life, whether as struggling lone parent or as absentee one.

> It is as if there are certain magic words, varying from person to person, that when spoken sincerely by a spouse, are able to alleviate the other's sense of moral injustice. The moral aspect addressed in this way can serve as a catalyst in the negotiations of the issue. (Milne and Folberg, 1988, p. 52)

There is frequent disagreement over whether and why the relationship has ended. Whether the focus of mediation is on the making of future arrangements for children, or the resolution of financial and property matters, there is unlikely to be progress unless there is first an opportunity for the parties to address powerful ethical and emotional concerns about fault and fairness, even to apologize (see Whatling, 2004). These concerns may include grievances not only about past actions and responsibility for the breakdown, but also about the present and the future, such as responsibility for the economic and social inequities arising from the family breakdown. It is the common experience of mediators that what the parties want in these circumstances is not necessarily judgment by a third party on who is right and who is wrong, but rather the opportunity to have their views heard and acknowledged, not by the mediator but by their former partner.

Safeguarding a fair process

As a process of consensual, joint decision-making, mediation requires high practice standards and high standards of provision and delivery. This means:

- the proper selection, training, supervision and accreditation of mediators;
- quality assurance procedures (including quality control mechanisms, quality audit and quality assessment);
- an independent and neutral environment for the provision of mediation, free of stigma, coercion or confusion with other professional interventions;
- pre-mediation screening out of unsuitable cases (for example, domestic violence or other serious imbalances of power or incapacity);
- rigorous adherence to the principles of mediation (voluntariness of participation, in particular);
- equal access to full and accurate information necessary for informed decision-making (legal, tax, welfare rights, and so on);
- independent legal or other advice and review, where necessary.

Mediators also need constantly to bear in mind, and address in practice, the vital questions raised about their authority and power. These are:

- How can the authority of the mediator be exercised in ways that serve the essential objectives of the process and protect its fundamental characteristics and principles?

- When does the exercise of that authority cease to serve those objectives, becoming instead an abuse of power with the mediator exerting unacceptable pressures upon one or both of the parties who then act (or fail to act) in ways they would not otherwise have done?

These questions are part of a larger question – of how mediation can retain its independence, distinct both from the practice of therapy, counselling, and welfare interventions on the one hand, and from legal process on the other; distinct, in particular, from attempts to refurbish court process and adjudication. One of the chief tasks of training is to assist trainee mediators to distinguish mediation clearly from those forms of intervention that may appear, at first sight, to be similar, such as settlement-seeking by officers of the court (such as CAFCASS officers) and judges; conciliatory negotiations by lawyers including collaborative lawyering; interventions into family functioning by family therapists; welfare interventions of social workers; and the personal and interpersonal focus of counsellors and psychotherapists.

Given that mediation is, by its nature, a private and informal process, and that the issue of authority in mediation is so fundamental, it is argued here that it is only by its independence from these other forms of intervention that the essential professional and ethical principles that give mediation its unique value and that fully safeguard the interests of an efficacious and just process can be realized.

It is necessary to ensure that the safeguards to protect fairness in mediation are in place. There are several ways in which fairness may be safeguarded (though not necessarily guaranteed) in mediation.

The safeguard of voluntariness

The voluntariness of participation in mediation is one of mediation's four fundamental characteristics (see UK College of Family Mediators' Code of Practice, General Principles, section 4; and the European legal instrument on family mediation, Recommendation no R (98)1, 1998. Principle 11, both of which unequivocally uphold voluntary participation as an essential principle and safeguard for the safe practice of family mediation). Voluntariness can be a vital safeguard against pressurization or coercion or inappropriate referral (for example, in cases of violence or incapacity). For it to be effective, voluntariness needs to be an explicit tenet of mediation practice at the outset and throughout the process. The parties do usually know one another and so are in a position to make a choice as to whether or not they are prepared to attempt a mediated solution (for a detailed presentation of the arguments against mandation and for voluntary participation in mediation, see Roberts, 2006).

With the growing interest on the part of the courts in actively pursuing settlement as its primary object, it is not at all surprising that this may be associated with a growing pressure toward mandatory mediation,[7] in response to an overloaded family justice system having to deal with the increased number of litigants in person (because of the stringencies of legal aid) and many complex and difficult family conflicts.[8]

While it has been argued that court officials and mediators may have a common interest in shifting business, this should not be at the expense either of the defining principles that distinguish the different dispute resolution domains or of the clarity of the boundaries that distinguish them – of acute relevance particularly at the juncture where referrals to mediation are made by the court or the court welfare service and where these are likely to be experienced as ordered by the court.[9]

In principle, what distinguishes mediation and constitutes its chief benefit is respect for the parties' decision-making authority. This defining principle is incompatible with an approach that denies the parties the right to make their own informed decision as to whether or not they want to participate in the process in the first place. Not only are these approaches incompatible in principle, but serious incompatibilities arise in relation to practice – to coerce participation in unsuitable cases could be, not only inappropriate, but also unethical and possibly dangerous. Research reveals the frequency with which parties choose not to disclose issues of abuse to mediators (Keys Young, 1996).

---

7   Mandation in relation to mediation can take a number of forms – indirect compulsion (for example, financial pressure) and direct compulsion (compulsion to attend mediation before the parties are entitled to a court hearing) as referred to here (see Ingleby, 1993). At present, compulsion attaches only to the pre-mediation meeting to determine suitability for mediation for parties seeking legal aid for legal representation (Access to Justice Act 1999, section 11). Informed unwillingness to mediate is recognized to be an index of unsuitability.

8   For a useful presentation of the debate on fairness in mediation in the US, with arguments in favour of 'lawyer participation' as representatives of the parties in mandatory mediation to ensure fairness, see McEwen et al., 1995.

9   Judges have no formal power to order mediation, although the Family Law Act 1996 gave judges the power to require the parties to attend a meeting for the purpose of receiving an explanation about facilities available for mediation and of providing an opportunity for each party to agree to take advantage of those facilities (sections 13.1(a) and (b)). Judicial opinion, on the whole, supports encouragement for mediation rather than compulsion (see Lord Chancellor's Department, 1995a; Woolf, 1995; the Court of Appeal judgment in *Halsey* v. *Milton Keynes NHS Trust* [2004] 1 WLR 3002).

The skill and integrity of the mediator

Reliance on party control does not absolve the mediator from the ethical responsibility to ensure that both parties participate actively and freely in discussion and reach a mutually acceptable outcome. Attempts at bullying or overreaching must be prevented by the mediator as far as possible. Furthermore 'some things cannot and should not be compromised' (Folberg and Taylor, 1984, p. 247). If necessary, the mediator should bring the session to an end rather than countenance unfairness.

Where a situation of manifest inequality occurs, resort to mediation could be inappropriate or even unethical. One such example is when the capacity of one or other party to think or plan clearly and rationally is seriously impaired, as in cases of clinical depression or other mental disorder, serious emotional distress (for example, at an early stage of relationship breakdown), or incapacitation through drink or drugs. Another is when fear or intimidation characterizes and distorts relationships – for example, where there is or has been violence or other forms of abuse.

The mediator needs to understand the situation of each party so that imbalances, where these exist and are not recognized, or are recognized insufficiently, may be pointed out and talked about (for a discussion of useful interventions for power-balancing, see Kelly, 1995).[10] Open discussion is necessary if each party is to make a proper evaluation of their own situation, consider all the relevant factors and practicable alternatives and so reach reasoned, informed consensual decisions. Imbalances in negotiating skill must also be taken into account – for example, where one party is less articulate, slower to grasp what is happening, or lacking in confidence. An understanding of the situation of each party requires, in addition to an understanding of gender inequality, an awareness and understanding of cultural dynamics – the specific cultural, religious and regional perspectives and responses of different communities in relation to attitudes to conflict and disputes (Shah-Kazemi, 1996, 2000).

Structural and procedural protections

These are necessary both to offset the kinds of inequalities that can arise – for example, from a failure to structure sessions fairly – and to enhance

---

10   Those who argue in favour of mandatory mediation need to be aware that compulsion can create new imbalances in power and new vulnerabilities – for the willing party and for the unwilling party (see Roberts, 2006). What is appropriate for one party may not be appropriate for another, and mandated referral to mediation could result in the official privileging of one party. Another effect is in creating rules against litigation (see Ingleby, 1993).

the control of the parties and of women in particular (Kelly and Duryee, 1992). The framework of the mediation session should be designed to achieve fairness. The separate opportunity for each party to talk alone to the mediator at an early stage of every session is one important structural safeguard that should in no circumstances be dispensed with if full and free disclosure is to be protected. The research of Cobb and Rifkin (1990) at five dispute-resolution programmes in Western Massachusetts, covering a range of civil, criminal and family disputes, found that the order in which the disputants state the issue, and the ways in which they do so, can mirror the adversarial mode. The first disputant can 'negatively position' the second disputant. The research suggests that people may not have equal access to the mediation process, nor may they be able to participate fully or equally as a result of the structural arrangements of the session.

The Coogler model of structured mediation adopted and adapted by some independent family mediation services, expressly addresses the issues of party autonomy, mediator power and the protection of a fair process, by means of structure (see Chapter 7). Coogler's (1978) emphasis on the importance of a clear structure, composed of the integration of three structural components, was designed to protect the parties procedurally, ethically and emotionally.

Screening for domestic Abuse

Domestic abuse[11] highlights, perhaps in its starkest form, central concerns about fairness and power in all dispute resolution processes, and that of mediation in family disputes, in particular. Domestic abuse, therefore, imposes special demands and heavy responsibilities on mediators to be clear about the limits and boundaries of the process and to ensure that the necessary safeguards are in place – safeguards of principle, structure, and procedure as well as of external review. Fairness requires that there be relative equality of bargaining power between the parties. Where there is a situation of manifest inequality between the parties, particularly one associated with domestic abuse, resort to mediation would be inappropriate, if not dangerous, for the abused party and/or their children.

Latest figures in the UK (corresponding to those in the US and Australia) confirm that the high incidence of domestic violence makes it a key criminal justice issue – two women a week are murdered by current or former

---

11   The term 'domestic abuse' has been preferred to that of 'domestic violence', because it reflects the *range* of behaviours that make up intimidatory, oppressive and coercive behaviour, not just physical violence. The public usually associate 'domestic violence' with physical violence only (see Domestic Abuse Screening Policy, UK College of Family Mediators, 2000b).

partners and domestic abuse accounts for 16 per cent of all violent crime in England and Wales. British Crime Survey (2005) figures show that there are almost 13 million incidents against women and 3 million against men every year (for a study of gender differences in domestic abuse incidence, see Nazroo, 1995). Research findings show that the incidence of domestic abuse is especially high in the divorcing and separating population as well as the link between domestic abuse and the abuse of children (Hester and Radford, 1996; Hester et al., 1995, 2007).[12]

In the 1980s, much of the discussion on the issue of domestic abuse and mediation was firmly polarized. There were those, including feminist legal academics, who argued against the use of mediation in family disputes involving domestic abuse. Others, including some mediators, argued that mediation could be a valuable and effective process in *some* cases of domestic abuse. Much of the debate occurred at 'the extremes', with perhaps insufficient understanding, on each side, both about mediation practice and about the complexity of domestic abuse, as well as its effects on those who have been abused.

In the 1990s, there was evidence of a shift in approach and in the literature, which indicated that, with growing awareness, many of the concerns and criticisms about mediation were being addressed by the adoption of policies and practice guidelines on domestic abuse.[13] There was now broad consensus in the field, that mediation was likely to be most effective where the parties had relative equality of bargaining power and had had the opportunity to make a free and informed choice about whether or not they wanted to engage in the process. As Grillo (1991, p. 3) wrote in the context of voluntary mediation:

> Entering into such a process with one who has known you intimately and now seems to threaten your whole life and being has great creative, but also enormous destructive, power. Nonetheless, it should be recognized that when two people themselves decide to mediate and they physically appear at the mediation sessions, that decision and their continued presence, serve as a rough indication that it is not too painful or too dangerous for one or both of them to go on.

---

12   The amendment made to the Children Act 1989, in section 120 of the Adoption and Children Act 2002, expands and clarifies the meaning of 'harm', making explicit that 'harm' includes, not only the child being ill-treated themselves, but also impairment suffered by a child from seeing or hearing the ill-treatment of another.

13   Initially National Family Mediation (NFM) (later followed by the UK College of Family Mediators) responded to these developments and current research (for example, Hester and Radford, 1992, 1996; Hester and Pearson, 1993; Pagelow, 1990) by making an unequivocal statement of policy and recommending best practice guidelines to address the issue of domestic abuse in relation to mediation. In order to fulfil this policy, all NFM services *must* routinely screen for domestic abuse *before* mediation starts, and that if mediation does take place, procedures must be in place to ensure client protection, child protection and mediator safety so that continuing attention is paid throughout mediation to the possible existence of domestic abuse.

One concern at that time, was associated with the anticipated introduction of the Family Law Act 1996, which endorsed mediation as the preferred approach (and as a voluntary process), to settling family disputes following divorce and separation. This was related to the expected increase in the numbers of couples likely to be encouraged to use mediation. It was feared that this created two risks:

- that people would experience being pressured into mediation;
- that cases that were inappropriate for mediation, such as in cases of domestic abuse, would be referred to mediation.

However, one of the overarching general principles of the Family Law Act 1996 was:

> that any risk to one of the parties to a marriage, and to any children, of violence from the other party should, so far as reasonably practicable, be removed or diminished. (FLA 1996, section 1(d))

The Act required, in particular, that in publicly funded mediation, the mediator complied with a code of practice that included 'arrangements designed to ensure – (a) that parties participate in mediation only if willing and not influenced by fear of violence or other harm; (b) that cases where either party may be influenced by fear of violence or other harm are identified as soon as possible' (sections 27(6) and 27(7)).

Current policy on domestic abuse in the UK (Domestic Abuse Screening Policy, UK College of Family Mediators, 2000b) is distinguished both by the approach it adopts – including the pre-eminence that it attaches to the meanings and experiences of the individuals concerned – and by the wide definition of domestic abuse upon which it rests. It is the *impact* of domestic abuse as experienced by each/any of the individuals involved, and the fact that this is viewed from the perspectives of the recipient of the abuse (that is the abused person), that are significant:

> Domestic abuse is behaviour that seeks to secure power and control for the abuser and the *impact* of which is to undermine the safety, security, self-esteem and autonomy of the abused person. Domestic violence contains elements of the use of any or all of physical, sexual, psychological, emotional, verbal or economic intimidation, oppression or coercion. (UK College of Family Mediators, 2000b; emphasis added)

This approach may be contrasted with the North American one, which involves the making of a diagnostic judgment on the part of the professional, based on a typology of domestic violence profiles (for example, Johnston, 1993).

The policy stipulates the following requirements (Domestic Abuse Screening Policy, UK College of Family Mediators, 2000b).

- Each participant must make a fully informed and voluntary decision to enter mediation. This requires that each participant is sufficiently informed and has sufficient time to make the decision to attempt mediation after all safety issues, including screening for domestic abuse, have been fully considered.
- Safety issues include not only the participants in mediation but any other significant member of the family of either party.
- Assessment for domestic abuse and/or child protection is a continuing requirement that lasts throughout the whole of the mediation process.
- Implementation of this policy requires a written procedure for the safe and effective screening for domestic abuse.

The practical implication of this policy for those who undertake screening (intake worker or mediator) means that in reaching a decision about whether or not to proceed (and the mediator, ultimately, has the final say), priority must be given to the individual's *perception* of violence rather than the making of any judgment about levels of severity or types of violence. The beauty of the policy of the UK College of Family Mediators (and the original NFM 1996 version) is that it accords both with recent scholarly approaches to the subject (for example, Astor, 1994) *and* with the basic precepts of mediation.

Review by mediation

There should be an opportunity to return to mediation to review or renegotiate an agreement if it is thought to be unfair or does not work out in practice. Changes of circumstance may make revision necessary, and in some cases an agreement may only be acceptable to the parties if it is provisional, to be reviewed subject to a trial implementation of limited duration.

Co-working

An early research study indicated that co-working could increase the risks of mediators exerting unacceptable pressure, for example, by underlining each other's interventions rather than by counteracting bias or omission (Dingwall, 1988). No gender implications of co-working were explored in this research. Consumer research (Davis and Roberts, 1988) also found that the use of co-workers of each sex did help prevent any one gender outlook predominating. The presence of a male mediator was found to be reassuring to some women fearing intimidation by their former spouses. Co-workers could monitor each other, limiting bias or omission (see Chapter 5). One of the key findings of a project piloting mediation in international child abduction cases, is that these cases, given their complexity and the complementary expertise required, should always be co-mediated. However, from the parents' perspectives, a mixed gender pair of co-mediators was not regarded as necessary, rather 'the key requirement is the expertise, professionalism and neutrality of the mediators' (Reunite, 2006, p. 49).

Independent legal review

Another check on unfairness arising in mediation is that afforded by independent legal advice and review. Both parties should know what their legal rights are, including the fact that resort to mediation jeopardizes none of these rights. Where someone is not legally represented they should be urged to consult a solicitor where appropriate. If agreements are reached in mediation which may be legally binding – for example, where any financial or property matters form part of an agreement over residence or contact, the parties should submit their Memorandum of Understanding to their respective solicitors for independent review. It is essential that the full tax and legal implications of any agreement are clearly understood by the parties, that nothing important has been omitted, and that the agreement is expressed in terms that are faithful to the parties' understanding and meaning. The parties must still 'own' their agreement, but with the reassurance of informed partisan confirmation.

Training

The mediator's own potential to exceed, even abuse, his/her role has to be recognized explicitly in the training of mediators (Roberts, 1988). Findings have identified inadequate training as responsible for failures of practice – for the mediator's failure both to recognize the problem and to do anything about it (Cobb and Rifkin, 1990).

Training needs to include anti-discriminatory practice and the study of the impact of culture on disputes, both because mediation practice should fulfil its potential to the wider community by being accessible and by meeting specific cultural needs, and because of the likelihood of increasing numbers of cross cultural mediations, either where the disputants come from different cultures or where the mediator is from a culture different from that of one or both parties (see Chapter 6 for further discussion on different approaches to this subject; see also NFM *Cross-cultural Policy and Practice Guidelines*, 1998).

Supervision/professional practice consultancy (ppc)

Supervision[14] has always been the primary approach to the quality control of family mediation practice (for a study showing the uniqueness of the model of supervision within family mediation, see Allport, 2005). Supervision fulfils three main functions:

- support and professional guidance;
- professional development;
- monitoring, assessment of and accountability for the quality of practice.

The crucial importance of this approach to quality control of practice is recognized both in the standards of the professional body for family mediators (UK College of Family Mediators, 2000a, 2003) and in the Legal Services Commission *Quality Mark Standard for Mediation* (2002, p. 155, D4.2) which states:

> Effective systems of supervision are *critical to quality service provision*, as they ensure that proper support is available to all staff to help them deliver a consistently high-quality service, and because they should allow you to identify problems before they become significant or systemic.

Direct observation of practice by the supervisor or professional practice consultant (ppc), while not a requirement of the Quality Mark Standard for Mediation, is considered to be:

> a particularly valuable means of fulfilling the quality control function of the supervisor. It shows how the mediator manages the mediation session and allows the quality of management to be assessed ... Direct observation is a simple and effective way of demonstrating and recording the quality of practice independently and objectively. (Legal Services Commission, 2002, p. 155, D4.2)

---

14   With the advent of the UK College of Family Mediators, the task of *supervision* was redefined as *professional practice consultancy* in order to achieve its greater acceptability, particularly for mediators with a legal background.

Professional regulation

Nearly 30 years of family mediation practice in the UK have seen it transformed from its pioneering grassroots into a highly regulated professional activity, both self-regulated voluntarily from its earliest beginnings, by mediators themselves, and, since the 1990s, subject to government regulation with the advent of public funding for family mediation (for an account of this trajectory and the tensions that have shaped it, see Roberts, 2005b).

The imperatives of professionalization have grounded attention on some of the fundamental preoccupations for mediators – that is, the nature of their intervention, on what constitutes good practice, on transparency and accountability, and on fairness. In addressing these central issues of their craft, mediators have had to grapple with the abiding paradox of mediation as a professional intervention – representing the re-assertion of *party* control over decision-making, in the place of *professional* control. This objective, based on certain core values has drawn on a tradition of humanist ideas about autonomy and respect (see Chapter 1). In pursuit of that objective, the intervention of the mediator, however powerful its impact is recognized to be, has required an unobtrusive and modest stance, in contrast to the usual role of the professional, that of the dominant expert. Yet, despite the modest ambition of mediation to support party decision-making, it remains a complex and expert intervention requiring, at least, the normal safeguards of professional regulation. These safeguards assume even greater significance in the light of the privacy and informality inherent in the practice of mediation. These safeguards are essential both for the protection of the public and for ensuring the credibility of mediation as a professional activity.

If the objectives of mediation are modest, the objectives of professional regulation have been ambitious. First, fundamental question have had to asked and answered: what are the qualities of the good mediator? What constitutes competent practice? Second, starting from scratch, extensive detailed work has been done, over many years, identifying, analysing and assessing generic mediation standards of quality and translating these in to the objective criteria of actual performance (see CAMPAG, 1998). These have included standards both for professional competence, as well as for organizational provision and delivery.

Prior to the launch in 1996 of the UK College of Family Mediators, family mediation providers (NFM in particular) created their own extensive and stringent quality control mechanisms for establishing appropriate national standards for practitioners and for evaluating practice against these standards. In the 1990s, National Family Mediation, the not-for-profit provider of family mediation, set out to achieve these goals expressly through its national professional and organizational framework, consisting of affiliation criteria for services, a code of practice for regulating ethical and professional standards of practice, its equal opportunities policy and equal opportunities monitoring, and national procedures for the selection, training, supervised practice and accreditation of mediators (on the basis of competence).[15] In addition to this regulatory framework, further monitoring of standards of provision was secured by means of the publication of annual statistics, reports and guidelines; external monitoring of developments through research and consultancy; links with Institutions of Higher Education and European bodies;[16] and built-in evaluation and reviewing procedures (see also Roberts, 1994).

The rapid growth in the market of a number of mediation training bodies brought associated problems, not least that of maintaining a proper balance between the supply of mediators and the demand for mediation. This proliferation of training bodies also highlighted the risk of unregulated practice and the urgent need – in the interests of protecting the public – for a uniform regulatory framework of standards for all practitioners, whatever their professional background or sector of provision, private, statutory or not-for-profit (see Astor and Chinkin, 2002, for an overview of Australian professional developments in the field).

The advent of public funding for family mediation (initiated by the Family Law Act 1996) brought to the fore the demand for (and the dilemmas of) external regulation for the first time. There was a statutory requirement that any contract entered into by the Legal Aid Board (now the Legal Services Commission) for the provision of mediation 'must require the mediator to comply with a code of practice' (section 27(6)). Such a code required the mediator to have 'arrangements designed to ensure', among other things, pre-mediation screening for domestic violence, as well as the consultation of children in mediation (sections 27 (7) and (8)).

In 1996, in response to these developments (with the political and financial support of government), a single professional body, the first and only regulatory body of its kind in the UK, was established by the three main family mediation providers. The UK College of Family Mediators was launched with three main objectives:

---

15   In so far as NFM's national professional framework recognized the necessity of all its components – personal aptitude for mediation, training, supervised practice *and* performance evaluation based on competence – it met the major challenges that were raised about the North American *Interim Guidelines for Selecting Mediators*, published by the National Institute for Dispute Resolution (NIDR 1993) (see for example, Kolb and Kolb, 1993; Baruch Bush, 1993; Menkel-Meadow, 1993b; McEwen, 1993).

16   As a signatory to the European Charter on Training, for example.

- to advance the education of the public in the skills and practice of family mediation;
- to set, promote, improve and maintain the highest standards of professional conduct and training for those practising in the field of family mediation;
- to make available the details of registered mediators qualified to provide family mediation (UK College of Family Mediators, 1997, p. A3).

The UK College also has a responsibility to ensure that mediation is accessible to all members of the community regardless of their cultural, religious or ethnic background.

Membership of the UK College is based on the demonstration of professional practice competence, amongst other requirements (such as professional practice consultancy/supervision and continuing professional development), and full membership of the UK College, following successful completion of its competence assessment process is a requirement for doing publicly funded mediation[17] (Legal Services Commission, 2002, p. 70, D5a.1). At its height, membership of the UK College exceeded 700 although this has declined (by 15 per cent between 2002 and 2005) with fewer mediators doing a greater volume of work (UK College of Family Mediators, 2006a, 2006b).[18]

The establishment of the UK College marked the formal arrival in the UK of family mediation as a new profession. The three hallmarks characterizing the achievement of professional status were now officially in place:

- a recognized and distinct body of knowledge;
- mechanisms for the transmission of that body of knowledge;
- mechanisms for self-regulation, evaluation and accountability.

In establishing its own disciplinary and complaints committees, the UK College officially acknowledged the necessity for addressing bad practice by means of formal and transparent procedures.

---

17 The UK College of Family Mediators decided in late 2007 to expand its membership to include community and other mediators, and renamed itself accordingly, 'The College of Mediators'. The College of Mediators is a provisional member of the nascent Family Mediation Council (FMC), which is made up of family mediation provider bodies and which has been recognised by the Legal Services Commission for the purposes of conferring the Quality Mark Standard for Mediation on suitably qualified family mediators.

18   In 2005, the total number of family mediations carried out were in the region of 17,000 to 18,000, with wholly privately funded cases accounting of around 20 per cent of the total. 32 per cent of mediation cases involved a mix of public and private funding (UK College of Family Mediators, 2006b).

The UK College also approves independent provider bodies, 'Approved Bodies' to carry out the functions of recruitment, selection, training (including continuing professional development courses) and ppc/ supervision, according to its standards. In this way, the requisite separation of standard-setting and monitoring on the one hand, and the provision of functions such as training and service delivery, has been secured. However, structural tensions arising from these conflicts of function, have always posed a threat to the stability of the UK College as a regulatory body of individual members (the provider bodies having nominated representatives with voting powers on the governing board of the UK College). This threat, exacerbated by competition for membership in a small field, risks damaging the fruits of ten years of collaboration and professional achievement and a return to the destructive proliferation of bodies that brought about the need for the UK College in the first place.

While publicly funded family mediation provision is, properly, to be subject to stringent quality assurance standards, difficult questions arise and need to be addressed: to what extent will the security of external funding, inevitably bringing with it demands of accountability and quantifiable measures of effectiveness, lead to a stifling, or even loss, of autonomy, flexibility and creativity and peer professional control of family mediation? How can the benefits of a variety of models and individual practice styles, and of consistency and uniformity of high standards, be balanced? How can a proper balance be achieved too, between external regulation by government and the law agencies (such as the Law Society) and regulation by the profession itself?

Research

A large, cross-disciplinary body of literature, much of it North American, valuably informs understandings both about the nature of ADR and of mediation in particular. This literature encompasses a range of perspectives and conclusions, some of which raise serious questions about the political implications of informal justice, about power, about justice and fairness, about neutrality and coercion, about styles and models of practice, and about assessment of effectiveness – concerns that 'mediators themselves debate and worry over' (Rifkin, 1994, p. 204). Notwithstanding this range, there has also been a conspicuous lack in the literature, of the practitioner perspective, particularly one based on actual mediation experience, within or across fields of practice (exceptions include Kolb et al., 1994, and Roberts, 2007).

Peculiar to this field perhaps, the relationship between the theory and practice of mediation has been characterized, explicitly in North America, as a problematic one, involving a theory/practice divide (Rifkin, 1994). In particular, the interaction between research and practice has been perceived to be restricted – with exchanges relatively rare and with limited impact (Rifkin, 1994). When exchanges have occurred, these have been considered to be less than productive, with a consequent loss of benefit to both researchers and practitioners. A number of reasons for this have been posited:

- the absence of explicit theories of practice underpinning mediation training programmes, which are unable, as a consequence, to incorporate innovative theoretical perspectives;
- the problem of practitioners continuing to be shaped by the professional training of their professions of origin;
- the lack of consensus among practitioners and their professional organizations as to what constitutes 'good practice';
- the failure of scholars, few of whom offer recommendations for the transformation of practice; this, it is argued, goes beyond the boundaries of their aims;
- the lack of opportunities for researchers and practitioners to collaborate in exploring the practical implications of research studies.

The larger question has also been raised as to whether and to what extent it is possible or desirable for there to be a productive exchange between researchers and practitioners (see Roberts, 1992b; Dingwall and Greatbatch, 1993, 1995; Roberts, 1994; Shah-Kazemi, 2000; Davis et al., 2000; Walker et al., 1994, 2004). While the interests of researchers and practitioners do not necessarily coincide, common understanding would seem to be important if practice is to be informed by reputable research and there is to be the co-operation and confidence of practitioners necessary for research to take place in the field.

An alternative narrative posits a different, less oppositional experience of the interaction between theory and practice in respect of mediation. The ADR field is acknowledged to be an 'experiential' field exemplifying the concepts and practices of the 'theories-in-use' school in the development of professional education (for example, Schön, 1983; Menkel-Meadow et al., 2005). The importance of 'grounded theory' also highlights the recognition that good practice and the reflections of experienced practitioners constitute a rich resource of the development of the best models and theories (Jones, 2001, p. 133).

The situation in the UK has been more encouraging in this regard. A number of practitioners involved in mediation policy and practice in this country have been engaged with researchers in productive exchange expressly focused on identifying models of good mediation practice informed both by research findings and practice experience. This has covered research work on mediation in relation to children and divorce

(Simpson, 1989; Cockett and Tripp, 1994), all-issues mediation (Walker et al., 1994) and domestic violence (Hester and Pearson, 1993; Kaganas and Piper, 1993) and, more generally, in relation to child abduction, child maintenance and child protection (King, 1999). Furthermore, developments in family mediation, under the auspices of NFM in the 1990s, demonstrated the close collaboration of researchers and practitioners in joint working parties, constructing a range of policies and practice guidelines such as on domestic abuse, the role of children in mediation, cross-cultural mediation, selection criteria and procedures, and mediation models for dealing comprehensively with decisions relating to all issues associated with family breakdown – those concerning finance, property as well as children.

While tension can arise between the academic and the practitioner, it is clear that it is not theory that poses problems for practice; on the contrary, a rich source of theory, generating new intellectual and experiential insights, is welcomed for providing fresh and imaginative directions for thinking about the field (Schaffer, 2004). The greater the theoretical range, the more responsive the mediator can be to differing needs. A progression of thinking, in culturally diverse directions and involving innovative, flexible and relevant approaches to practice, is taking place, for example, in relation to mediation in the international Ismaili Muslim community (see Whatling and Keshavjee, 2005).

Research in the US has proved valuable for mediators (see for example, Kelly, 2004; Emery et al., 2005). Research is much needed in the UK, to fill the gaps of understanding that exist on relevant topics – research that does justice to its complex, difficult and, at times, ambivalent demands, as well as the socio-cultural context in which it takes place. More knowledge is needed if the inherent limitations in the process are to be offset and failures in practice are to be mitigated or avoided. Research is necessary to explore the impact of cultural difference and its implications for recruiting and training mediators, and should include consumer evaluation, with a focus on the perspectives and meanings of the parties. What is needed, in addition to academic research and theory, and critical debate, is analysis of practice by practitioners themselves. This involves no diminution of the import of other researchers' contributions to the field.

Theory and research are recognized to have significance in practitioners' understandings about their work – across fields of mediation (Roberts, 2007). Practitioners acknowledge too the rich variety of sources of theory that contribute to their work – collegiate exchange, practitioners' own teaching, training, writing and reflections on their work, as well as the academic literature dealing with 'pragmatic' and theoretical issues. Research and theory, taking many forms, can interweave constructively with practice in a recursive relationship of mutual influence and significance, influencing, informing and advancing understanding and, therefore, practice experience.

Epilogue[1]

... I think the beauty of it was they [the mediators] let you make your own decisions. They weren't forcing their opinions on you. They were just giving you another side of an argument perhaps. They were exposing the whole thing so you could look at it logically. *Mother with residence*

We were fair to each other ... there was a fairness and the [mediator] represented a certain kind of fairness, exuded a sort of reasonableness. *Non-resident father*

By the time we came back the second time, really the problems had been solved at that first meeting, simply by saying 'Well, OK, you know this is the agreement.' And from then on it was much smoother too – it sounds almost miraculous – but emotionally it became much less fraught. We'd solved the problem over access and a lot of other things at the same time ... *Non-resident father*

Her dad and I, oh, we have our ups and downs still, we have our little ... I feel sometimes I could say something, I think, no we've got to keep the peace for the children. I never ever pull her dad down and hope he hasn't ... [since] mediation we've been able to communicate more, which I think has helped Linda [daughter] tremendously. *Non-resident mother*

We came to an amicable agreement [at the mediation session] my wife and I, over it [access] ... We was [sic] trying to both be very sensible about it and not let our feelings get in the way of trying to do what was best for the children, which was the whole point, I think. I tried to make sure that the children weren't hurt if it could be helped. It's bad enough for them without having their mother there, without causing arguments in front of them. *Father with residence, subsequently reconciled*

Unless we went there we'd most likely end up in court. And that they [the mediators] felt the sort of service that they were doing and the sort of service they were offering was keeping people out of court – keeping decisions between the partners and not involving all the legal machinery. And I would actually agree with that, as far as we're concerned anyway. And it seems so simple, what they were doing in fact. I mean, it's like anything. It was really simple. *Mother with residence*

---

1   Quotes of those who experienced mediation (see Davis and Roberts, 1988).

Bibliography

Abel, R.L. (1982), 'The contradictions of informal justice', in R.L. Abel (ed.), *The Politics of Informal Justice*, Vol. 1 (New York: Academic Press).

ACAS (Advisory, Conciliation and Arbitration Service) (n.d.), *The ACAS Role in Conciliation, Arbitration and Mediation*, ACAS Reports and Publications.

Acland, A.F. (1995), *Resolving Disputes without Going to Court* (London: Random Century Books).

Advice Services Alliance (2006), *Notes for Advisers* (London: Advice Services Alliance).

Albin, C. (1993), 'The role of fairness in negotiation', *Negotiation Journal*, 9, 223–39.

Allport, L. (2005), *Supervision in Mediation: Linking Practice and Quality* (Sion: Institut Universitaire Kurt Bosch).

Amundson, J.K. and Fong, L. (1993), 'She prefers her aesthetics; he prefers his pragmatics: A response to Roberts and Haynes', *Mediation Quarterly*, 11(2), 199–205.

Anderson, H. (2001), 'Post-modern collaboration and person-centred therapies: What would Rogers say?', *Journal of Family Therapy*, 23, 341–58.

Astor, H. (1994), 'Violence and family mediation policy', *Australian Journal of Family Law*, 18(1), 3–21.

Astor, H. and Chinkin, C. (2002), *Dispute Resolution in Australia*, 2nd edn (Chatswood, Australia: Butterworth).

Auerbach, J.S. (1983), *Justice Without Law?* (New York: Oxford University Press).

Bainham, A. (1990), 'The privatisation of the public interest in children', *Modern Law Review*, 53, 206–21.

—— (2000), 'Children law at the millennium', in S.M. Cretney (ed.) *Family Law: Essays for the New Millennium* (Bristol: Jordans).

Baruch Bush, R.A. (1993), 'Mixed messages in the interim guidelines', *Negotiation Journal*, 9(4), 341–7.

Benians, R.C. (1976), 'Marital breakdown and its consequences for children', address to the Medico-Legal Society, Royal Society of Medicine, London, 14 October.

—— (1980), 'Impact of marital breakdown on children', *The Journal of Maternal and Child Health*, Parts I and II, October and November.

Benjamin, M. and Irving, H.H. (1995), 'Research in family mediation: Review and implications', *Mediation Quarterly*, 13(1), 53–82.

Berger, B. and Berger, P.L. (1983), *The War over the Family: Capturing the Middle Ground* (London: Hutchinson).

Bernard, J. (1971), 'No news but new ideas', in P. Bohannan (ed.), *Divorce and After* (New York: Doubleday).

—— (1973), *The Future of Marriage* (New York: Bantam).

Bohannan, P. (ed.) (1971), *Divorce and After* (New York: Doubleday).

Bohmur, C. and Ray, M.L. (1994), 'Effects of different disputes resolution methods on women and children after divorce', *Family Law Quarterly*, 28(2), 223–45.

Booth Committee (1985), *Report of the Committee on Matrimonial Causes* (London: HMSO).

Bordow, S. and Gibson, J. (1994), *Evaluation of the Family Court Mediation Service*, Research Report No.12, Melbourne: Family Court of Australia.

Bottomley, A. (1984), 'Resolving family disputes: A critical view', in M.D.A. Freeman (ed.), *State, Law and the Family* (London: Tavistock).

—— (1985), 'What is happening to family law? A feminist critique of conciliation', in J. Brophy and C. Smart (eds), *Women in Law* (London: Routledge and Kegan Paul).

Bottomley, A. and Olley, S. (1983), 'Conciliation in the USA', *LAG Bulletin*, January, 9.

Bowling, D. and Hoffman, D. (2000), 'In theory: Bringing peace into the room: The personal qualities of the mediator and their impact on the mediation', *Negotiation Journal*, 5, 5–27.

Brasse, G. (2006), 'Its payback time! *Miller, McFarlane* and the Compensation Culture', *Family Law*, August, 36, 647–54.

Bridge, S. (2006), 'Money, marriage and cohabitation', *Family Law*, August, 36, 641–6.

—— (2007), 'Financial relief for cohabitants: How the law commissions scheme would work', *Family Law*, 37, 998–1003.

British Crime Survey (2005), London.

Brophy, J. and Smart, C. (eds) (1984), *Women in Law* (London: Routledge and Kegan Paul).

Brown, H. (1991), *Alternative Dispute Resolution: Report*, Courts and Legal Services Committee (London: Law Society, Legal Practice Directorate).

Brown, J. and Day Sclater, S. (1999), 'Divorce: A psychodynamic perspective', in S. Day Sclater and C. Piper (eds), *Undercurrents of Divorce* (Aldershot: Ashgate).

Burgoyne, J. (1984), *Breaking Even: Divorce, Your Children and You* (Harmondsworth: Penguin).

Burrows, D. and Orr, N. (2007), *Stack* v. *Dowden: Co-ownership of Property by Unmarried Parties*, Special Bulletin (Bristol: Jordans).

Bush, R.A.B. and Folger, J.P. (1994), *The Promise of Mediation: Responding to Conflict through Empowerment and Recognition* (San Francisco: Jossey-Bass).

—— (2005), *The Promise of Mediation: The Transformative Approach to Conflict*, 2nd edn (San Francisco: Jossey-Bass).

Butler, I., Robinson, M. and Scanlan, L. (2005), *Children and Decision-Making* (York: Joseph Rowntree Foundation).

Butler-Sloss, E. (2001), 'Contact and domestic violence', *Family Law*, May, 31, 355–8.

CAFCASS (Children and Family Court Advisory and Support Service) Consultation Papers. Draft National Standards (2000); 'Contact: Principles, practice guidance and procedures' (2004); 'Every day matters: New directions for CAFCASS: A consultation paper on a new professional and organisational strategy' (undated paper published in 2005).

CAFCASS (2003), *Seeking Agreement: A Thematic review of CAFCASS Schemes in Private Law Proceedings* (London: MCSI).

—— (2005), *Every Day Matters*, Consultation Paper (London: HMSO).

CAMPAG (1998), *Standards in Mediation* (London: The National Training Organisation for Employment).

Campbell, D., Draper, R. and Huffington, C. (1989), *Second Thoughts on the Theory and Practice of the Milan Approach to Family Therapy* (London: D.C. Associates).

Campbell, D., Reder, P., Draper, R. and Pollard, D. (1983), 'Working with the Milan Method: Twenty Questions', Occasional Papers on Family Therapy, No. 1 (London: Institute of Family Therapy).

Caplan, G. (1986), 'Preventing psychological problems in children of divorce: General practitioner's role', *British Medical Journal*, May, 292.

Caplan, L. (1995), 'The milieu of disputation: Managing quarrels in East Nepal', in P. Caplan (ed.), *Understanding Disputes: The Politics of Argument* (Oxford: Berg).

Caplan, P. (1995), 'Anthropology and the study of disputes', in P. Caplan (ed.), *Understanding Disputes: The Politics of Argument* (Oxford: Berg).

Children Act Sub-Committee (2002), 'Making contact work', A Report to the Lord Chancellor by the Children Act Sub-Committee (CASC) of the Lord Chancellors Advisory Board on Family Law.

Chin-A-Fat, B. and Steketee, M. (2001), Summary of Dutch Report (trans.) Bemiddeling in Uitvoering: Evaluatie experimenten scheidings-en-omgangsbemiddeling. Free University, Amsterdam and Verwey-Jonker Institute, Utrecht.

Christie, N. (1977), 'Conflicts as property', *Bristol Journal of Criminology*, 17, 1.

Clarke, L. and Berrington, A. (1999), 'Socio-demographic predictors of divorce: High divorce rates; the state of the evidence on reasons and remedies', *Research Series*, 1, 2, papers 1–3, (London: LCD).

Clulow, C. (ed.) (1995), *Women, Men and Marriage* (London: Sheldon Press).

Cobb, S. and Rifkin, J. (1990), 'Rethinking neutrality: Implications for mediation practice', unpublished.

—— (1991), 'Practice and paradox: Deconstructing neutrality in mediation' *Law and Social Inquiry*, 16(1), 35–62.

Cockett, M. and Tripp, J. (1994), *The Exeter Family Study: Family Breakdown and its Impact on Children* (Exeter: University of Exeter Press).

Collinson, J. and Gardner, K. (1990), 'Conciliation and children', in T. Fisher (ed.), *Family Conciliation Within the UK: Policy and Practice* (Bristol: Jordan).

Commonwealth Department of Family and Community Services Report (2002), *Through a Child's Eyes: Child Inclusive Practice in Family Relationship Services* (Commonwealth of Australia).

Conciliation Project Unit (1989), *Report to the Lord Chancellor on the Costs and Effectiveness of Conciliation in England and Wales* (London: LCD).

Conneely, S. (2002), *Family Mediation in Ireland* (UK: Ashgate).

Consultation Paper (1993), *Looking to the Future: Mediation and the Ground for Divorce*, Cm2424, London: HMSO.

Coogler, O.J. (1978), *Structured Mediation in Divorce Settlement* (Lexington, MA: Lexington Books/D.C. Heath).

Corbin, J. (1994), *Gaza First: The Secret Norway Channel to Peace between Israel and the PLO* (London: Bloomsbury).

Cormick, G.W. (1977), 'The ethics of mediation: Some unexplored territory', unpublished paper presented to The Society of Professionals in Dispute Resolution, Fifth Annual Meeting, October, Washington DC.

—— (1981), 'Environmental mediation in the US. Experience and future directions I', unpublished paper presented to the American Association for Advancement of Science Annual Meeting, Toronto, Canada.

—— (1982), 'Intervention and self-determination in environmental disputes: A mediator's perspective', *Resolve*, Winter, 260–65.

Council of Europe (1998), Recommendation No. R (98) 1 of the Committee of Ministers to Member States on Family Mediation, Strasbourg.

Cretney, S.M., Masson, J.M. and Bailey-Harris, R. (2003), *Principles of Family Law*, 7th edn (London: Sweet and Maxwell).

Cross, R. and Tapper, C. (2007), *On Evidence*, 11th edn (Oxford: Oxford University Press).

Cross, R. and Wilkins, N. (1996), *Outline of the Law of Evidence*, 7th edn (London: Butterworths).

Dallos, R. and Draper, R. (2000), 'An introduction to family therapy: Systemic theory and practice', in R. Woolfe, W. Dryden and S. Strawbridge, *Handbook of Counselling Psychology*, 2nd edn (Buckingham: Open University Press).

Davis, A.M. (1984), 'Comment', in *A Study of Barriers to the Use of Alternative Methods of Dispute Resolution*, Vermont Law School Dispute Resolution Project (South Royalton, VT: VLSDRP).

Davis, A.M. and Gadlin, H. (1988), 'Mediators gain trust, the old fashioned way – we earn it!' *Negotiation Journal*, 1, 55–62.

Davis, G. (1981), 'Report of a research to monitor the work of the Bristol Courts Family Conciliation Service in its first year of operation', *30th Legal Aid Annual Reports, 1979–80* (London: HMSO).

—— (1983), 'Conciliation and the Professions', *Family Law*, 13, 1.

—— (1985), 'The theft of conciliation', *Probation Journal*, March, 32, 1.

—— (1988), *Partisans and Mediators: The Resolution of Divorce Disputes* (Oxford: Oxford University Press).

—— (2001a), 'Mediation and legal services – the client speaks', *Family Law*, February, 31, 110–14.

—— (2001b), 'Family mediation – where do we go from here?', *Family Law*, April, 31, 265–9.

Davis, G. and Bader, K. (1985), 'In-court mediation: The consumer view', Parts I and II, *Family Law*, March and April, 15(3), 42–9, 82–6.

Davis, G., Bevan, G., Clisby, S., Cumming, Z., Dingwall, R., Fenn, P., Finch, S., Fitzgerald, R., Goldie, S., Greatbatch, D., James, A. and Pearce, J. (2000), 'Monitoring publicly funded family mediation', Final Report to the Legal Services Commission, July.

Davis, G., Cretney, S.M. and Collins, J. (1994), *Simple Quarrels* (Oxford: Clarendon Press).

Davis, G., MacLeod, A. and Murch, M. (1983), 'Divorce: Who supports the family?', *Family Law*, 13(7), 217.

Davis, G., Matthews, S. and Wyer, M. (1991), 'Child custody mediation and litigation: Further evidence on the differing views of mother and fathers', *Journal of Consulting and Clinical Psychology*, 59, 410–18.

Davis, G. and Roberts, M. (1988), *Access to Agreement: A Consumer Study of Mediation in Family Disputes* (Milton Keynes: Open University Press).

—— (1989a), 'Mediation in disputes over children: Learning from experience', *Children and Society*, 13(3), 275–9.

—— (1989b), 'Mediation and the battle of the sexes', *Family Law*, August 19, 305.

Day Sclater, S. (1999), 'Experiences of divorce', in S. Day Sclater and C. Piper (eds.), *Undercurrents of Divorce* (Aldershot: Ashgate).

Deech, R. (1995), 'Divorced from reality', *The Spectator*, 4 November, 12–16.

Della Noce, D.J., Bush, R.A.B. and Folger, J.P. (2001), 'Myths and misconceptions about the transformative orientation', in *Designing Mediation: Approaches to Training and Practice within a Transformative Framework* (US: Institute for the Study of Conflict Transformation).

Department of Health (1989), *Rights of the Subject: The Access to Personal Files (Social Services/Regulations No.206)* (London: HMSO).

—— (1998), *Working Together to Safeguard Children: A Guide to Inter-agency Working to Safeguard and Promote the Welfare of Children* (London: HMSO).

Deutsch, M. (1973), *The Resolution of Conflict: Constructive and Destructive Processes* (New Haven, CT: Yale University Press).

Dingwall, R. (1986), 'Some observations on divorce mediation in Britain and the United States', *Mediation Quarterly*, 11, 5–24.

—— (1988), 'Empowerment or enforcement? Some questions about power and control in divorce mediation', in R. Dingwall and J. Eekelaar (eds), *Divorce Mediation and the Legal Process* (Oxford: Oxford University Press).

Dingwall, R. and Eekelaar, J. (1986), 'Judgments of Solomon: Psychology and family law', in M. Richards and P. Light (eds), *Children of Social Worlds: Development in a Social Context* (Cambridge: Polity Press).

—— (eds) (1988), *Divorce Mediation and the Legal Process* (Oxford: Clarendon Press).

Dingwall, R. and Greatbatch, D. (1993), 'Who is in charge? Rhetoric and evidence in the study of mediation', *Journal of Social Welfare and Family Law*, 15, 367–85.

—— (1995), 'Family mediation researchers and practitioners in the shadow of the Green Paper: A rejoinder to Marian Roberts', *Journal of Social Welfare and Family Law*, 17(2), 199–206.

Douglas, A. (1957), 'The peaceful settlement of industrial and intergroup disputes', *Journal of Conflict Resolution*, 1(1), 69–81.

—— (1962), *Industrial Peacemaking* (New York: Columbia University Press).

Douglas, G. and Lowe, N. (2006), *Bromleys Family Law*, 10th edn (Oxford: Oxford University Press).

Eckhoff, T. (1969), 'The mediator and the judge', in V. Aubert (ed.), *Sociology of Law* (Harmondsworth: Penguin).

Eekelaar, J. (1978), *Family Law and Social Policy* (London: Weidenfeld and Nicolson).

—— (2006), 'Property and financial settlement on divorce – sharing and compensating', *Family Law*, September, 36, 754–8.

Eekelaar, J. and Maclean, M. (1986), *Maintenance after Divorce* (Oxford: Oxford University Press).

Eekelaar, J. et al. (1977), *Custody after Divorce* (Oxford: Centre for Socio-Legal Studies and Social Science Research Council).

Effron, J. (1989), 'Alternatives to litigation: Factors in choosing', *Modern Law Review*, 52(4), 480–97.

Emery, R.E. (1994), *Renegotiating Family Relationships: Divorce, Child Custody and Mediation* (New York: Guilford Press).

Emery, R.E., Laumann-Billings, L., Waldon, M., Sbarra, D.A. and Dillon, P. (2001), 'Child custody mediation and litigation: Custody, contact and co-parenting twelve years after initial dispute resolution', *Journal of Consulting and Clinical Psychology*, 69, 323–32.

Emery, R.E., Matthews, S. and Wyer, M. (1991), 'Child custody mediation and litigation: Further evidence on the differing views of mothers and fathers', *Journal of Consulting and Clinical Psychology*, 59, 410–18.

Emery, R.E., Sbarra, D. and Grover, T. (2005), 'Divorce mediation: Research and reflections', *Mediation in Practice*, May, 7–18.

Epstein, E.S. and Loos, V.E. (1989), 'Some irreverent thoughts on the limits of family therapy: Towards a language-based explanation of human systems', *Journal of Family Psychology* 2(4), 405–21.

European Parliament and the Council of the European Union (2008), *Directive 2008 on Certain Aspects of Mediation in Civil and Commercial Matters*.

Falk Moore, S. (1995), 'Imperfect communications', in P. Caplan (ed.), *Understanding Disputes: The Politics of Argument* (Oxford: Berg).

Family Policy Studies Centre (1987), *One Parent Families*. Fact Sheet (London: FPSC).

—— (1996), *The Family Law Bill*. Family Briefing Paper No. I, March (London: FPSC).

Felstiner, W.L.F., Abel, R.L. and Sarat, A. (1980–81), 'The emergence and transformation of disputes: Naming, blaming, claiming …', *Law and Society Review*, 15(3), 631–54.

Felstiner, W.L.F. and Sarat, A. (1992), 'Enactments of power: Negotiating reality and responsibility in lawyer–client interactions', *Cornell Law Review*, 77(6), 1447–98.

Felstiner, W.L.F. and Williams, L. (1985), 'Community mediation in Dorchester, Mass', in S.B. Goldberg, E.D. Green and F.E.A. Sander (eds), *Dispute Resolution* (Boston and Toronto: Little, Brown).

Filkin, Lord (2004), 'Improving justice for families', News Release 1 July 2004, 350/04 (London: Department for Constitutional Affairs).

Finer Report (1974), *Report of the Committee on One Parent Families*. Cmnd 5629 (London: HMSO).

Fisher, R. and Ury, W. (1981), *Getting to Yes* (Boston: Houghton-Mifflin).

Fisher, T. (1986), *Family and Industrial Conciliation: Identifying Common Practice* (Unpublished).

—— (ed) (1992), *Family Conciliation Within the UK: Policy and Practice*, 2nd edn (Bristol: Family Law).

Fiss, O.M. (1984), 'Against settlement', *Yale Law Journal*, 93, 1073–90.

Folberg, J. (1983), 'Divorce mediation – Promises and problems', paper prepared for midwinter meeting of American Bar Association Section on Family Law, St Thomas.

——— (1984), 'Divorce mediation – the emerging American model', in J.M. Eekelaar and S.N. Katz (eds), *The Resolution of Family Conflict, Comparative Legal Perspectives*, pp. 193–211 (Toronto: Butterworths).

Folberg J. and Milne, A. (eds) (1988), *Divorce Mediation: Theory and Practice* (New York: Guilford Press).

Folberg, J. and Taylor, A. (1984), *Mediation: A Comprehensive Guide to Resolving Conflicts Without Litigation* (San Francisco: Jossey-Bass).

Folger, J.P. and Bush, R.A.B. (2001), 'Transformative mediation and third party intervention: Ten hallmarks of transformative mediation practice', in *Designing Mediation: Approaches to Training and Practice within a Transformative Framework* (Institute for the Study of Conflict Transformation).

Forster, J. (1982), *Divorce Conciliation: A Study of Services in England and Abroad with Implications for Scotland* (Edinburgh: Scottish Council for Single Parents).

Francis, D. (2002), *People, Peace and Power: Conflict Transformation in Action* (London: Pluto Press).

Freeman, M.D.A. (1983), *The Rights and Wrongs of Children* (London: Frances Pinter).

——— (1984), 'Questioning the delegalization movement in family law: Do we really want a family court?', in J.M. Eekelaar and S.N. Katz (eds) *The Resolution of Family Conflict: Comparative Legal Perspectives* (Toronto: Butterworths).

——— (2006), 'Review of Reece, H. (2003) Divorcing responsibly', *Modern Law Review*, 69(1), 120–23.

Fuller, L.L. (1971), 'Mediation – its forms and functions', *Southern California Law Review*, 44, 305–39.

Galanter, M. (1984), 'What else is new? The emergence of the judge as mediator in civil cases 1930–1980', Working paper, Disputes Processing Research Programme, Madison: University of Wisconsin.

Gale, D. (1994), 'The impact of culture on the work of family mediators', *Family Mediation* 4, 2.

Garwood, F. (1989), *Children in Conciliation: A Study of the Involvement of Children in Conciliation by the Lothian Family Conciliation Service* (Edinburgh: Scottish Association of Family Conciliation Services).

Genn, H., Fenn, P., Mason, M., Lane, A., Bechai, N., Gray, L. and Vencappa, D. (2006), 'Twisting arms: Court referred and court linked mediation under judicial pressure', *Ministry of Justice Research Series* 1/07, May.

Gilligan, C. (1982), *In a Different Voice* (Cambridge MA: Harvard University Press).

Glasser, C. (1994), 'Solving the litigation crisis', *The Litigator*, 1, 14.

Goethe von, J.W. (1809, trans. 1971), *Elective Affinities* (Harmondsworth: Penguin).

Goldstein, J., Freud, A. and Solnit, A.J. (1973), *Beyond the Best Interests of the Child* (New York: Free Press).

Goldstein, S. (1986), *Cultural Issues in Mediation: A Literature Review*. PCR Working Paper (Honolulu: University of Hawaii).

Goolishan, H. and Anderson, H. (1992), 'Strategy and intervention versus non-intervention: A matter of theory?', *Journal of Marital and Family Therapy*, 18, 5–15.

Grant, B. (1981), *Conciliation and Divorce: A Father's Letters to his Daughter* (Chichester and London: Barry Rose).

Green Paper (1993), *Looking to the Future: Mediation and the Ground for Divorce*, Cm2424 (London: HMSO).

—— (1995), *Legal Aid: Targeting Need*, Cm2854 (London: HMSO).

—— (2003), *Every Child Matters: New Directions for CAFCASS*, Cm 5860 (London: HMSO).

Grillo, T. (1991), 'The mediation alternative: Process dangers for women', *Yale Law Journal*, 100(6), 1545–640.

Guggenheim, M. (2005), *What's Wrong with Children's Rights?* (Cambridge MA: Harvard University Press).

Gulliver, P.H. (1971), *Neighbours and Networks* (Berkeley: University of California Press).

—— (1977), 'On mediators', in I. Hamnett (ed.), *Social Anthropology and Law* (London: Academic Press).

—— (1979), *Disputes and Negotiations: A Cross-Cultural Perspective* (New York: Academic Press).

Haley, J. and Hoffman, L. (1967), *Techniques of Family Therapy* (New York: Basic Books).

Hamnett, I. (ed.) (1977), *Social Anthropology and Law* (London: Academic Press).

Hampshire, S. (2000), *Justice is Conflict* (Princeton, NJ: Princeton University Press).

Haynes, J.M. (1980), 'Managing conflict: The role of the mediator', *Conciliation Courts Review*, 18(2), 9–13.

—— (1981), *Divorce Mediation: A Practical Guide for Therapists and Counsellors* (New York: Springer).

—— (1982), 'A conceptual model of the process of family mediation: Implications for training', *American Journal of Family Therapy*, 10, 4.

—— (1983), 'The process of negotiation', *Mediation Quarterly*, 1, 75–92.

—— (1985), 'Matching readiness and willingness to the mediators strategies', *Negotiation Journal*, January, 79–92.

—— (1992), 'Mediation and therapy: An alternative view', *Mediation Quarterly*, 10(1), 21–34.

—— (1993), *The Fundamentals of Family Mediation* (London: Old Bailey Press).

Hester, M. and Pearson, C. (1993), 'Domestic violence, mediation and child contact arrangements', *Family Mediation*, 3(2), 3–6.

Hester, M., Pearson, C., Harwin, N. with Abrahams, H. (2007), *Making an Impact: Children and Domestic Violence* (London and Philadelphia: Jessica Kingsley Publishers).

Hester, M. and Radford, L. (1992), 'Domestic violence and access arrangements for children in Denmark and Britain', *Journal of Social Welfare and Family Law*, 1, 57–70.

—— (1996), *Domestic Violence and Child Contact Arrangements in England and Denmark* (Bristol: Policy Press).

Hetherington, E.M. and Kelly, J. (2002), *For Better or for Worse: Divorce Reconsidered* (New York: W.W. Norton).

Home Office (1994), *National Standards for Probation Service Family Court Welfare Work* (London: HMSO).

—— (2003), *Safety and Justice: The Governments Proposals on Domestic Violence* (London: HMSO).

—— (2004), Letter to the UK College of Family Mediators, 6 February, 2004.

Howard, J. and Shepherd, G. (1982), 'Conciliation – new beginnings?', *Probation Journal*, 29(3).

—— (1987), *Conciliation, Children and Divorce: A Family Systems Approach* (London: B.T. Batsford).

Hunt, J. with Roberts, C. (2004), 'Child contact with non-resident parents', Family Policy Briefing, 3, January (Oxford: University of Oxford).

—— (2005), 'Intervening in litigated contact: Ideas from other jurisdictions', Family Policy Briefing, 4, September (Oxford: University of Oxford).

Ingleby, R. (1992), *Solicitors and Divorce* (Oxford: Clarendon Press).

—— (1993), 'Court sponsored mediation: the case against mandatory participation', *Modern Law Review*, 56, 441–51.

—— (1994), 'The legal process in family disputes and the alternatives', in J. Eekelaar and M. Maclean (eds), *A Reader on Family Law* (Oxford: Oxford University Press).

James, A.L. (1988), '"Civil work" in the probation service', in R. Dingwall and J. Eekelaar (eds), *Divorce Mediation and the Legal Process* (Oxford: Clarendon Press).

James, A.L. and Hay, W. (1993), *Court Welfare in Action: Practice and Theory* (Hemel Hempstead: Harvester Wheatsheaf).

James, A.L. and Wilson, K. (1984), 'Towards a natural history of access arrangements in broken marriages', in J.M. Eekelaar and S.N. Katz (eds), *The Resolution of Family Conflict* (Toronto: Butterworths).

—— (1986), *Couples, Conflict and Change: Social Work with Marital Relationships* (London: Tavistock).

Johnston, J. (1993), 'Gender, violent conflict and mediation', *Family Mediation*, 3, 2.

Jones, T.S. (2001), 'Editor's introduction', *Conflict Resolution Quarterly*, 19(2), 131–4.

Joseph Rowntree Foundation (1996a), *The Impact of the Child Support Act on Lone Mothers and their Children*, Social Policy Research 92, March (York: Joseph Rowntree Foundation).

—— (1996b), *Lone Mothers and Work*, Social Policy Research 96, May (York: Joseph Rowntree Foundation).

—— (2004), *Together and Apart: Children and Parents Experiencing Divorce*, March (York: Joseph Rowntree Foundation).

——(2006a), *What Will it Take to End Child Poverty? Findings: Informing Change* (York: Joseph Rowntree Foundation).

—— (2006b), *Monitoring Poverty and Social Exclusion in the UK 2006, Findings* (York: Joseph Rowntree Foundation).

Joseph Rowntree Foundation Research (1994), *Comprehensive Mediation* (York: JRF).

Kaganas, F. and Piper, C. (1993), 'Towards a definition of abuse', *Family Mediation*, 3(2), 7–8.

Kallipetis, M. and Bartle, P. (2005), *Mediators and the Proceeds of Crime Act 2002* (Bristol: ADR Group).

Kelly, J.B. (1995), 'Power imbalances in divorce and interpersonal mediation assessment and intervention', *Mediation Quarterly*, 13, 2.

—— (2004), 'Family mediation research: Is there empirical support for the field?', *Conflict Resolution Quarterly*, 22(1–2), 3–35.

Kelly, J.B. and Duryee, M.A. (1992), 'Women's and men's views of mediation in voluntary and mandatory mediation settings', *Family and Conciliation Courts Review*, 30(1), 34–49.

Kelly, J.B. and Emery, R.E. (2003), 'Children's adjustment following divorce: Risk and resilience perspectives', *Family Relations*, 52, 352–62.

Keys Young (1996), *Research/Evaluation of Family Mediation Practice and the Issue of Violence*, August (NSW: Attorney-General's Department).

King, M. (1987), 'Playing the symbols: Custody and the law commission', *Family Law*, June, 17, 186.

—— (1997), 'Representing the interests of child victims of divorce – to what end?', *Family Mediation* 7,3, 7–8.

—— (1999), 'The future of specialist child care mediation', *Child and Family Law Quarterly*, 11, 137–49.

—— (2007), 'The right decision for the child', *Modern Law Review*, 70(5), 859–73.

King, M. and Trowell, J. (1992), *Children's Welfare and the Law: The Limits of Legal Intervention* (London: Sage Publications).

Kirby, B. (2006), 'CAFCASS: Productive conflict management research and the impetus for change', *Family Law*, November, 36, 970–74.

Kolb, D.M. (1985), *The Mediators* (Cambridge, MA: MIT Press).

—— (ed.) (1994), *When Talk Works: Profiles of Mediators* (San Francisco: Jossey-Bass).

Kolb, D.M. and Kolb, J.E. (1993), 'All the mediators in the garden', *Negotiation Journal*, 9(4), 355– 9.

Kressel, K. (1985), *The Process of Divorce* (New York: Basic Books).

Kressel, K. and Pruitt, D.G. (1985), 'Themes in the mediation of social conflict', *Journal of Social Issues*, 41(2), 179–98.

Labour Party Report (1995), *Access to Justice: A Consultation Paper on Labour's Proposals for Improving the Justice System* (London: Labour Party).

Landsberger, H.A. (1956), 'Final Report on a research project in mediation', *Labour Law Journal*, August, 7, 501–510.

Lang, M.D. and Taylor, A. (2000), *The Making of a Mediator: Developing Artistry in Practice* (San Francisco: Jossey-Bass).

Lansdown, G. (1995), *Taking Part: Children's Participation in Decision-Making* (London: Institute of Public Policy Research).

Larner, G. (1995), 'The real as illusion: Deconstructing power in family therapy', *Journal of Family Therapy*, 17, 191–217.

Law Commission (1988), *Facing the Future – A Discussion Paper on the Ground for Divorce*, Law Com. No.170 (London: HMSO).

—— (1990), *Family Law: The Ground for Divorce*, Law Com. No. 192 (London: HMSO).

—— (2006), *Cohabitation: The Financial Consequences of Relationship Breakdown* (London: HMSO).

—— (2007), *Cohabitation: The Financial Consequences of Relationship Breakdown*, Law Com. No. 307 (London: HMSO).

Law Society (1993), *Guide to the Professional Conduct of Solicitors* (London: Law Society).

—— (2002), *Family Law Protocol* (London: Law Society).

Law Society, Legal Practice Directorate (1991), 'Alternative Dispute Resolution Report', prepared by Brown, H.

Legal Services Commission (2000), *Monitoring Publicly Funded Mediation: Final Report to the Legal Services Commission* (London: LSC).

—— (2002), *Quality Mark Standard for Mediation*, December (London: Community Legal Service).

Lemmon, J.A. (1985), *Family Mediation Practice* (New York: The Free Press).

Lord Chancellor (1995), House of Lords, Hansard, 30 November, 567, 10, 704.

Lord Chancellor's Department (1995a), *Looking to the Future: Mediation and the Ground for Divorce*, Cm 2799 (London: HMSO).

—— (1995b), *Notes to Accompany Draft New Rules*, Ancillary Relief Working Party, Rules Committee Working Party (London: LCD).

—— (2002), *The Government's response to the Children Act Sub-committee Report, 'Making Contact Work'*, (London: Family Policy Division 2 LCD).

—— (2003), *Facilitation and Enforcement Group, Final Report Response to Making Contact Work* (London: LCD).

Lord Chancellor's Advisory Committee on Legal Education and Conduct (ACLEC) (1999), *Mediating Family Disputes: Education and Conduct Standards for Mediators*, December (London: LCD).

Lowe, N. and Douglas, G. (2006), *Bromley's Family Law*, 10th edn (Oxford: Oxford University Press).

Lukes, S. (1973), *Individualism* (Oxford: Basil Blackwell).

—— (1974), *Power: A Radical View* (Basingstoke: Macmillan Education).

Lund, M. (1984), 'Research on divorce and children', *Family Law*, 14, 198–201.

Maccoby, E.A. and Mnookin, R.H. (1992), *Dividing the Child: Social and Legal Dilemmas of Custody* (Cambridge, MA: Harvard University Press).

Macfarlane, J. (2002), 'Culture change? A tale of two cities and mandatory court-connected mediation', *Journal of Dispute Resolution*, 241, 1–70.

Maclean, M. and Eekelaar, J. (1984), 'The economic consequences of divorce for families with children', in J.M. Eekelaar and S.N. Katz (eds), *The Resolution of Family Conflict* (Toronto: Butterworths).

Maidment, S. (1977), 'Access and family adoptions', *Modern Law Review*, 40, 3.

—— (1984), *Child Custody and Divorce* (Beckenham: Croom Helm).

Mather, L. and Yngvesson, B. (1981), 'Language, audience and the transformation of disputes', *Law and Society Review*, 15, 775–821.

Mather, L., Maiman, R.J. and McEwen, C.A. (1995), 'The passenger decides on the destination and I decide on the route: Are divorce lawyers expensive cab drivers?', *International Journal of Law and the Family*, 9, 286–310.

Matthews, R. (ed.) (1988), *Informal Justice?* (London: Sage).

Mayer, B. (1989), 'Mediation in child protection cases: The impact of third party intervention on parental compliance attitudes', *Mediation Quarterly*, 24.

Mayer, J.E. and Timms, N. (1970), *The Client Speaks: Working Class Impressions of Casework* (London: Routledge and Kegan Paul).

McAllister, F. (1999), *High Divorce Rates: The State of the Evidence on Reasons and Remedies*, Vol. 1: Paper 2 – *Effects of Changing Material Circumstances on the Incidence of Marital Breakdown*, Research Report (London: LCD).

McCarthy, P. and Walker, J. (1996a), 'Involvement of lawyers in the mediation process', *Family Law*, 26, 154–8.

—— (1996b), *Evaluating the Longer Term Impact of Family Mediation* (Newcastle-upon-Tyne: Relate Centre for Family Studies, University of Newcastle-upon-Tyne).

McCrory, J.P. (1981), 'Environmental mediation – another piece for the puzzle', *Vermont Law Review*, 6(1), 49–84.

—— (1985), 'The mediation process', paper delivered at the Bromley Conference, April 1985 (Bromley: South East London Family Mediation Bureau).

—— (1988), 'Confidentiality in mediation of matrimonial disputes', *Modern Law Review*, 51(4), 442–66.

McCulloch, J. (2007), 'Comment: Setting the agenda', *Family Law*, 37, 381.

McDermott, F.E. (1975), 'Against the persuasive definition of self-determination', in F.E. McDermott (ed.), *Self-Determination in Social Work* (London: Routledge and Kegan Paul).

McEwen, C.A. (1993), 'Competence and quality', *Negotiation Journal*, 9(4), 317–19.

McEwan, C.A., Rogers, N.H. and Maiman, R.J. (1995), 'Bring in the lawyers: Challenging the dominant approaches to ensuring fairness in divorce mediation', *Minnesota Law Review*, June, 79, 6.

McIntosh, J. (2000), 'Child inclusive mediation: Report on a qualitative research study', *Mediation Quarterly*, 18(1), 55–69.

Meehan, A. (2006), 'Miller and McFarlane: An opportunity missed?', *Family Law*, 36, 566–74.

Menkel-Meadow, C.J. (1985a), 'Portia in a different voice: Speculation on a women's lawyering process', *Berkeley Womens Law Journal*, 1(39), 50.

—— (1985b), 'Feminist discourse, moral values and the law – a conversation', *Buffalo Law Review*, 34, 11.

—— (1993a), 'Lawyer negotiations: Theories and realities – what we learn from Mediation', *Modern Law Review* (special issue: *Dispute Resolution: Civil Justice and its Alternatives*) 56, 3.

—— (1993b), 'Measuring both the art and science of mediation', *Negotiation Journal*, 9(4), 321–5.

—— (ed) (1995), *Mediation: Theory, Policy and Practice* (Dartmouth, Aldershot: Ashgate).

—— (2001), 'Ethics in ADR: The many Cs of professional responsibility and dispute resolution', *Fordham Urban Law Journal*, 28(4), 979–90.

—— (2004), 'Remembrance of things past? The relationship of past to future in pursuing justice in mediation', *Cardoza Journal of Conflict Resolution*, 5(97), 97–115.

Menkel-Meadow, C.J., Love, L.P., Schneider, A.K. and Sternlight, J.R. (2005), *Dispute Resolution: Beyond the Adversarial Model* (New York: Aspen Publishers).

Merry, S.E. and Rocheleau, A.M. (1985), *Mediation in Families: A Study of the Children's Hearing Project* (Cambridge, MA: Cambridge Family and Children's Service).

Meunch, G.A. (1960), 'A clinical psychologist's treatment of labour management conflicts', *Journal of Humanistic Psychology*, 3, 92–7.

Meyer, A.S. (1950), 'Some thoughts about mediation', mimeographed paper.

—— (1960), 'Functions of the mediator in collective bargaining', *Industrial and Labor Relations Review*, 13, 159–65.

Milne, A. and Folberg, J. (1988), 'The theory and practice of divorce mediation: An overview', in J. Folberg and A. Milne (eds), *Divorce Mediation – Theory and Practice* (New York: Guilford Press).

Minuchin, S. (1974), *Families and Family Therapy* (London: Tavistock).

Mitchell, A. (1985), *Children in the Middle: Living Through Divorce* (London: Tavistock).

Mnookin, R.H. (1984), 'Divorce bargaining: The limits on private ordering', in J. Eekelaar and S.N. Katz (eds), *The Resolution of Family Conflict: Comparative Legal Perspectives* (Toronto: Butterworths).

Mnookin, R.H. and Kornhauser, L. (1979), 'Bargaining in the shadow of the law: The case of divorce', *Yale Law Journal*, 88, 950–97.

Moore, C. (1996), *The Mediation Process: Practical Strategies for Resolving Conflict*, 2nd edn (San Francisco: Jossey-Bass).

Munby, Mr Justice (2005), 'Families old and new – the family and Article 8', *Child and Family Law Quarterly*, 17(4), 487–509.

Murch, M. (1980), *Justice and Welfare in Divorce* (Sweet and Maxwell).

National Audit Office (NAO) (2007), *Legal Services Commission: Legal Aid and Mediation for People Involved in Family Breakdown*, Report by the Comptroller and Auditor General (London: NAO).

National Family Mediation (1998), *Cross-Cultural Mediation Policy and Practice Guidelines* (London: NFM).

—— (2007), Private communication from Chief Executive of NFM to the author. 1 May 2007.

National Family Mediation Report (1994), *Giving Children a Voice in Mediation* (London: NFM).

National Family Mediation and the Tavistock Clinic (1998), *Alternative Dispute Resolution Project Final Report* (London: Department of Health).

National Institute for Dispute Resolution (NIDR) (1993), *Interim Guidelines for Selecting Mediators* (Washington DC: NIDR).

National Organisation for Education, Training and Standards Setting in Advice, Advocacy, Counselling, Guidance, Mediation and Psychotherapy (CAMPAG) (1998), *Mediation Standards*, October (London: CAMPAG).

Nazroo, J. (1995), 'Uncovering gender differences in the use of marital violence; the effect of methodology', *Sociology* 29(3), 475–94.

Neale, B., Flowerdew, J. and Smart, C. (2003), 'Drifting towards shared residence?', *Family Law*, 33, 904–908.

Newsline Extra (2007), *Family Law*, July, 37, 651–2.

Nichols, M.P. (1989), 'Some irreverent comments', *Journal of Family Psychology*, 2(4), 422–5.

Office of Population Censuses and Surveys (1995), *1993 Marriage and Divorce Statistics* (London: HMSO).

Ogus, A. (1998), 'Rethinking self-regulation', in R. Baldwin, C. Scott and C. Hood (eds), *A Reader in Regulation* (Oxford: Oxford University Press).

Ogus, A., McCarthy, P. and Wray, S. (1987), 'Court-annexed mediation programmes in England and Wales', in *The Role of Mediation in Divorce Proceedings: A Comparative Perspective*, Vermont Law School Dispute Resolution Project (South Royalton VT: VLSDRP).

O'Neill, O. (2002), 'A question of trust', *Reith Lectures*, BBC, Radio 4.

O'Quigley, A. (1999), *Listening to Children's Views and Representing Their Best Interests* (York: Joseph Rowntree Foundation).

Pagelow, M. (1990), 'Effects of domestic violence on children and their consequences for custody and visitation agreements', *Mediation Quarterly*, 7, 4.

Palmer, G., MacInnes, T. and Kenway, P. (2006), *Monitoring Poverty and Social Exclusion* (York: Joseph Rowntree Foundation).

Palmer, S. and McMahon, G. (eds) (2006), *Client Assessment* (London: Sage).

Parker, D. and Parkinson, L. (1985), 'Solicitors and family conciliation services – a basis for professional cooperation', *Family Law*, 15, 270.

Parkinson, L. (1983), 'Conciliation: Pros and cons', *Family Law*, 13, Parts I and II.

—— (1986), *Conciliation in Separation and Divorce: Finding Common Ground* (Beckenham: Croom Helm).

—— (2004), 'Family mediation in practice – "a happy concatenation?"', in J. Westcott (ed.) *Family Mediation: Past, Present and Future* (Bristol: Family Law).

Parliamentary Working Party on Child Abduction (1993), *Home and Away: Child Abduction in the Nineties* (London: reunite).

Pearson, J. (1993), 'Ten myths about family law', *Family Law Quarterly*, 27, 2.

Pearson, J. and Thoennes, N. (1989), 'Divorce mediation: Reflections on a decade of research', in K. Kressel et al. (eds), *Mediation Research: The Process and Effectiveness of Third Party Intervention* (San Francisco: Jossey-Bass).

Piper, C. (1993), *The Responsible Parent: A Study in Divorce Mediation* (London: Harvester Wheatsheaf).

Pirrie, J. and Fellowes, K. (2006), 'Reform of the role of the CSA', *Family Law*, 36, 585–7.

Population Trends (2003), 'Divorces in England and Wales during 2003', *Marriage, Divorce and Adoption Statistics* – Series FM2, no.28.

Post Adoption Centre (1995), *Interim Report* (Mediation Service, London: Post Adoption Centre).

Poulter, S. (1982), 'Child custody – recent developments', *Family Law*, 12(1), 5.

Pound, R. (1964), 'The place of the Family Court in the judicial system', *Crime and Delinquency*, October, 10, 4.

Power, M. (1994), *The Audit Explosion* (London: Demos).

Princen, T. (1992), *Intermediaries in International Conflict* (Princeton, NJ: Princeton University Press).

Private Law Programme (2004), *Guidance Issued by the President of the Family Division* (London: DCA).

Probert, R. (2007), 'Why couples still believe in common law marriage', *Family Law*, 37, 403–406.

Protocol (2003), *Judicial Case Management in Public Law Children Act Cases* (London: DCA).

Pruitt, D.G. (1981), *Negotiation Behaviour* (New York: Academic Press).

Pruitt, D.G. and Carnevale, P.J. (1993), *Negotiation in Social Conflict* (Buckingham: Open University Press).

Pugsley, J. and Wilkinson, M. (1984), 'The court welfare officers role: Taking it seriously?', *Probation Journal*, 31, 3.

Raiffa, H. (1982), *The Art and Science of Negotiation* (Cambridge MA: Belknap, Harvard University Press).

Reich, C.A. (1970), *The Greening of America: How the Youth Revolution is Trying to Make America Livable* (New York: Random House).

Reunite (2006), *Mediation in International Parental Child Abduction: The reunite Mediation Pilot Scheme* (Leicester: *reunite* International Child Abduction Centre).

Richards, M. (1981), 'Children and the divorce courts', *One Parent Times*, October, 7.

—— (1994a), 'Divorcing children: Roles for parents and the state', reprinted in J.M. Eekelaar and M. Maclean (eds), *A Reader on Family Law* (Oxford: Oxford University Press).

—— (1994b), 'Giving a voice or addressing needs? A comment on the report "Giving Children a Voice in Mediation"', *Family Mediation*, 4, 3.

Richbell, D. (1999), 'National standards for mediation', *Family Mediation*, 9(2), 15–17.

Rifkin, J. (1994), 'The practitioner's dilemma', in J.P. Folger and T.S. Jones (eds), *New Directions in Mediation* (London: Sage).

Riskin, L.L. (1984), 'Towards new standards for the neutral lawyer in mediation', *Arizona Law Review*, 26, 330–62.

Roberts, M. (1988), *Mediation in Family Disputes: A Guide to Practice*, 1st edn (Aldershot: Wildwood House).

—— (1991), *A Conciliator's Guide to the Children Act 1989* (Swindon: National Family Conciliation Council (NFCC)).

—— (1992a), 'Systems or selves? Some ethical issues in family mediation', *Mediation Quarterly*, 10, 1.

——(1992b), 'Who is in charge? Reflections on recent research on the role of the mediator', *Journal of Social Welfare and Family Law*, 5, 372–87.

—— (1994), 'Who is in charge? Effecting a productive exchange between researchers and practitioners in the field of family mediation', *Journal of Social Welfare and Family Law*, 4, 439–54.

—— (1996), 'Family mediation and the interests of women – facts and fears', *Family Law*, April, 26, 239–41.

—— (1997), *Mediation in Family Disputes: Principles of Practice*, 2nd edn (Aldershot: Arena, Ashgate).

—— (2003), 'Third persons in family mediation: Towards a typology of practice,' *Mediation in Practice*, April, 33–40.

—— (2005a), 'Hearing both sides: Structural safeguards for protecting fairness in family mediation,' *Mediation in Practice*, May, 23–32.

—— (2005b), 'Family mediation: The development of the regulatory framework in the United Kingdom', *Conflict Resolution Quarterly*, 22(4), Summer, 509–26.

—— (2006), 'Voluntary participation in family mediation', *Family Law*, 36, 57–62.

—— (2007), *Developing the Craft of Mediation: Reflections on Theory and Practice* (London and Philadelphia: Jessica Kingsley Publishers).

Roberts, S.A. (1979), *Order and Dispute: An Introduction to Legal Anthropology* (Harmondsworth: Penguin).

—— (1983a), 'Mediation in family disputes', *Modern Law Review*, 46(5), 337–57.

—— (1983b), 'The study of dispute: anthropological perspectives', in J.A. Bossy (ed), *Disputes and Settlements: Law and Human Relations in the West* (Cambridge: Cambridge University Press).

—— (1986), 'Towards a minimal form of alternative intervention', *Mediation Quarterly*, 11, 25–41.

—— (1992), 'Mediation in the lawyers' embrace', *Modern Law Review*, 55(3), 258–64.

—— (1993a), 'Mediation and "the family justice system"', *Family Mediation*, 3, 1.

—— (1993b), 'Alternative dispute resolution and civil justice: An unresolved relationship', *Modern Law Review*, 56(3), 452–70.

—— (1995a), 'Litigation and settlement', in A.A.S. Zuckermann and R. Cranston (eds), *Reform of Civil Procedure: Essays on Access to Justice* (Oxford: Clarendon Press).

—— (1995b), 'Decision making for life apart', *Modern Law Review*, 58, 5, 714–22.

—— (2001), 'Family mediation after the act', *Child and Family Law Quarterly*, 13(3), 265–73.

—— (2002), 'Institutionalized settlement in England: A contemporary panorama', *Willamette Journal of International Law and Dispute Resolution*, 10, 17–35.

—— (2006), Seminar Paper (unpublished).

Roberts, S.A. and Palmer, M. (2005), *Dispute Processes: ADR and the Primary Forms of Decision-Making* (Cambridge: Cambridge University Press).

Robinson, M. and Parkinson, L. (1985), 'A family systems approach to conciliation in separation and divorce', *Journal of Family Therapy*, 7, 357–77.

Rodgers, B. and Pryor, J. (1998), *Divorce and Separation: The Outcomes for Children* (York: Joseph Rowntree Foundation).

Rose, P. (1985), *Parallel Lives* (Harmondsworth: King Penguin).

Rosen, L. (1989), *The Anthropology of Justice: Law as Culture in Islamic Society* (Cambridge: Cambridge University Press).

Ross, J. (1986), 'The Scottish scene: A summary of recent developments in conciliation throughout Scotland', *Mediation Quarterly*, 11.

Rubin, J.Z. and Brown, B.R. (1975), *The Social Psychology of Bargaining and Negotiation* (New York: Academic Press).

Rwezaura, B. (1984), 'Some aspects of mediation and conciliation in the settlement of matrimonial disputes in Tanzania', in J.M. Eekelaar and S.N. Katz (eds), *The Resolution of Family Conflict: Comparative Legal Perspectives* (Toronto: Butterworths).

Ryan, J.P. (1986), 'The lawyer as mediator: a new role for lawyers in the practice of nonadversarial divorce', *Canadian Family Law Quarterly*, 1(1), 130–31.

Salter, D. (2006), '*Martin-Dye* v. *Martin-Dye*: The unanswered questions', *Family Law*, 36, 666–74.

Sander, F.E.A. (1984), 'Towards a functional analysis of family process', in J.M. Eekelaar and S.N. Katz (eds), *The Resolution of Family Conflict: Comparative Legal Perspectives* (Toronto: Butterworths).

Saposnek, D.T. (1985), *Mediating Child Custody Disputes* (San Francisco: Jossey-Bass).

Sarat, A. (1994), 'Patrick Phear: Control, commitment, and minor miracles in family and divorce mediation', in D.M. Kolb (ed.), *When Talk Works: Profiles of Mediators* (San Francisco: Jossey-Bass).

Sarat, A. and Felstiner, W.L.F. (1995), *Divorce Lawyers and their Clients: Power and Meaning in the Legal Process* (Oxford: Oxford University Press).

Schaffer, L. (2004), 'Why mediators need theory', *Mediation Matters*, 77, 14–15.

Schelling, T.C. (1960), *The Strategy of Conflict* (Cambridge MA: Harvard University Press).

Schön, D.A. (1983), *The Reflective Practitioner: How Professionals Think in Action* (New York: Basic Books).

Seidenberg, R. (1973), *Marriage between Equals: Studies from Life and Literature* (New York: Doubleday Anchor Press).

Selvini Palazzoli, M., Boscolo, L., Cecchin, G. and Prata, G. (1978), *Paradox and Counterparadox: A New Model in the Therapy of the Family in Schizophrenic Transaction* (New York: Jason Aronson).

Sennett, R. (2003), *Respect: The Formation of Character in an Age of Inequality* (London: Penguin/Allen Lane).

—— (2006), *The Culture of the New Capitalism* (New Haven and London: Yale University Press).

Shah-Kazemi, S.N. (1996), 'Family mediation and the dynamics of culture', *Family Mediation*, 6(3), 5–7.

—— (2000), 'Cross-cultural mediation: A critical view of the dynamics of culture in family disputes', *International Journal of Law, Policy and the Family*, 14, 302–25.

Shapiro, M. (1981), 'Judging and mediating in Imperial China', in *Courts: A Comparative and Political Analysis* (Chicago: University of Chicago Press).

Shepherd, G. and Howard, J. (1985), 'Theft of conciliation? The thieves reply', *Probation Journal*, 32, 2.

Shepherd, G., Howard, J. and Tonkinson, J. (1984), 'Conciliation: Taking it seriously?', *Probation Journal*, 31, 1.

Silbey, S.S. and Merry, S.E. (1986), 'Mediator settlement strategies', *Law and Policy*, 8(I), 7–32.

Simmel, G. (1908a), *The Sociology of Georg Simmel*, trans. K.H. Wolff (1955) (New York: Free Press).

—— (1908b), *On Individuality and Social Forms*, in D.N. Levine (ed.) (Chicago: University of Chicago Press, 1971).

Simpson, B. (1989), 'Giving children a voice in divorce: The role of family conciliation', *Children and Society*, 3, 3.

—— (1994), 'Bringing the "unclear" family into focus: Divorce and remarriage in contemporary Britain', *Man* (The Journal of the Royal Anthropological Institute), New Series, 29, 3.

Smart, C. (1982), 'Justice and divorce: The way forward?', *Family Law*, 12(5), 135.

—— (1984), *The Ties that Bind* (London: Routledge and Kegan Paul).

Smart, C., Neale, B. and Wade, A. (2001), *The Changing Experience of Childhood: Families and Divorce* (Cambridge: Polity Press).

Smart, C. et al. (2003), *Residence and Contact Disputes in Court*, Vol. 1 (London: LCD).

Society of Professionals in Dispute Resolution (SPIDR) Commission (1989), *Qualifying Neutrals: The Basic Principles* (Washington DC: National Institute for Dispute Resolution).

Society of Professionals in Dispute Resolution (SPIDR) (1995), *Report of The SPIDR Commission on Qualifications, 1989. Ensuring Competence and Quality in Dispute Resolution Practice.* (Report no. 2) (Washington DC: SPIDR Commission on Qualifications).

Stenelo, L.-G. (1972), *Mediation in International Negotiations* (Malmo, Sweden: Nordens boktryckeri).

Stevens, C.M. (1963), *Strategy and Collective Bargaining Negotiation* (New York: McGraw Hill).

Strategic Partners P/L (1999), *Child Inclusive Practice in Family and Child Counselling and Family and Child Mediation*. Report for Family and Community Services, Commonwealth of Australia.

Strauss, A. (1978), *Negotiations: Varieties, Contexts, Processes and Social Order* (San Francisco: Jossey-Bass).

Street, E. (2003), 'Counselling psychology and naturally occurring systems/ families and couples', in R. Woolfe, W. Dryden and S. Strawbrige (eds), *Handbook of Counselling Psychology* (London: Sage).

Stulberg, J. (1981), 'The theory and practice of mediation: A reply to Professor Susskind', reprinted in S.B. Goldberg, E.D. Green and F.E.A. Sander (eds), *Dispute Resolution* (Boston and Toronto: Little, Brown).

—— (1987), *Taking Charge/Managing Conflict* (Lexington, MA: Lexington Books).

Sturge, C. and Glaser, D. (2000), 'Contact and domestic violence – the experts' report', *Family Law*, 30, 615–29.

Sutton, A. (1981), 'Science in court', in M. King (ed), *Childhood, Welfare and Justice* (London: B.T. Batsford).

Tannen, D. (1990), *You Just Don't Understand: Women and Men in Conversation* (New York: Morrow).

—— (1998), *The Argument Culture: Moving from Debate to Dialogue* (New York: Random House).

Tapper, C. (2007), *Cross and Tapper on Evidence*, 11th edn (Oxford, Oxford University Press).

Thoennes, N.A. and Pearson, J. (1985), 'Predicting outcomes in divorce mediation: The influence of people and process', *Journal of Social Issues*, 41(2), 115–26.

Tilley, S. (2007), 'Recognizing gender differences in all issues mediation', *Family Law*, April, 37, 352–5.

Timms, J. (1995), 'Safeguarding the interests of children in divorce', *Representing Children*, 8, 4.

Trinder, L., Beek, M. and Connolly, J. (2002), *Making Contact: How Parents and Children Negotiate and Experience Contact after Divorce* (York: Joseph Rowntree Foundation).

Trinder, L. et al. (2006), *Making Contact Happen or Making Contact Work? The Process and Outcomes of In-Court Conciliation*, DCA Research Series 3/06, March (London: DCA).

UK College of Family Mediators (1997), *Directory and Handbook 1997/98* (London: FT Law and Tax).

—— (2000), *Code of Practice and Standards for Mediators and Approved Bodies* (London: UKCFM).

—— (2002a), *Children, Young People and Family Mediation: Policy and Practice Guidelines* (London: UKCFM).

—— (2002b), *Domestic Abuse Screening* Policy (London: UKCFM).

—— (2003), *Professional Practice Consultancy for Family Mediators: A Guide to Roles and Responsibilities*, January (London: UKCFM).

—— (2006a), *Strategy Review*, October (London: UKCFM).

—— (2006b), *Privately Funded Work in Family Mediation: Calculating the Volume of Privately Funded Family Mediation Cases*, December (London: UKCFM).

—— (2006c), *Guidance on the Proceeds of Crime Act 2002* (London: UKCFM).

UN Convention on the Rights of the Child (1989).

Updike, J. (1965), *Of the Farm* (London: Penguin).

Utting, D. (1995), *Family and Parenthood: Supporting Families, Preventing Breakdown* (York: Joseph Rowntree Foundation).

Vermont Law School Dispute Resolution Project (1984), *A Study of Barriers to the Use of Alternative Methods of Dispute Resolution* (South Royalton VT: VLSDRP).

Wade, A. and Smart, C. (2002), *Facing Family Change: Children's Circumstances, Strategies and Resources* (York: Joseph Rowntree Foundation).

Walczak, Y. with Burns, S. (1984), *Divorce: The Childs Point of View* (London: Harper and Row).

Walker, J.A. (1986), 'Assessment in divorce conciliation: Issues and practice', *Mediation Quarterly* 11, 43.

—— (1987), 'Divorce mediation – an overview from Great Britain', in Vermont Law School Dispute Resolution Project, *The Role of Mediation in Divorce Proceedings: A Comparative Perspective* (South Royalton VT: VLSDRP).

Walker, J. (ed.) (2000), *Information Meetings and Associated Provisions within the Family Law Act 1996: Final Evaluation of Research Studies* (Newcastle Centre for Family Studies, University of Newcastle).

Walker, J., McCarthy, P. and Timms, N. (1994a), *Mediation: The Making and Remaking of Cooperative Relationships: An Evaluation of the Effectiveness of Comprehensive Mediation* (Newcastle-upon-Tyne: Relate Centre for Family Studies).

Walker, J. and Robinson, M. (1992), 'Conciliation and family therapy', in T. Fisher (ed.), *Family Conciliation within the UK: Policy and Practice* (Bristol: Jordan and Sons Limited).

Walker, J. et al. (2004b), *Picking Up the Pieces: Marriage and Divorce Two Years After Information Provision* (London: DCA).

Wallerstein, J. and Kelly, J.B. (1980), *Surviving the Break Up* (London: Grant McIntyre).

Walrond-Skinner, S. (1976), *Family Therapy: The Treatment of Natural Systems* (London: Routledge and Kegan Paul).

—— (1987), Introduction in S. Waldrond-Skinner and D. Watson (eds), *Ethical Issues of Family Therapy* (London: Routledge and Kegan Paul).

Walsh, E. (2006), *Working in the Family Justice System* (Bristol: Jordans Publishing Limited).

Watson, D. (1987), 'Family therapy, attachment theory and general systems theory: Separation may be no loss', in S. Walrond-Skinner and D. Watson (eds), *Ethical Issues in Family Therapy* (London: Routledge and Kegan Paul).

Wegelin, M.M. (1984), 'The policing of motherhood and fatherhood after divorce in the Netherlands', paper given at the Second International Interdisciplinary Congress on Women, University of Amsterdam.

Weingarten, H.R. (1986), 'Strategic planning for divorce mediation', *Social Work*, May–June, 31, 3.

Whatling, T. (2004), 'Apology matters – the power of apology in family mediation', *Mediation in Practice*, December, 7–10.

Whatling, T. and Keshavjee, M.M. (2005), 'Reflective learning from the training programmes of the Ismaili Muslim conciliation and arbitration boards, globally', *Mediation in Practice*, December, 23–8.

White Paper (1995), *Looking to the Future: Mediation and the Ground for Divorce*, Cm 2799 (London: HMSO).

—— (1996), *Striking the Balance: The Future of Legal Aid in England and Wales*, Cm 3303 (London: HMSO).

Wikely, N. (2006), 'Child support: Liability orders after Farley,' *Family Law*, 36, 675–7.

Wilkinson, M. (1981). *Children and Divorce* (Oxford: Basil Blackwell).

Williams, J.C. (1989), 'Deconstructing gender', *Michigan Law Review*, 87, 797.

Wishik, H. (1984), 'Family disputes: Problems arising from the regulation of the legal practice', in Vermont Law School Dispute Resolution Project, *A Study of Barriers to the use of Alternative Methods of Dispute Resolution* (South Royalton VT: VLSDRP).

Woolf, Lord (1995), *Access to Justice: Interim Report to the Lord Chancellor on the Civil Justice System in England and Wales* (London: HMSO).

—— (1996), *Access to Justice: Final Report to the Lord Chancellor on the Civil Justice System of England and Wales* (London: HMSO).

Woolfe, R., Dryden, W. and Strawbrige, S. (eds) (2003), *Handbook of Counselling Psychology* (London: Sage).

Index

Tapper, C. 189–90
Tavistock Clinic 210
techniques, family therapy
    adoption of as strategy difficulty in
        mediation 172
therapy, family
    adoption of as strategy difficulty in
        mediation 172
    comparison with process of
        mediation 21–7
Thoennes, N. 175, 223
training, mediator 234–5
transition, negotiation
    as strategy difficulty in mediation 170
Trinder, L., 44
Trowell, J. 210
trust, as driver for successful mediation
    176–7

UN Convention on the Rights of the
    Child 38, 191

viewpoints, unlocking of
    as successful mediation strategy 164–6
violence, domestic
    definition and provision under
        Family Law Act 66
    influence on parent-child contact
        80–81

voluntarism
    as characteristic of mediation 10
    safeguarding of in family mediation
        227–8

Wade, A. 116–17
Walker, J. 118
Wallerstein, J. 197
Walsh, E. 67
welfare, child
    as principle of Children Act 67
    as principle influencing family
        mediation court decisions 76
welfare officers, court 42–7, 188–9
Welfare Reform and Pensions Act
    (1999) 87
willingness, as driver for successful
    mediation 176–7
women, perceptions about family
    mediation process 221–4
Woolf, Lord 181, 220
Working Party on Child Abduction,
    Parliamentary (PWPCA) 207
Working Together of Safeguard Children
    (2006) 75

young people *see* children